Hit Him Where It Hurts

THE TAKE-NO-PRISONERS

GUIDE TO DIVORCE—

ALIMONY, CUSTODY, CHILD

SUPPORT, AND MORE

SHERRI DONOVAN

Divorce Clinic Specialist, Service Fund of the
National Organization for Women, NYC

ADAMS MEDIA
AVON, MASSACHUSETTS

I dedicate this book to my daughter,
Jasmine Rachael Clarke,
my Miracle Child.

Published by
Adams Media, an F+W Publications Company
57 Littlefield Street, Avon, MA 02322. U.S.A.
www.adamsmedia.com

ISBN 10: 1-59337-739-8
ISBN 13: 978-1-59337-739-7

Printed in the United States of America.

J I H G F E D C B A

Library of Congress Cataloging-in-Publication Data
Donovan, Sherri.
Hit him where it hurts / Sherri Donovan.
p.   cm.
Includes index.
ISBN-13: 978-1-59337-739-7
ISBN-10: 1-59337-739-8
1. Divorce suits—United States—Popular works. 2. Separated women—United
States—Handbooks, manuals, etc. 3. Divorced women—United States—
Handbooks, manuals, etc. I. Title.
KF535.Z9D65 2007
346.7301'66—dc22
2006032607

Cover image ©2004 PictureArts
This book is available at quantity discounts for bulk purchases.
For information, please call 1-800-289-0963.

Contents

Acknowledgments

THE WORK ON THIS book would not have been possible without the patient understanding and precocious wisdom of my daughter, Jasmine, who allowed me the time and space to get it done.

Behind every strong woman there are more strong women. So I am grateful for the support of my women friends. For making certain that my practice stayed on track and for the years of dedicated service to our firm and our mission, I thank Jane Chua and Judy Edwards Greene, my long term paralegals for their expertise, loyalty, and assistance. For knowing how to get things done efficiently and properly, I thank Natashia De Graaf, my administrative assistant. I thank my many law student interns over the years, who provided their intelligent curiosity and research assistance, in particular Joy Rosenthal, Dawn Orsati, and Deena Kalai.

I give thanks to my parents, Judy Sutter and Sidney Sutter, and to the rest of my family who always encouraged my endeavors and achievements.

I thank my book agent, Lori Perkins, who had faith in this project from the beginning. My great appreciation for her impeccable talent and tireless work in record breaking time goes to my editor, Colleen Sell. I also thank Shari Michaels, my first editor who greatly assisted me in organizing the early draft of the book. Credit goes to my publisher, Adams Media, and in particular, Paula Munier and Laura Daly, for giving birth to this book.

I give honor and thanks to all of the women who allowed me to represent them and learn from their experiences, grow from their strengths, understand their difficulties, and advocate where they were weak. I thank the present and past presidents of the National Organization for Women, New York City for acknowledging a need for my services on behalf of women for over 16 years at N.O.W.'s pro bono divorce clinic. Lastly but not least, I thank my adversaries upon whom I sharpened my skills, and the judges I have appeared before, who provided guidance and wisdom.

Introduction

YOU MARRIED THE LOVE of your life, your best friend, and sweetheart rolled into one, with the hope and expectation of living happily ever after, vowing until death you do part. Now, here you are, months or years or decades later, flattened by a deathblow to your heart, as the harsh reality or strong possibility of divorce strikes you with its merciless fist.

Maybe it's been a long while brewing and you've finally reached the end of your rope, no longer willing or able to hang in there, waiting for things to change or for a better time to end it. Maybe you both saw it coming and worked hard to prevent it, but now you've realized you're beating a dead horse and you've got nothing left to give. Maybe the blow caught you by surprise, knocking the wind out of you and sending you reeling to the floor—your spouse's out-of-the-blue confession that he wants out. Or worse, a stranger showed up unannounced and handed you a piece of paper telling you that, ready or not, like it or not, the end of your marriage has already begun . . . without you. Then again, maybe you've simply come to the liberating conclusion that, for whatever reason, you're just not into it anymore.

No matter how or why or when you got to this crossroads, divorce is tough. Really tough. Mike Tyson, George Foreman, Mohammad Ali tough. And anyone who tells you otherwise isn't telling you the truth. The simple truth is this: More often than not, divorce is a scrappy fight to the finish that can turn your one-time sweetheart and best friend into a sour brute and your worst enemy. And divorce is anything but simple. It involves and impacts every aspect of your life—not to mention the lives of any children involved—not only during and immediately after the divorce, but for years afterward, often the rest of your lives. Even when a split is "amicable," you can sustain a beating and not even realize the extent of the damage until after the fact, when it's too late to even the score.

To survive a divorce—to get through, over, and beyond it without losing your sanity or your shirt—you've got to approach it like a prizefighter. You've got to condition and prepare yourself to go the full nine rounds and leave the ring intact, on your feet, and ready for a rematch. You've got to assemble a solid team in your corner to keep you healthy, safe, and motivated—so you can stay focused on the fight and the prize. You've got to hook up with a professional coach who can help you to anticipate and avert your opponent's blows and guide you to a decisive victory.

How do I know this simple, if vicious, truth? Because I've experienced it firsthand, in different capacities: twice as a contender, once as an up-close-and-personal ringside spectator, and more times than I can count as a coach. During the more than twenty years I've practiced matrimonial law, I've represented almost 2,000 women in their divorces and been involved with or studied the cases of countless others. I've also battled through my own two divorces and witnessed the dissolution of my parents' marriage. Divorce has been a central part of my life for a long time, and very rarely in my experience has the woman not had to fight for her rights and future.

Granted, not all divorces become Battles Royale. Some, the minority, are relatively civil and straightforward, mere fistcuffs that leave hurt feelings and minor bruises but no serious or lasting damage. Others, the majority, are contentious and complicated bouts decided only after several rounds of knockdown drag-outs, leaving both sides saddled with penalties and injuries.

Then there are the malicious, extreme-competition matches that no one truly "wins" and that leave the participants, including the sparring couple's children, battered and scarred. One of those is too many for any lifetime, and I do everything within my power as an attorney to spare my clients that kind of bloodbath.

In contrast, the divorces in my personal life have been relatively benign—in large part due to the judicious manner in which they were handled. Still, they were painful. And both my parents' divorce and my own divorces left an indelible mark on me, which has enabled me to empathize with the women I've represented and to go to battle for them and their children.

"What about the kids?" is the question foremost on the minds of most women facing divorce. As numerous studies have shown, the way in which people conduct themselves immediately before, during, and after a divorce plays a major role in how well children recover from divorce. Of course, no child of divorce is completely unaffected by it, including me.

I was sixteen when my parents split up, at a time in life when fitting in seemed paramount and a time in society when the word *divorce* was spoken in hushed tones. None of my friends had mothers who'd moved out, leaving their husbands to raise the children, as mine had. My father did an admirable job of raising my two sisters and me, and my mother continued to be an important part of our lives. Still, my family stuck out like a sore thumb in our suburban neighborhood, and the transition to our reconstructed life was sometimes bumpy. What I didn't realize then but came to appreciate later was that it could have been a lot worse had my parents not come to terms without going to court or stayed in a dysfunctional marriage.

Nevertheless, I left home for college swearing I'd never marry. Then love walked in the door, and at age nineteen I said "I do." Four years later, we said our goodbyes. We were naive, without assets, and childless. I got lucky: the bout was short and clean, and I walked away relatively unscathed.

Soon after, I finished my law degree and opened my matrimonial law practice. Over the last two decades, I have represented a broad cross-section of clients, primarily women and their children, in divorce and other family law actions. I've also served as the attorney for the National Organization for Women's (NOW) divorce clinic in New York City for over sixteen years, written articles on divorce law for numerous publications, and I lecture on divorce law. This extensive experience, coupled with my personal thirst for justice and my competence in the courtroom, usually results in victory for my clients. Even when facing a large law firm—in what might seem like a featherweight taking on a heavyweight—I've frequently been able to successfully champion my client's cause, often to the surprise of my less-agile opponent.

Though my career has been a focal point of my life, I eventually met my second husband. We wed four years into our relationship, and after the pain and loss of several miscarriages, we celebrated the miracle of our daughter's birth. We raised her together for eight years, until our marriage crumbled. My husband and I worked out joint custody arrangements in which our daughter has ongoing input. She spends a substantial amount of time with her father, with whom I remain on good terms.

My second divorce wrenched my heart and was more involved than the first. But it went as smoothly and successfully as I could have hoped—for several reasons: because my child's father is a reasonable man whose primary interest, like mine, is our daughter's well-being. Because I had the emotional support and legal expertise I needed to face any foe. Because I knew my rights and my child's rights—and was ready, willing, and able to fight for them. Because I knew—from years of hammering out complex divorce settlements and battling adversarial spouses in court on my clients' behalf—exactly what the stakes were and how to fight to win.

You deserve no less. And doing any less would be a disservice, at best, and could be disastrous to you and your children. Entering a divorce ring without the right attitude, preparation, and professional coaching puts you at a serious disadvantage. One that could leave you lying on the mat with the stuffing knocked out of you, wondering what the heck happened. One that could leave you walking around for years to come, nursing the wounds and wearing the telltale scars of a horribly mismatched fight.

"Well, my divorce won't be like that," I can almost hear some of you say (only because I've heard the divorce stories of so many women). "My husband and I have agreed to work this out fairly and squarely. Neither of us wants this to drag on or to drag each other through the muck. No one wants to hurt anybody here." *Riiight.* And it could be right. But odds are it's not. This country is filled with women whose lives have been seriously compromised or ruined because they did not aggressively fight for the divorce outcome they deserved and had the legal and moral right to. This harsh reality is substantiated by a slew of divorce statistics and studies and by legal, financial, and psychological experts. In my own experience, some of the most brutal divorce cases I've handled are those of women who sought legal counsel late in the game, after they'd already taken a beating and lost several rounds.

But for the sake of argument, let's say that your husband is a really great guy with the best intentions and that the two of you have talked it over and pledged to end your marriage peacefully and equitably. Given the stakes involved—your and your children's welfare and futures—this is one time when *better safe than sorry* is a lot more than a tired old cliché. It should be your mantra, your guiding force, as you decide whether, when, and how to put up your dukes in the divorce arena.

The three biggest and most common mistakes that women facing divorce make are:

1. Underestimating their opponent (namely, their spouse and their spouse's lawyer)

2. Underestimating the lasting impact divorce will have on their and their children's futures
3. Underestimating their own power in determining the outcome of their divorce

In other words, by "playing nice," they often get hammered and come out on the short end of the stick. That is why I've written this book, a bout-by-bout, round-by-round, blow-by-blow guide to Championship Divorcing that lays out how to hit him where it hurts—smack dab on the side of justice. Think of this book as your personal divorce trainer, coaching you on how to prepare, proceed, and prevail—regardless of who takes the first swing and who's "at fault." Regardless of whether you have children, a prenup, a job, a business, extreme wealth, or extreme debt. Regardless of whether you're in a marriage or an unmarried domestic partnership.

As a child of divorce, a divorcee, the mother of a child of divorce, and a seasoned divorce attorney who's successfully represented women in every conceivable matrimonial dispute, I know what you're going through and what you're up against. And I know that with the right preparation and representation, you can get through this in one piece, claim your victory, and move on to a better, brighter future.

So put on your spunkiest tank top and boxing shorts (it's amazing what a feisty attitude can do!) and meet me in chapter one for your first training session at the Take No Prisoners Divorce Camp.

—*Sherri Donovan, Esq.*

Chapter 1

Are You Ready to Rumble?

"In true courage there is always an element of choice, of an ethical choice, and of anguish, and also of action and deed. There is always a flame of spirit in it, a vision of some necessity higher than oneself."

—Brenda Ueland, *Strength to Your Sword Arm*

DIVORCE DOES NOT BEGIN when you or your spouse files a legal petition to dissolve your marriage. Nor when one of you moves out. Nor even when one (or both) of you throws down the gauntlet and announces, "I want a divorce." Divorce begins when either (or both) of you decide, silently and within yourself, that you no longer want to be in the marriage. That agonizing decision arises from an internal evaluation process in which you study the situation from several angles and weigh all your thoughts and feelings about it—like a prizefighter getting ready for a championship bout. This crucial sizing-up stage marks the start of any divorce or separation process. And it is to your advantage to do it before you jump into the ring.

When facing the reality or possibility of divorce, you will be forced to make tough decisions. And you must make these choices alone—without your husband's input or consensus—based solely on what is best for you. This might feel unnatural and uncomfortable to you, given that you're probably accustomed to making major life decisions with your mate and, if

1

you're like most women, to putting your needs at the bottom of the list. But it is absolutely imperative.

First and foremost, you must decide whether you're going to fight (or fight back) . . . or just take it on the chin and let fate—or your opponent and his attorney—decide how the bout will be fought and how you will live in its aftermath.

POW!

ON THE FENCE? YOU'RE NOT ALONE
At any given moment, 28 million people (one-fifth of American adults) are debating whether to stay in or leave a marriage.

The Brutal Truth about Divorce

Marriage is an emotional, moral, social, and spiritual commitment. It is also a lifestyle, a cohabitation agreement, and a business partnership. Dissolving such a complex relationship—sorting out how each aspect of a shared life will now be sliced, diced, and divvied up—is a complicated and lengthy process packed with raw emotion. Stripped down to its boxer shorts, it is a civil lawsuit against one's mate. Just the thought of that can make you weak in the knees. But don't let it derail you. When a marriage is embattled, the last place you want to be is hanging on the ropes, where the aggressor can move in unchallenged and pummel you to a pulp before you realize what hit you.

Though every marriage and every divorce is unique, the starting bell for all separations and divorces rings when one partner decides to call a time out, or just call it quits—and then makes it official by filing a petition in court. Once that first decision is made, a flurry of others soon follows:

- Who goes and who stays in your current residence?
- Who gets custody of any children and pets?
- Will you need to defend your parental fitness?

- Will you have to sell your home?
- How will you survive financially during the divorce?
- How will you pay your legal fees?
- Do you need a protective order to prevent your spouse from harming you, your children, your assets, your reputation, your credit?
- Who pays which bills?
- Who gets what property?
- What about child support? Who pays? How much? When? How? For how long?
- Will you need, or be required to pay, spousal maintenance or palimony?
- How will insurances, pensions, wills, and taxes be handled?
- How will the divorce impact any inheritance you or your spouse might have?
- How will you split or sell or otherwise handle any business you own together?

If you are not properly informed and prepared—emotionally, mentally, physically, financially, and legally—you cannot make good decisions, much less fight for them. And odds are that you'll have to fight for the outcome you want, deserve, and are entitled to.

Statistics show that the majority of divorces are adversarial—meaning, one or both parties consider the other to be an adversary who opposes (or is expected to oppose) the divorce, the grounds for divorce, the settlement terms, or all of the above. What do couples fight over? You name it, and some couple somewhere has gone to blows over it in divorce court. But the most common "fighting words" are *children* and *money*.

To add insult to injury, the fight isn't always fair. Some spouses go a little bonkers in the divorce ring and do vengeful and bizarre things you'd never expect from a rational human being—like biting their opponent's rear (figuratively and financially) by driving up debt and selling and hiding assets or lying to assassinate their spouse's character in a child custody battle. Overzealous and unscrupulous attorneys (which, fortunately, are few and far between, but, unfortunately, are out there) will do almost anything to win, especially when the client has given his attorney license to maim. To further complicate matters, some divorce laws are biased or vague; matrimonial laws change; and some judges play favorites. So if you don't possess or hire the legal expertise you need to take on the complex and less-than-perfect judicial system, you can get seriously worked over.

The more extensive, convoluted, and protracted your case, the longer it will take to resolve. The longer and the more legal proceedings it takes to resolve, the higher the cost, not only in legal expenses but also in terms of the toll it takes on you and your family. The cost of not putting up a good fight, however, can far exceed your attorney's fees (which, by the way, your husband may be required to pay, as discussed in Chapter 4). In fact, failing to arm yourself with adequate legal power can undermine your financial security and your family's well-being for years to come.

Questions to Ask Yourself Before Throwing in the Towel

Think about the following things before proceeding:

- Is it safe for you (and your children, if you have them) to stay?
- Do you believe that ending your marriage is your best or only option?
- Do you think or know your spouse wants out?
- What are the advantages of staying?
- What are the disadvantages or risks of staying?
- What are the advantages of leaving?
- What are the disadvantages or risks of leaving?

- Is there another option to divorce or separation, such as marriage counseling, that you and your spouse are both willing and able to try?
- Are you ready, willing, and able to stand up and fight for the outcome you want?

Why So Many Women File for Divorce

The United States has the highest divorce rate in the world, with about 50 percent of first marriages and 60 percent of second marriages ending in divorce.

Of the more than 1 million divorces granted each year, 60 to 85 percent are initiated by women—more than two to three times the number initiated by men. The opposite was true back in what folks in certain quarters refer to as the "good old days," when virtually all divorces were initiated by men and women essentially had the legal rights and social status of chattel—property belonging to their husbands. When women finally gained certain civil liberties and began joining the work force in large numbers, they also gained the economic ability, legal protection (such as child and spousal support laws), and confidence to recover from divorce. Consequently, the rate of divorces initiated by women increased dramatically, and accordingly, so did the rate of divorce overall.

Some social critics blame the high rate of divorce and divorces initiated by women on the "walk-away wife syndrome," a moniker coined by journalist Paul Akers in 1996 to describe what he viewed as the cavalier manner in which many modern women end their marriages. He and others have claimed that many American women divorce for frivolous reasons—for example, out of boredom or simple Mars-Venus differences.

While there are, always have been, and always will be people—both men and women alike—who seek to dissolve their marriages for selfish and superficial reasons, the majority of women have ample grounds for divorce. Adultery. Incompatibility. Domestic violence. Neglect. Desertion. Fraud. Insanity. Emotional detachment. Incarceration. Substance abuse. Mental cruelty. Financial irresponsibility.

The dirty-laundry list goes on and on, and each offense is an assault on the marriage.

Rarely does a single act of misconduct by one's spouse or a short period of marital discord instigate a divorce. Most divorces result from a history of detrimental behavior, thoughts, and emotions. And the decision to divorce is made—yes, usually by the woman—only after considerable effort to "fix" things and careful consideration of all involved.

Sometimes a single event does trigger the decision to divorce: Discovering your husband is cheating on you. Getting shoved against the wall for the first (or final) time. Being humiliated by your spouse's drunken antics at a social function. Seeing your child's face crumple in pain when his father (or stepfather) flings cruel words at him, or worse. Not being considered, much less consulted, before your spouse makes a major purchase or career decision.

In reality, these and other divorce-invoking incidents are the last blow to an already fractured marriage. Then suddenly the truth hits you like a closed fist: *I want out.* Or your spouse beats you to the punch and hands you your walking papers.

By the time you've reached that turning point, you're apt to feel like you've already been through a nasty street fight. You may feel emotionally, physically, and spiritually spent. You may have withdrawn from family and friends and withheld your marital problems from them, making you feel all the more vulnerable, like you're standing alone in the ring. Your financial footing may also be shaky. In that condition, the thought of engaging in a whole new fight—one with huge stakes and lots of unknowns—may fill you with fear and dread.

So you might vacillate and hesitate, wondering what to do next, pondering all the what-ifs, and avoiding making a decision.

At least, that's what most women on the verge or in the throes of divorce do. We women tend to be masters of worry, empathy, and guilt—both by nature and because of our assigned and assumed roles in society. We also tend to gather and process as much information as possible before making major life decisions, which is a good thing when it comes to divorce. On the flip side, women have a tendency to let emotion override reason in matters of the heart. And letting your emotions get the better of you in a divorce can cost you big time.

Don't get me wrong: Emotion, if properly channeled, can serve you well, giving you the gumption to stand up for and look out for yourself and your kids. But if emotion—whether anger or anxiety or affection—isn't accompanied by a clear mind and solid muscle, it can disable you from making good decisions and following through with them.

Signs You Might Be Heading for the Divorce Ring
Here are some telltale signs to watch for:

- One or both of you are being verbally and/or physically abusive toward the other.
- One or both of you are having an affair.
- You and your spouse argue vehemently and cast blame over unresolved conflicts, with little or no regard for the other's feelings and with no real effort or seeming desire to resolve problems.
- You and your spouse bicker frequently about petty things.
- One or both of you is highly critical of the other.
- One or both of you are indifferent toward and make a concerted effort to avoid the other.
- The level of intimacy between the two of you has decreased significantly.
- Exchanges of affection, compliments, inside jokes, and sexual relations between you and your spouse have diminished.

- You and your spouse spend little time together, are absent from the family home more than normal, and attend few family gatherings and social events together.
- One or both of you is pursuing new interests and friends independent of the other.
- One or both of you are evasive, secretive, or controlling about finances.
- When you're not around your spouse, you feel more confident, relaxed, happy, and more "yourself."
- One or both of you has envisioned, threatened, or taken steps toward a separation or divorce.

POW!

AN EASY DECISION? NOT EVEN CLOSE

Many women feel trapped in abusive or unhappy marriages because they believe or fear that:

- They cannot afford to leave and make it on their own.
- Their husband will get custody of their children.
- Their spouse will never go away and leave them alone.

How Women and Children Fare After Divorce

The bare-knuckled truth is that no one comes out of a divorce unscathed. Divorce hurts. A lot. And it injures everyone involved. So does a miserable or dysfunctional marriage, especially one in which conflict and chaos are a way of life or a family member is being neglected, mistreated, or abused.

Here are some facts, stats, and expert opinions about the outcome of divorce that you might want to consider when determining your best moves from this point forward:

- Eight-five percent of mothers are awarded custody.
- The number of custodial fathers has increased 25 percent since the 1980s.

- After a divorce or separation, the standard of living for the average woman decreases 30 to 45 percent, while the average man's standard of living increases 10 percent.
- Fifty percent of custodial parents are awarded child support.
- Less than half of custodial parents who are awarded child support receive the full amount; 25 percent receive little or nothing.
- Nearly 45 percent of children living with a divorced mother live at or near the poverty level.
- Five percent of women are stalked by their estranged or former spouses.
- Women remarry later and less often than do men.
- Two-thirds of women and half of men report being "more content with life" five years after a divorce than they'd been before divorce.
- Divorce is most damaging to children when there is chronic conflict between the estranged parents.
- Years after divorce, one-third of ex-spouses still fight over their children.
- Most teens eventually adjust to divorce, but about one-third do not. In those cases, the nastiness of the divorce is the primary cause of unhealthy responses in affected teens.
- Children sustain deep emotional scars when one or both parents grossly neglects or abandons their parental roles postdivorce.
- The parent-child relationship diminishes over time when children see their noncustodial parent less than 35 percent of the time.
- After three years, 52 percent of noncustodial parents rarely see their children.
- Men who have joint legal custody and play active roles in their children's lives are more compliant with child support.
- Single custodial parents are often closer to their children than they were during marriage.

In general, women experience less stress and transition more smoothly to their postdivorce lives than men do. This is mainly due to three factors:

1. Their self-esteem increases after a divorce.
2. They feel relief that marital problems have ended.
3. They are more likely to seek and accept comfort and support from family and friends.

Divorce Ain't for Sissies

Divorce is not simply a move-out followed by a few meetings, papers to sign, and a parting of ways. Once you get through the evaluation and decision-making process, which alone can bring you to your knees, you've still got eight more rounds to slug your way through.

The eight phases of divorce or separation are:

1. Evaluation
2. Preparation
3. Planning
4. Filing
5. Negotiating
6. Settling
7. Finalization by judge/court
8. Transition

You'll learn more about each of these stages in later chapters. What you need to know up front is that divorce takes a lot of energy, effort, time, fortitude—and a whole lot out of you. Going the whole nine rounds can sap you emotionally, physically, and financially. That is why it is wise to prepare yourself for the fight of a lifetime, so that you can walk away victorious, with minimal injuries and the strength left to rebuild and enjoy your life.

Emotional Blows

Divorce can feel like an unruly, unwelcome intruder that comes storming in with a gym bag full of disturbing and often clashing emotions that it summarily dumps right on you. In fact, some psychologists claim that the only experience more emotionally devastating to adults is the death of a loved one. The emotional storm of divorce typically begins before divorce papers are served and lingers after the final decree is signed, sealed, and delivered. However, emotions tend to be most volatile from the time the legal action is initiated until a settlement is reached.

During a divorce, it is normal to feel angry, sad, anxious, depressed, insecure, or any number of feelings—including love, affection, desire, and, yes, pure hatred, for the estranged spouse. Emotional mishmash comes with the territory—regardless of who throws the first punch.

Initiators of divorce are apt to feel fear, doubt, guilt, resentment, detachment, and impatience—along with longing, exhilaration, and relief. Those on the receiving end often feel shocked, betrayed, insecure, resentful, wistful, apprehensive, victimized, paranoid, and bitterly angry. Some become obsessed with reconciling or with retaliating—and either response bodes trouble in divorce proceedings.

Just as it takes two to tango, it takes two to tangle. You cannot control how your spouse responds to his emotions; you can control only how you respond to your emotions and to his reactions. It is vitally important to attend to your divorce blues so they won't:

- Prevent you from providing vital emotional support to your children
- Distort the reality of your marital truth
- Cloud your judgment, causing you to make bad decisions
- Detract your focus from the fight

Physical Wear and Tear

Divorce not only delivers a double whammy to your heart and psyche, it can also wear you down physically. According to the National Institute of Mental Health, marital disrupt is the most powerful predictor of stress-related physical and emotional illness.

The stress that typically accompanies divorce combined with the sheer exertion of "doing it all"—working more to earn money and taking on household responsibilities previously handled by your spouse—often lead to exhaustion and health problems for women going through a divorce. By the time your divorce is finalized, you'll be past due for a respite—only to be faced with the daunting task of rebuilding your and your family's lives. Though that initial adjustment period might last only a few months, the full transition usually takes one to four years.

The good news is, you can lighten your load, conserve your strength, and protect your health by preparing yourself for the fight ahead.

Financial Hits

Meanwhile, regardless of how emotionally spent and physically drained you might be, you'll need to maintain your "normal" life. That typically means working full- or part-time while also taking care of yourself and your children, household, social obligations, any pets, and finances. For most women, money is a major concern during a divorce, second only to the welfare of their children, and the chief concern is usually, "Will I have enough?"

Unless you are independently wealthy, the loss of or a reduction in your spouse's financial contribution to your household will impact your ability to meet your and your children's normal living expenses. During the break up of a marriage, money also tends to disappear. So it is wise to have your own money for emergencies. You may also need money for other reasons, such as to leave an abusive situation, to establish a new home, to cover bills your spouse should have taken care of but didn't, and to pay legal fees. Even if your lawyer feels confidant you'll be awarded support, you may need money to hold you over until your husband is ordered to pay and then actually does.

Divorce Is Not a Spectator Sport

When it comes to your family and friends, divorce is like a pebble—or boulder, as the case may be—tossed into a lake, its effects rippling out to everyone with whom you and your spouse have shared relationships. To those so affected by a divorce, sitting ringside and watching powerlessly as two people tear apart their marriage can be hurtful and uncomfortable. Some will be compelled to take sides. Some will remain loyal to you and your spouse. And some will turn away from you both.

It is impossible to predict how everyone in your life will respond to your divorce, and you will undoubtedly take a few surprise jabs along the way. But knowing what to expect and how to (and not to) respond can help you to minimize the impact of your divorce on people you care about. In subsequent chapters, we'll talk about how to stay above the fray and how to defend yourself and your family when you can't. Now, let's look at some probable effects of divorce on the people closest to you.

Impact on Children

The greatest tragedy of divorce, in my opinion, is its effect on children. Divorce is *never* easy or "good" for children. That said, the most recent and reliable studies indicate that children of divorce stand as good a chance as any other kids of leading happy, healthy, productive lives—provided the parents conduct themselves properly before, during, and after the divorce.

The thing that really messes up children is chronic conflict between parents and within the family unit. Conflict wreaks havoc on kids whether the couple stays together or splits up, and living in a home in which there is continuous conflict and stress between the parents can be worse for children than a divorce.

The other thing that wounds children of divorce is having an absentee or neglectful parent. By the same token, growing up in an intact family in which one or both parents grossly neglects or shows little interest in and has little involvement with the child can cause serious harm, too.

Poverty or financial duress during or following divorce can also undermine a child's emotional, psychological, and physical health, particularly when it results in inadequate nutrition and/or health care. A drop in their standard of living can also be confusing, embarrassing, frightening, and demeaning to children, eroding their sense of well-being and self-worth.

It goes without saying that *any* abuse—verbal, physical, psychological, sexual—is devastating to children, especially when directed at the child but also when the child witnesses the abuse of a sibling or parent. Abuse is far more damaging to children than divorce, and if the abuse continues after the divorce, the emotional cost to kids is doubled.

Even when none of these harmful factors are present in a divorce, it's an emotionally trying experience for kids. Most children cannot understand how parents can stop loving each other or wanting to be together. Many feel somehow responsible, especially if the child and/or parenting issues have been a source of conflict between the parents. Children of divorce often feel betrayed and left out, have difficulty trusting, and fear being rejected or abandoned by one or both parents.

Teens tend to cope better during divorce and to adjust better after divorce than do younger children, and girls usually do better than boys. (This assumes the aforementioned harmful factors do not exist.) But all kids are emotionally affected by divorce, including any stepchildren and grandchildren, and even adult children.

As a rule of thumb, putting the children's interests first and taking the high ground will ensure that you've done all within your power to minimize the impact on your kids.

Impact on Extended Families

Divorce inevitably changes the relationships between you and your in-laws, between your spouse and members of your family, and between the two families. Not surprisingly, divorce usually splits the extended family into two camps: yours and his. That does not mean the two camps are always or frequently at odds, and it certainly is better, especially for the children of the divorcing couple, if everyone stays on mostly friendly terms. But it usually means that any closeness you might have shared with his family and vice versa will diminish.

That can be a huge loss for close-knit extended families, and some might not take well to it. When parents think of their son-in-law or daughter-in-law "like a son" or "like a daughter" or siblings have a brotherly or sisterly connection with an estranged in-law, they are likely to miss that person greatly and worry about his or her well-being. They might also want to keep in contact. Most important, in-laws remain grandparents, aunts, uncles, and cousins to a divorced couple's children for life, so they will always have an emotional stake in those relationships.

Most extended family members feel concern, confusion, empathy, and sadness. Some will be shocked, particularly if they were under the impression (however close or far from reality it might be) that you and your spouse are "the perfect couple." Some will disapprove, because they don't understand or accept the reasons for the decision or because of religious or moral beliefs. There may be pressure and even interference to stay together "for the sake of the children."

Some family members might be angry, disappointed, and judgmental. Others might blame and fling accusations and insults at you or your spouse or both. It is also not uncommon for family members, including your own, to avoid you and exclude you. As hurtful as this is, try to remember that they're hurting, too, and that retaliating can only do more harm. Remember, too, that getting sucked into unnecessary family dramas can drain strength you'll need to fight for a brighter tomorrow for you and your children.

Most of the time, though, the majority of blood relatives—once they've been given the facts of the situation and the time to adjust to the idea—are compassionate and accommodating. They remain loyal and close to their daughter (or son) and usually become her (or his) strongest and most helpful supporters.

Impact on Close Friends

Just as extended families divide into his and her camps, so, too, will some of the people with whom you and your spouse have socialized as a couple. So be prepared to lose a few friends and for your relationships with others to change.

Friends, colleagues, fellow church members, neighbors, and others within your and your husband's social circle are likely to experience a range of emotions upon learning of your divorce. Feelings of betrayal, shock, and sadness are common. So are blame and fault-finding, as well as guilt (if your or your husband's relationship with that person has been a point of contention for your spouse or you).

Unlike family members, social familiars might not make it obvious whose camp they're in or might ride the fence until circumstances force the issue. Those who don't come forward early on as clear supporters may hold back for a variety of reasons: a) they are uncomfortable with the situation and don't know how to handle it, b) they have chosen your spouse's friendship over yours, c) they believe it's none of their business, or (d) they are deliberately distancing themselves from you and/or your spouse.

Try not to jump to conclusions or take it personally when friends aren't as open and friendly as usual, exclude you from social activities, or don't stay in close contact. Be cordial with these folks but don't spill your guts to them either—because only time will tell whether these fence-sitters are friend or foe.

Your closest and "true" friends will eventually weigh in with exactly where they stand, and you can count on them to be in your corner, even if they adore your spouse or question your decision. Some will be relieved, and others who disliked or had a strained relationship with your spouse may grow even closer to you after the split. Your best friends will also understand if you're not as available to them or as pleasant to be around during the divorce. But try not to neglect these friendships, because you'll need their support to see you through.

Impact on Spouse

The temptation might be to say, *Who cares how he feels?* But you probably do care. Most women have at least some degree of empathy for the spouse they are divorcing or who is divorcing them. After all, this is the man you once loved truly, madly, deeply . . . and maybe still do. But even if your partner has been a total dirtbag, and now, frankly, you don't give a damn how he feels, you should. Here are three good reasons why:

1. If you understand where your spouse is coming from, you can better anticipate his motivation and his moves— and be ready to respond with the most effective offensive or defensive tactic.
2. Contempt breeds contempt. Meaning, if you don't know or care what his hot buttons are, you're more likely to push them. Then he's more likely to push yours. And that can start a senseless flailing match that complicates and prolongs divorce settlements. And that increases legal costs, makes everyone more miserable, and irritates judges.
3. The kids. He's still their dad. They love him and care about him. If he hurts, they hurt. If he's upset, they're upset. If he's angry, they're in the line of fire.

Divorce can be an emotional snake pit for men. The loss of intimacy, time with their kids, social identity, disposable income, and often their homes is a big, nasty pill to swallow all at once, often making the emotional adjustment to divorce more difficult for men than for women. When faced with the possibility or threat of divorce, men also tend to resist initially and to invest more energy into saving the marriage. Divorce, then, can feel like an assault on their character, a callous rejection, and a personal failure. It can fill a man with self-doubt and self-loathing, and just as well, fill him with rage and resentment toward his soon-to-be ex.

Whatever your feelings toward your spouse, remember that he has feelings, too. Being aware of and sensitive to them will help you to make better decisions regarding the divorce or separation. It will help make things go smoother and come out better for all of you. Just don't let your empathy for him blindside you and undermine your and your children's futures.

A FOCUSED SHE-WARRIOR EMERGES VICTORIOUS

By all appearances, Deborah and Eric were living the American dream. Married fifteen years, they had three great kids, a beautiful home, and a wide circle of friends. Eric had a successful dental practice, which Deborah had helped him start and grow. Deborah was a supportive wife, a devoted and involved mom, and a consummate homemaker. In addition to handling virtually all the parenting and household responsibilities, she also handled all the family finances.

Deborah was devastated when she discovered Eric was having an affair with his young dental hygienist. Nevertheless, she approached her divorce with the same efficiency with which she ran her home. First, she sought emotional support with close friends and a good therapist. Next, she hired an attorney. Then she diligently gathered all of the information and documentation I needed to represent her.

First, she checked her family's bank accounts, investments, and retirement funds to make sure nothing was missing. (Luckily, nothing was.) She checked health and life insurance policies to make sure Eric would be unable to close or alter them before a settlement was signed. She compiled a complete history of their finances, including tax returns, creditor statements, and stock-broker statements. She also wrote out a detailed history of her marriage and her contributions to the family, including her role in establishing Eric's practice.

Deborah is every divorce attorney's dream client. She arrived on time and never missed an appointment. She reviewed all legal documents thoroughly and promptly. She asked questions and followed instructions. She attended every negotiation session and court hearing, even when she was not required to, which demonstrated to the judge that she was reliable, diligent, and interested in the outcome of her case. Despite the emotional duress she was under and all the responsibilities she had at home, she was focused, responsive, cooperative, and courteous.

Consequently, her case was settled in only a few months, rather than years. She got a favorable settlement, including full custody of her children, an excellent financial package, her family's home, child and spousal support, and substantial retirement funds in the bank. Eric, too, received a fair share of the couple's assets and ample visitation with his children, and Deborah graciously complied with the terms.

Though the settlement could not allay the emotional anguish Deborah suffered as a result of her husband's betrayal and the breakup of her marriage, the settlement alleviated her financial concerns so she could focus on her family and on moving on. Eventually, she became a teacher and began dating. ∎

Decision Time

The decision you now face—what to do next in response to the threat or reality of divorce or separation—is one of the most important and difficult choices you'll ever make. Every decision regarding a marital breakup is difficult, and the consequences of each choice you make and each step you take are profound and lasting to you and your family. So you need as much information, as much preparation, and as much courage as you can muster. And it all begins by digging deep to answer two pivotal questions:

1. What is your truth about your marriage?
2. What is your vision of your future?

Everyone goes into marriage with a romantic notion of how it's going to be, and the reality of marriage never perfectly matches up with that ideal. So when I talk about "your marital truth," I'm not talking about that fantasy. I'm talking about real life—*real* being the operative word. Before you can decide whether and how to end your marriage or domestic partnership, you first need to get real about the relationship and how you feel about it. Not how you want it to be, or it used to be, or it could be. Not how you long to feel, or once felt, or would feel "if only." When considering or facing something as life altering as divorce, only the truth can set you free.

I'd lay odds that, deep down, you already know the truth about your marriage—the "why" that's brought you to the option or reality of divorce or separation. You probably also know, or have some concept of, your vision of your future—the "what" you hope to achieve once you're through the divorce or separation process. Now, you just need to dial into yourself, tune out all the static, and hone in on that voice inside that knows what is really going on, what you really want and are capable of, what your spouse wants and is capable of, and what is in the best interests of you and your family.

If you and/or your spouse are contemplating or have initiated a divorce or separation, your best chance of surviving and securing a decent future for you and your family is to do whatever inner work it takes to get crystal clear about what you want and why you want it. This will enable you to keep your eye on the prize throughout what promises to be the fight of your life. And it will give you the "fire in the belly" you'll need to proceed, persevere, and prevail.

TKO!

DIVORCE MISTAKE #1
Signing a legal agreement without understanding it completely, discussing it with a trusted friend, getting professional legal counsel, and carefully thinking it through.

Chapter 2

Choose Your Corner

"When it comes to the cause of justice, I take no prisoners and I don't believe in compromising."

—Mary Frances Berry, *I Dream a World*

AT SOME POINT IN the process of contemplating and finalizing a divorce or separation, you must take, or will be forced into taking, a stance as either an aggressor or a challenger. That is, to fight offensively, like a champion, or defensively, like the underdog. Regardless of where you stand now—even if your husband has taken the lead with fists flying and got you on the ropes, barely deflecting his blows—you *can* get the upper hand. It's never too late to upset your opponent and take the bout, not when your spouse has filed first, not when a settlement has been reached, not even after a judge has finalized the divorce. It might take some intense conditioning, fast footwork, and powerful blows under the direction of a skilled coach, but you can get through and come out of this in good shape. And the sooner you get into the ring with the right stuff in your corner, the better your chances of claiming your rightful and desired victory.

Sizing Up Your Opponent
One of the biggest and most common mistakes divorcing women make is to "play nice," assuming (or hoping) their spouse will, too. In an effort to "fight fair," women tend to hold punches (for

example, by withholding detrimental information about their husbands that could weigh in their favor had the judge known) and compromise their positions (for example, by making undue peace offerings to placate a disgruntled spouse). Smart, assertive women who are barracudas in their professions or other aspects of their lives can turn to kowtowing mush-balls in the divorce ring and subsequently get creamed. Fiercely protective mothers stymied by a haze of guilt can let their guard down, giving their opponents a clear shot at their most vulnerable spot. Practiced tacticians can forsake the cardinal rule of negotiation: start high, negotiate down, but never compromise your bottom line . . . and end up on the short end of the stick.

When it comes to divorce—in which the stakes are your and your family's futures—you simply cannot afford to pussyfoot around or be a patsy. You must fight tough and fight smart. And to do that, you've got to get a handle on, and get real about, your opponent.

Answering the following questions about your spouse should give you (and your attorney) an idea of what you're up against:

- Has he threatened or mentioned divorce or separation to you or anyone else?
- Is there any other indication he is or might be contemplating a divorce or separation? For example, has he sought information through books, the Internet, or people he knows?
- Has he made any plans or preparations for a divorce or separation?
- Has he sought legal counsel or hired an attorney?
- Has he filed or do you think he might file a suit or counter-suit for divorce or separation?
- Has he filed or do you think he might file for sole or joint custody of any minor children?
- Where does he stand with regard to the living and visitation arrangements of any minor children?

- Is he a fit and capable parent in whose custody or care any minor children will be safe and their welfare assured?
- Has or might he hide or sell money, property, or other assets?
- Has or might he make new debt without your knowledge and/or in his name only.
- What tactics and to what length might he go to prevent you from realizing the results you want and/or to get the results he wants?
- Does he have the financial means to engage in a long and nasty legal battle?
- Do you anticipate him resisting the divorce or any terms of divorce you might designate?
- Is there any history or risk of him being abusive to you and/or your children?

In answering these questions, don't rely solely on your intuition and whatever evidence might be right in front of you. Dig deeper into your memory. Turn over every stone and really look at what's under there. Check out your suspicions. Investigate the seemingly impossible. Ask trusted confidantes for information. Gather and record as many details and substantiating documents as you can, and put them where your spouse won't find them.

Do *not* tell your husband what you're doing or thinking about. Take care not to say or do anything that might tip him off, and don't say anything to anyone who might tell him. No matter how strong the urge might be to confront your spouse or to discuss your concerns or plans with him, doing so at this point could put your case, and even your safety, in jeopardy. Discretion during this sizing-up stage can also minimize the expense and trauma of the divorce proceedings. There is a right time and a right way to let your husband know you've taken your corner, but it is not here and now, before you've thoroughly prepared yourself and outlined a winning strategy.

Aggressor Versus Challenger

Divorce and legal separation are civil lawsuits, as are most other legal actions relating to family law, such as court orders involving child custody, child support, child visitation, alimony, palimony, spousal maintenance, and distribution of property and debts. As such, each of these civil suits has a *plaintiff* (or *petitioner*) who initiates the action, and a *defendant* (or *respondent*) against whom the suit is filed and who has an opportunity to respond to the lawsuit. The defendant may also file *counterclaims* against the plaintiff for specific actions within the civil suit (such as child custody).

Many people assume the plaintiff is automatically and always the aggressor and the respondent the challenger. In reality, the defendant can be a ferocious aggressor and the plaintiff a total pushover. Whichever corner you find yourself in, it is almost always in your best interests to take an aggressive and offensive, rather than a passive and defensive, stance in a divorce or separation. This is especially true if the breakup involves minor children, significant assets, substantial debt, and/or the presence or risk of domestic violence.

The mere thought of being an aggressor, especially with one's spouse, may be off-putting. It might help to know that being aggressive in a divorce does *not* mean being illegal or immoral, or being unkind or unjust to anybody. It does not mean being a "gold-digger" or "ball-breaker," as women are often called, almost always unfairly, in a divorce situation. Being an aggressor means taking a stand and fighting for what is best and just for you and your family, and refusing to back down to any bully, intimidator, manipulator, or avenger. It means using the knowledge, preparation, and support you need to get the results you want.

Whether you start out as the plaintiff or defendant in a divorce or separation, you must decide whether to be the aggressor or the challenger in the bout.

If You Take the First Swing

One of the advantages of being the plaintiff, the one who initiates the divorce or separation, is that it enables you to set forth the terms you desire in the *summons and complaint*. This typically includes:

- **Grounds for divorce or separation**—fairly straightforward in no-fault states but it can be complicated in states where no-fault is rare or impossible
- **Legal custody of any minor children**—whether one or both parents shall be responsible for making major decisions regarding their welfare
- **Residential arrangements of any minor children**—whether they will reside solely or primarily with one parent or with each parent at specified intervals
- **Day-to-day care of any minor children**—including how their basic living expenses, clothing and other material needs, and health care needs will be met
- **Child support**—who pays whom, how much, when, how, for how long
- **Distribution of personal and marital property** and other assets
- **Distribution of personal and marital debt**
- **Issues regarding health insurance, life insurance, pensions, retirement funds, taxes,** and all other business aspects of the marital/domestic partnership
- **Alimony/palimony, spousal support**—who pays whom, how much, when, and how

The initiator may also submit emergency orders to the court, such as for temporary child custody, temporary child support, and protective orders in the presence or risk of domestic violence.

The permanent terms and conditions of the divorce or separation are subject to one of the following:

1. The plaintiff and defendant agreeing on each and every
   item
2. The plaintiff and defendant negotiating and compromising until the two parties reach agreement
3. Going to litigation (court) if the two parties cannot agree
   and having an arbitrator or a judge decide the outcome
   (or a jury, when the grounds for divorce are unresolved)

Needless to say, the first scenario is typically the fastest, easi-
est, and least costly in terms of legal expenses. It is also the
least likely to occur and the least likely to yield an equitable and
appropriate settlement—particularly for women with children.
Litigation—the most protracted, difficult, and expensive of the
three scenarios—occurs in about 5 percent of cases and results
in an equitable settlement more than half the time. Negotiated
settlements, which might be reached with or without a mediator,
are the most common—but can, and often do, end up with the
wife receiving a raw deal financially and making undue concessions with regard to her children's welfare. Why? Usually it's
because she did not seek or receive good legal counsel and/or
failed to follow the advice of her attorney in being aggressive in
fighting for her (and her children's) best interests.

In most cases, the person who initiates the legal action to
divorce or separate has an advantage, at least initially. In terms of
preparation and conditioning, the plaintiff is often a step or two
ahead of the respondent, having already done some of the emotional and practical work toward ending the relationship and
beginning a new life. This is significant when you consider that a
civil suit of this nature is certain to stir up a hornet's nest of emotions and to shake up and rearrange every important part of your
life. By thinking out your moves and preparing for contingencies

in advance, you'll be better able to make good decisions, ward off wild swings, sustain less damage from any hits you take, and stay on your feet during the entire bout. Conversely, being caught off guard is more apt to knock the wind out of you or knock you flat on your back, either of which will take time and effort to recover from and could affect the outcome of your case.

One of the downsides of being the first to file a divorce action is that it can be a confusing, scary, and overwhelming endeavor. Knowing you are launching a major and disruptive change in your and your family's lives is frightening enough. Not knowing exactly what to do and what to expect then increases that angst many times over. You might also be afraid of your husband's reaction, worried that he might lash out at you or your children in some way, resist the divorce, countersue, fight you on every major issue, or embark on an all-out campaign to make the whole ordeal as difficult as possible.

Again, advance preparation, including getting good legal counsel, will help give you the muscle to initiate the legal dissolution of your marriage or partnership—if that is your decision and your husband doesn't file first. It will also help give you the focus and stamina you'll need to fight aggressively for the outcome you want. And it will better your odds of achieving that outcome, regardless of whether you're the plaintiff or the defendant.

POW!

BATTLE OF THE ROSEBUDS
Every year, 150,000 divorcing couples cannot agree on child custody.

If You Get Sucker-Punched

In about 18 out of 100 divorces, the man initiates the divorce or legal separation. In most of these cases, the husband is very secretive and gives the wife no indication he's bailing out of the marriage until he lambastes her with divorce papers. That's what's known as a sucker-punch. And it can flatten you. Even when you've suspected your spouse might file for divorce, even when he's told you so ahead of time, even when you've been contemplating or planning to file, too, finding out he's initiated the divorce still feels like a blow to the gut. And it makes you feel vulnerable.

While being forced into the defendant's corner can cost you a round or two, you *can* pull it together, even out the odds, and come out on top—but only if you put on the aggressor's gloves at that point and prepare yourself to fight aggressively to the end.

POW!

EQUITY SCHMEQUITY
The average divorced woman earns 22 percent less than the average divorced man—but typically receives a smaller percentage of the marital assets than the man does. Why? In most cases, it's because the woman didn't ask and didn't fight for her fair share.

If your husband does beat you to the punch in filing for divorce, you have two options: answer his petition or file a counterclaim for those issues you disagree with. Whichever route you take, it is imperative not to respond immediately, emotionally, or without first obtaining legal council, preferably by way of hiring a kick-ass matrimonial attorney. Even if you agree with every aspect of your spouse's summons and complaint, you should think it over carefully and have it reviewed by an experienced lawyer before signing anything. Remember, almost every divorce stipulation can be refused or negotiated, and no one has the legal right to coerce you into anything.

If any part of the agreement is unclear, doesn't sit right with you, or seems not to be in your (or your children's) best interests, don't agree to it—period. If in doubt, retain the services of a good attorney and seek the advice of close confidantes who have only your welfare in mind. Compromise only when it is prudent to do so. Otherwise, don't buckle to pressure from your spouse or your spouse's attorney. Be ready and willing to fight like a champion to hammer out an agreement you truly can live with.

Taking a Stance

Once you're certain you want to split up with your husband, or he makes his wishes known to you, you'll need to decide your opening move. In an ideal world, you would have a heart-to-heart with your husband and either reveal your plans or decide together whether to move forward with a trial separation, a legal separation, an annulment, or a divorce. You would discuss or decide together who will initiate the petition and how all the major issues—such as how child custody, residency, and support, as well as debts and assets—will be handled.

But in the real world, this is rarely the best move and is sometimes a bad move. Before broaching the topic with your husband, I strongly suggest that you first consult with an attorney or at least thoroughly evaluate your situation and investigate your options. Then, you will be better able to make an informed and thoughtful decision about which legal action to take and whether to inform your husband by:

- Telling him yourself
- Having your lawyer send him a letter stating you've retained an attorney to represent you in the dissolution of your marriage and asking for the name of his attorney
- Having your spouse served with your petition for divorce or separation

After thinking things through and talking it over with your husband, close confidantes, attorney, and/or counselor, you might instead decide to live apart without taking any legal action.

Informal Separation

Some married couples choose to live apart on either a trial or permanent basis, without obtaining a formal separation or divorce through the court. The most common reasons for doing this are:

- To make one last-ditch effort to save the marriage
- To let the other spouse down more gently and/or to prepare emotionally for divorce
- To continue health insurance until one spouse can arrange for insurance independently
- To give everyone concerned an opportunity to test out and adapt to the possibility of divorce, including children and extended family members, before going to the trauma and expense of a divorce
- To get a resistant spouse to move out or to allow the other party to move out with less difficulty
- To buy time to prepare for a divorce or legal separation—for example, to give one spouse the opportunity to obtain medical insurance or gainful employment
- To adhere to religious covenants forbidding divorce

While any of these objectives may be valid, there are also some drawbacks to consider before deciding to live apart for a while or indefinitely without the benefit of a formal separation or divorce. One of the main problems is an imbalance of power. Most of the time, the person initiating the split is six to twenty-four months ahead of the other party in doing the inner work, making the decisions, and taking the practical steps to separate. And usually, that person has already either made the decision to divorce or is leaning strongly in that direction. That gives the initiator an unfair advantage in determining the terms and timetable of the divorce. Often, when they're ready to proceed, the other party is not.

Frequently, the person who suggests living apart is simply using the separation to get his ducks in a row (making his wife a sitting duck), so he can move swiftly and decisively when the time is right. This is particularly important to consider if you reside in a state that requires a married couple to live separately for a specified period of time before a no-fault divorce can be granted.

Using a trial separation as merely a decoy for a certain divorce—whether to connive for position or due to one's lack of courage—can also give the other party false hope. And that's just mental and emotional cruelty—which, by the way, is grounds for divorce in many states.

In retaliation for being duped and hurt, the unsuspecting spouse may also become inordinately combative and vindictive once legal action is taken to dissolve the marriage. This only makes a difficult situation worse, driving up both the emotional and financial costs of the breakup.

There are also a few legal ramifications you should consider before initiating or agreeing to live apart rather than divorcing or legally separating:

- In most states, when a couple lives apart temporarily, with the intent or possibility of getting back together, the assets and debts they accumulate during the trial period are usually considered jointly owned.
- In most states, once a couple in a trial separation decides to make the separation permanent, all assets received and most debts made from that point on are usually considered the separate property or responsibility of the spouse incurring them.
- In some states, when a married couple live apart with no clear effort toward or intention of reuniting—and with no explicit trial or permanent separation agreement between them—all

property and debts incurred from the time of the split are usually considered the separate property of the person who incurred them.

One last potential downfall: the spouse who leaves the family home during a trial separation may not be able to return to it or remove marital property from the home later.

If divorce is truly an uncertainty or encumbrance at this time and you decide to separate for a while without making it "legal," it is best not to do it on the fly. You must have a plan and a time-table, even if you need to change them several times down the road. If the plan or timetable that you are considering involves living separately for even one second more than thirty days, you should seriously consider having a written separation agreement.

You should also consider paying an attorney to draw up a *working arrangement* that itemizes the financial and parenting arrangements to which you and your spouse have agreed. This is easier to reverse and less expensive than a legal separation filed in court, and it offers some legal protection, but not nearly as much as either a divorce or legal separation. While you're living under such an arrangement, your husband could turn around and file for divorce, using the working agreement as the basis of the settlement. If the agreement is not one you could live with after the divorce, you would be in the difficult position of having to convince the courts that the terms you agreed to temporarily are no longer satisfactory. So make sure the informal separation agreement reflects what you'd want in a divorce, should it come to that. Never separate without some form of written and nota-rized agreement. And never sign anything on the spot before thinking it over carefully and running it by your lawyer.

Legal Separation

Couples whose marriages seem to be heading toward divorce might initially (or instead) choose a legal separation, for the same reasons they might go for an informal separation. In a legal separation, the terms under which the married couple lives apart are stipulated by a written agreement that is notarized and filed with the court. The agreement may be approved or decided by a judge, but it doesn't have to be.

If you and your husband are going to live separately for more than a few weeks, you need to ensure that your standard of living during the time you are living apart remains as close as possible to what it was when you lived together. You must also consider how your bills are going to be paid, ensure that your family assets won't be unfairly or unnecessarily depleted, and resolve all issues of child custody and visitation during the separation.

Make sure to also include health insurance in your separation agreement. One of the reasons some couples split up under a separation agreement rather than a divorce is because it saves money on health insurance. If you remain technically married, even though you are legally separated, you may be able to remain on your spouse's health plan (or he on yours). Because health insurance can be very expensive, the cost of the premiums should be considered in all separation negotiations.

Before you agree to anything, even in casual conversation, think it through carefully and consult with your lawyer. I also strongly advise you to have your lawyer draw up the separation agreement or to at least use the standard legal separation forms for your county and state, rather than just a homemade document you and/or your spouse put together. Don't sign anything without thinking it through carefully, reviewing it with your lawyer, and amending it to reflect the terms you'll need not only during the separation but also in a divorce.

In most cases and in most jurisdictions, the court will not allow you to make any changes to your separation agreement once you have signed it. Not only that, but the separation agreement will become the blueprint for your divorce settlement. If you fail to include specific items, such as who gets your car and who pays off which debts, these sometimes cannot be added later. So if the credit card debt for the family expenses is left out of the separation agreement that then becomes the divorce agreement, you will be stuck with that debt and any resulting credit history problems.

In several states the terms of the legal separation agreement automatically become the terms of the divorce agreement, once the divorce action is initiated. In other states the separation agreement serves as the basis of the divorce settlement, and it can be difficult or impossible to add, remove, or change any of the terms. So you must negotiate a separation agreement as carefully as you would a divorce agreement.

A separation agreement is a legally binding contract only if it:

- Is in writing
- Signed and dated by both parties
- Notarized
- Filed with and accepted by the court

As with a divorce agreement, the couple must disclose all pertinent information and negotiate until they come to agreement on all terms of the separation agreement. Otherwise, the matter goes to court, where a judge decides. In states where establishing fault is an issue, the grounds for a separation decree are similar to the grounds for a divorce.

Not all states recognize separation agreements. If you are considering this option, check with your attorney or local divorce court to determine whether it is possible. If so, make sure the separation agreement reflects the outcome you want and are entitled to, in the event you end up in divorce court. Statistics show that the majority of couples who separate do eventually divorce, most within a year of separating.

On the optimistic side, should you and your husband find a way to work out your problems and get back together, you can always scrap the separation agreement (on advice of your lawyer, of course). On the other hand, if you and/or your husband decide to divorce, then the separation agreement will give you a leg up on that process and ensure that you've set up the best possible position for your and your family's future.

POW!

COMMON-LAW MARRIAGE

Once upon a time, common-law marriages were relatively common; today they are almost an anomaly. When an unmarried man and woman live together as husband and wife, presenting themselves as and behaving like a married couple, for a long period of time (*not* the mythical seven years), they eventually gain the legal status of marriage—in some states. Fifteen states and the District of Columbia recognize common-law marriage, but the provisions for the legal dissolution of such a relationship (property, child custody, etc.) tend to be complicated and rigid. Stepping into that ring without powerful legal representation in your corner would be setting oneself up for a humiliating and injurious defeat.

If you are reasonably certain divorce is your ultimate objective and that you and your spouse are both ready to split up, legal separation is probably *not* the best first move. Obtaining a legal separation first and a divorce later only increases the legal costs and prolongs the inevitable.

Divorce

The main advantage and disadvantage of divorce are one and the same: its permanence. A divorce ends a marriage, along with the negative things that perpetuated it, once and for all, enabling the two parties to move forward with their emotional healing and begin rebuilding their lives. It also nixes any chance of reinstating the marriage, save for remarrying (which rarely happens and even less rarely sticks). Then, too, all stipulations of the divorce—child custody, property distribution, etc.—are finally, after all the rigmarole it typically takes to reach agreement, pretty much cast in stone. On the plus side, that makes it next to impossible for your ex to renege on the deal once the judge decrees it final. Conversely, it also prevents you from correcting any inequities you encounter after the fact.

If you or your ex-spouse's circumstances change dramatically postdivorce or one or both of you fail to comply with the terms of the agreement, the case can be reopened or a new civil suit filed to address issues regarding children (but no other aspects of the divorce). However, it is usually much more difficult to undo or redo a divorce settlement, however warranted a change may be, than it is to get the outcome you want and deserve in the first place.

Another reason some people choose legal separation over or as a precursor to divorce—aside from wanting to leave the doors of reuniting open—is that they think separation will be easier or cheaper or both. It rarely is. Nor, in reality, is it any less permanent. The vast majority of couples who separate—more than 90 percent—end up divorcing anyway. Indeed, separation often merely prolongs the inevitable and increases both the emotional and financial costs of dissolving a marriage. All things considered, unless there is a legal or practical reason not to (such as living apart first to comply with state divorce laws), it usually is better to make a clear-minded decision about whether you want to end your marriage and then, if you do, proceed with a divorce.

Annulment

Only a small percentage of marriages are annulled—a legal procedure by which a marriage is "nullified" (dissolved) on the grounds that a valid marital relationship never existed. The grounds for annulment vary from state to state, but the most common are the following.

- Failure to consummate the marriage (refusal or inability of one or both spouses to engage in sexual intercourse with the other)
- Concealment of a drug/alcohol addiction, felony conviction, sexually transmitted disease, or impotency
- One or both have not reached the legal age of consent to marry
- Bigamy
- Incest

Most annulled marriages are of short duration (a few weeks or months), in which case property and debts are usually not subject to division. Some states do have provisions for distribution of assets and debts for annulled marriages of long duration (several years). Children of an annulled marriage, regardless of its duration, are always considered "legitimate," and most states have child custody and support provisions for such cases.

Ending a Domestic Partnership

When a married couple splits up, there are plenty of laws, legal precedents, and resources in place to assist and protect them. Not so for unmarried couples, especially same-sex partnerships.

Some states recognize common-law marriage (in which a heterosexual couple lives together as man and wife for a specified period of time) and treat it the same as a legal marriage in terms of property division and spousal support. In states that do not recognize common-law marriage, the spouse seeking a division of property, assignment of debts, and/or spousal maintenance must first establish that a written or verbal financial partnership existed between the husband and wife.

In states that recognize domestic partnerships, both gay and straight, certain benefits are granted to the partners if they split up. Such benefits might include health care, retirement funds, and inheritance rights. At this time, however, no federal benefits, such as tax, immigration, or Social Security, apply to domestic partnerships.

Currently, gay and lesbian marriages are legal in only one state, Massachusetts, and two states (Connecticut and Vermont) allow same-sex civil unions conveying the same legal rights as marriage. (You can get a current update on the Web site: *www.ncsl .org/programs/cyf/samesex.htm.*) In those states in which same-sex marriages are legal or such couples are given the legal equivalent of marriage, the divorce must take place in the state in which the couple was married. Theoretically, a partner in a same-sex marriage is supposed to receive the same rights in a divorce as a partner in a heterosexual marriage.

POW!

MARRIED WITHOUT A LICENSE

There are more than 4 million opposite-sex and more than half a million same-sex unmarried couples in the United States. According to one poll (Harris Interactive), 40 percent of U.S. adults live as unmarried, cohabiting couples at some time in their lives.

Children are always protected by child custody and support laws, whether or not the parents are married. For unmarried couples, however, it may be necessary to legally establish paternity or to verify the joint-adoption of any children in the relationship.

It is always wise for unmarried couples—whether gay or straight—to create a written, signed, and notarized financial/ property agreement early on in their relationship. Even with such a legal document, however, sorting out the financial details of a separation and then making them legal and enforceable in a court of law can be challenging.

Timing the First Bout

When do you step into the ring to initiate or respond to a legal action to divorce? For many women, that is a loaded question.

You don't want to strike until you've got all your personal, financial, and legal preparations in order. But neither do you want to delay the process, prolonging the misery of a difficult living situation or, worse, giving your spouse an opportunity to undermine or go ballistic on you before you can physically separate. Yet, if you're coming up on a holiday or special family event, such as Christmas or a high school graduation, or your family is in the midst of an unrelated crisis, such as the decline or death of a family member, you don't want to complicate matters.

Truth is, there is no good time to strike the starting bell of a divorce, but there are better and worse times. Carefully consider your options and how each might impact you, your spouse, your immediate family, and the divorce process itself. Discuss the timing of the divorce and any concerns you might have with your attorney and your closest confidantes. It is perfectly reasonable, and often prudent, to put your needs at the top of the list. Just be considerate of the other people involved. Above all, be safe.

You'll want your spouse to be as calm as possible when he gets the initial news. So hitting him with divorce papers when his mother is about to have major surgery or he is about to give a big presentation at work is probably not great timing. Neither is telling him in the heat of an argument or just before you leave him with the kids for a weeklong business trip.

POW!

UNMARRIED WITH CHILDREN
About 35 percent of all births are to unmarried women. The natural parents of 28 percent of American children never marry.

If you have any inkling your spouse could fly off the handle and become abusive toward you or your children when he learns you've filed or plan to file for divorce, don't risk it. Let your attorney arrange to have a letter of intent to divorce or the divorce summons delivered to him by a neutral third party, at a time when you and your children are not present. If need be, go to a safe place for a few days, where he will not be able to find you. Make sure to always inform your attorney of your actions and whereabouts so you do not do anything to harm your case.

POW!

OFF-SEASONS OF DIVORCE

Many couples physically separate and a large number of divorces are filed in January and late August through early September, just before the fall school session begins. Experts believe this is because these couples want to keep their families intact so as not to "ruin" and perhaps to enjoy one last holiday season (Thanksgiving through New Year's Eve) or summer vacation together.

A NICEY WIFEY (ALMOST) GETS WORKED OVER

Rose and Marshall were married for most of their adult lives, during which Marshall handled all of the couple's finances. They were in their seventies and their children grown when Marshall told Rose he wanted to separate and eventually divorce. As always, he "took care of the details" and had his business lawyer draw up a separation agreement. Rose dutifully signed the contract, reasoning that not hiring her own attorney would save money and trusting her husband of nearly thirty years.

Because Rose didn't retain her own legal counsel, didn't understand matrimonial law, and was upset and vulnerable at that time, she had no clue the separation agreement would be converted to the final divorce decree. She didn't realize the lawyer was looking out for Marshall's interests, not hers. She didn't know she was entitled to a complete list of all their marital assets, including bank accounts, brokerage accounts, and valuable property. She didn't even know Marshall had a pension, much less that she had a legal right to part of it. It never occurred to her that her husband might withhold such information or that she would need to enforce full disclosure.

Fortunately, once she'd recovered from the initial shock, Rose began to suspect that Marshall was hiding assets and that the separation agreement was unfair. So she wisely hired her own divorce attorney, who was able to convince the judge that:

- The agreement was one-sided.
- The lawyer who'd drawn up the separation agreement was biased and had shortchanged Rose in favor of Marshall.
- Rose's contributions to the marriage and financial dependency on Marshall had not been duly considered.
- Marshall had deliberately hidden assets that he was legally obligated to disclose.
- Rose was legally entitled to a substantially larger portion of the marital estate, including a portion of Marshall's pension as well as the mutual funds I discovered after a diligent search.
- Marshall was obligated to pay Rose monthly support payments.
- Because Rose had no money to pay for the legal assistance she clearly needed to prevent her dishonest spouse from working her over, Marshall would pay her attorney fees. ∎

Gloves Off! When Not to Hold Punches

There is one circumstance in which being aggressive is crucial, and that is when your or your children's safety is in question. No woman and no child should ever, under any circumstances, be subjected to the verbal, emotional, mental, physical, and/or sexual abuse of any spouse or domestic partner. Nor should they be put in harm's way by nature of that spouse's criminal activity or deviant behavior, such as substance abuse or animal abuse.

If there is any history, or a clear and present risk, of your spouse engaging in such behavior, you should take immediate and decisive action—though carefully—to secure and to ensure the safety and well-being of you and your children.

POW!

AN AMERICAN ABUSE EPIDEMIC

- At least one woman in every ten American couples is abused by her spouse.
- One-third of all women experience some form of physical assault by a romantic partner during adulthood.
- Twenty-eight percent of all violence against women is at the hands of their male partners.
- Four million women experience serious assault by a male partner during an average twelve-month period.

Circumstances Warranting a Swift Plan of Attack

If you are contemplating or are in the process of getting a divorce or separation and your spouse has engaged in any of the following harmful behaviors, I strongly advise you to take every legal and practical safety measure available to you:

- Physical violence or threatening to commit physical violence against anyone
- Spousal battery—verbal, emotional, psychological, physical, sexual
- Child abuse—verbal, emotional, psychological, physical, sexual
- Child endangerment—through the spouse's neglect or reckless, irresponsible, or deviant behavior
- Substance abuse
- Criminal activity
- Taking or threatening to take the child(ren) without the other parent's consent

- Attempted or threatened suicide
- Deliberate destruction of property or harming of pets in a tirade, out of spite, or as a form of punishment

Behavioral Cycle of an Abuser
The following phases often accompany an abuser:

Phase 1: Agitation—increased tension, anger, arguing, criticizing, blaming, complaining

Phase 2: Battering—verbal abuse; threatening physical harm; throwing, slamming, and/or breaking things; isolating; bullying; physically restraining; shoving, slapping, choking, kicking, and/or punching; sexual intimidation or abuse

Phase 3: Reparation—calm, often accompanied by "best behavior," apologizing, justifying, denying, "making up" with gifts and compliments, expressing remorse (crying), promising not to do it again and/or to get help

Such behavior is illegal and should not be tolerated under any circumstances. Perpetrators of domestic violence should not be given access to their victims and should be held accountable for their actions.

Priority One: Protecting Your Children and Yourself
The stress and strain of divorce can cause even a normally rational, stable, and kindhearted person to do and say nasty things. That does not give him (or her) license to cause harm to others or to put others in harm's way, and any such disruptive or hurtful behavior should be addressed directly and immediately. In the case of an otherwise benign and responsible person who does *not* have a history of abusive or deviant behavior, this can usually be accomplished simply by taking a temporary break

from one another and then discussing the situation and possible solutions later, after everyone has cooled off. Sometimes, a mediator may be necessary.

On the other hand, when the other spouse has a history or propensity for such detrimental behavior, a divorce or separation action is likely to incite him like a match to dynamite. In that case, legal steps and practical precautions should be taken before, during, and after the divorce/separation to protect all other family members.

Here are some general safety guidelines to follow when dealing with an unstable or volatile spouse:

- Keep your guard up for any signs of trouble and take reasonable measures to avert incidents that may be damaging to you or your children.
- Keep a journal of any incidents or threats of domestic violence, criminal activity, substance abuse, or other deviant behavior. Record the date, place, and specific nature of the incident or threat. Hide the journal where the perpetrator cannot access it.
- Establish an escape plan and an alternative escape plan—how you might leave (exit from home, method of transportation, time of day) and two places you might go (family, friend, neighbor, shelter) in the event you need to leave your home quickly.
- Have an extra set of house and car keys made and hide them where he is unlikely to find them but where you can get to them in the event he confiscates yours.
- Make a copy of important papers and keep the originals in a safe place, ready to grab and run with them, if necessary: birth certificates, Social Security cards, insurance policies, police records, passport, medical records, mortgage/lease, etc.
- Make sure you always have some cash, your driver's license, credit cards, ATM cards, current photos of children, address

book, medications, eyeglasses, hearing devices, and dentures on your person or within hand's reach.

- Pack a bag with enough clothing and personal supplies (for you and your children, if applicable) for a few days, and hide it in a safe place that you can easily access.
- Make an inventory (written, preferably with photos) of anything of real or sentimental value—photos, jewelry, family heirlooms, etc. Keep the list with your personal papers. Keep the items themselves in a safe place where you can easily retrieve them.
- Report any incidence of domestic violence or criminal activity to the authorities.
- Retain an excellent matrimonial attorney, preferably one with experience in representing clients in similar situations.
- Obtain a protective order.
- Physically separate from the perpetrator as soon as possible, using every available legal option and practical precaution.
- Ensure that the final divorce/separation agreement includes stipulations that protect you and your children after the divorce, as well as legal repercussions should violations occur.
- Report any postdivorce violations to the proper authorities.

Subsequent chapters discuss many of these safety measures in greater detail. But first, let's move on to next crucial step: preparing yourself for the journey ahead.

TKO!

DIVORCE MISTAKE #2

Letting emotions—guilt, loneliness, embarrassment, fear—affect your decisions.

Chapter 3

Conditioning for the Fight of Your Life

"Divorce is only less painful than the need for divorce."

—Jane O'Reilly, *The Girl I Left Behind*

WHEN YOUR MARRIAGE FALLS apart, it can feel like you and your whole world are falling apart, too. But in the throes of divorce, you simply cannot afford to break down and allow other aspects of your life to fall to the wayside. If left unchecked, the stress of a divorce can wear you out and break your heart, debilitating you to the point that you make poor decisions and expose your most vulnerable spots to your opponent. And you must believe that, once the process is in motion, your spouse *will* be your opponent. Letting your guard down or letting your emotions override your good judgment can have devastating consequences that affect the rest of your life.

As frightened and fragile as you might feel—and you'll probably, and justifiably, be very scared and shaken—it is imperative to your and your children's welfare that you keep yourself together, keep your wits about you, and keep your dukes up from start to finish. To ensure you'll have the strength and stamina to go the full nine rounds of divorce—while continuing to take care of your kids, home, bills, job, etc.—you'll need to get and stay in peak fighting condition, emotionally, physically, and financially. This means taking care of *you*—so that you can take care of business. Remember: you can't keep your life afloat and your kids from going under if you're too wiped out to swim and don't have a lifeline of your own.

Psyching Up for the Fight

What we believe and how we think greatly influence every important decision we make and every action we take in life—and divorce is no exception. For example, if you believe you are powerless or that being assertive is futile or unbecoming, you are likely to choose the path of least resistance and not fight for, or even recognize, what is in your best interests. If you feel like a victim—and, granted, it's hard not to when your spouse has cheated on you, mistreated you, messed up your finances, or done something else to harm you—you are apt to be so busy licking your wounds that you do little or nothing to thwart the attack, much less fight back. If you tell yourself the odds are stacked against you, that you're no match for your husband, that you haven't a prayer of holding your own, much less winning, you'll probably let your opponent pummel you . . . and get exactly the negative results you predicted.

Champions don't think like that. If you were to look inside the mind of any champion, you would see a clear image of her goal and the things she needs to do to reach it. You would also see her solid belief that she has a fighting chance of winning and her fierce determination to do whatever it takes to reach her goal. Champions get their heads and hearts in the right place, get physically and practically prepared for the bout, and then go for it.

In deciding to end your marriage (or how to respond to your spouse's decision to end it) and in envisioning the best possible outcome for you and your family, as outlined in Chapters 1 and 2, you've brought your goal into focus. Now, you'll need to move forward with the attitude, mindset, and focus of a champion.

For starters, it might help to believe and know that:

- You and your children can get through this and be okay—and so can your spouse.
- You have the resources—within yourself and available to you—to create a better, rather than a bitter, end.
- You deserve and are entitled to a safe and secure life during and after a divorce or separation.
- You are not solely responsible for the break up of the marriage—even if you're divorcing a "basically good guy." And the divorce isn't the result of a single incident—even if he's divorcing you for a "good reason."
- You are not responsible for your spouse's feelings, actions, or welfare—beyond following the letter of the law and common decency.
- You have the right to fair and civil treatment by your spouse, his attorney, and the courts.

Of course, all that is easier said than done when everything you've worked hard to build seems to be crashing down around you and your emotions are on a wild roller-coaster ride. That's why shoring up your defense and support systems now is so important.

Marshaling Your Resources

Rarely in life will you need more inner fortitude and outside support than when going through a divorce. Interestingly, many women seem to instinctively know this and start paying closer attention to their well-being—for example, by exercising, rekindling friendships, or pursuing personal interests. Some women, though, become withdrawn and depressed and often neglect their health, finances, appearances, and relationships. A few go to the other extreme, recklessly seeking comfort and self-gratification in all the wrong places—excessive partying, irresponsible spending, extramarital affairs. That kind of behavior can only be detrimental to the woman, her children, and her matrimonial case.

Just like a prizefighter, you'll gain the best advantage and sustain the least amount of damage by being fit and nimble and having a reliable team in your corner.

Strengthen Mind, Body, Spirit

Now is a good time to attend to any health issues, to eat nutritiously, and to engage in some form of regular physical activity. Exercise of any kind—be it walking, gardening, boxing, or mowing the lawn—helps reduce the negative biological and psychological effects of stress. Combined with eating properly, exercise will also help boost your confidence and energy, both of which you'll need in ample amounts.

Getting enough R and R is also of benefit when you're under duress. Any activity that enables you to de-stress and tune in to your "inner voice"—such as prayer, meditation, journaling, yoga, or simply taking a warm bath—will help you to make better decisions and to cope with the emotional rough patches that are part and parcel of divorce. Likewise, good self-help and inspirational books and magazines can help alleviate confusion and bolster your resolve.

Though having a good time might be the last thing on your mind right now, pleasure is one of the most effective anecdotes for emotional pain and turmoil. So make a point of doing things you enjoy—both in solitude and with people you care about. And when the pressure starts building, take a short time-out.

POW!

ONLY THE LONELY
A random poll of 8,600 adults revealed that 20.4 percent of the divorced respondents and 29.6 percent of the separated respondents felt *less* lonely than they had while married.

Your Personal Support Team

Around every champion is a circle of loyal supporters who believe in her, console her, and help her. When she gets knocked down, they pull her up. When she feels like giving up, they encourage her to go on. When she missteps, they set her straight and get her back on track. When she's overpowered, they step in to protect her. When she triumphs, they celebrate her victory.

You need the same kind of relief team of people you trust and count on for guidance, assistance, and emotional support. Choose and approach each with care and caution to make sure he or she is truly in your corner and there's no risk of that person switching sides or tipping off your husband, innocently or otherwise. If in doubt, leave that individual out. Definitely steer clear of people who like to gossip or have betrayed your trust in the past.

Your team should be people you know well and who know you well and have been supportive in other capacities. Think of the different types of support you might need—a safe harbor if things get heated; a shoulder to cry on; a wise counsel; a babysitter for your kids; a money lender in a financial pinch; a corroborative witness to testify on your behalf if the need arises. Identify the person you'd feel most comfortable turning to in each instance. Then have a confidential heart-to-heart with your team members to let them know what's going on and the type of support you might need from them and to ensure they're willing and able to help.

You'll need at least one confidante you can tell everything to and at least one levelheaded friend or family member to go to for advice. Your confidante and advisor can be the same person or different people; just make sure your support system includes people who can fulfill both of these needs.

In your confidante you'll want someone who will listen and provide comfort and reasoned opinions, but not necessarily direction. After all, dear friends and relations tend to tell us what we want to hear, which is not always what we need to hear, and that's okay. Everyone needs to vent and to have a cheer-leader sometimes.

But when it comes to legal, financial, or other practical advice, you need facts and unbiased, informed opinions. So among your advisors you'll want someone who will be brutally honest with you and who is intelligent, rational, insightful, and knowledge-able about the issue in question, whether legal or financial.

You don't need a mob standing at the ready to assist you, and you shouldn't broadcast your situation to a large number of people. Confide and rely only on the few people you really need to, and no one else, at least until the legal procedure is underway, if not final. Later, when the news becomes public, some of those friends and relations you did not confide in might feel slighted and may even be miffed at you. If you explain that you were merely following the advice of your attorney (or this one) and trying to do what was best for you and your family, most of your friends, certainly your true friends, will understand.

Sometimes, friends you didn't think to ask for support will come forward on their own to offer a lending hand or soft place to fall. It's interesting how during major transitions in life, like divorce, a new and unexpected relationship can blossom with someone you least expect—a casual acquaintance, distant fam-ily member, or even a coworker. When people take it upon themselves to help you, accept their support—but only if you're comfortable doing so and certain of their discretion and loyalty to you.

It is not uncommon for someone going through a divorce to feel a connection with her attorney. While your lawyer should be sensitive and empathetic, her job is to provide legal—not personal—counsel. No attorney is qualified to be a surrogate therapist, and seeking emotional support from an attorney is not only ineffective and inappropriate, it's expensive. You pay for your attorney's time; use it wisely and appropriately.

Never allow yourself to become romantically involved with anyone helping you through a divorce or separation—especially not an attorney, social worker, financial advisor, or other professional involved in the proceedings. You should also use caution when entering into or conducting an existing romantic relationship with anyone. There is usually no harm in dating, in terms of its effect on your divorce, provided you are already physically separated from your spouse, behave appropriately in front of any children, and don't misuse any marital property.

TKO!

DIVORCE MISTAKE #3
Not asking for or allowing help from family, friends, and others.

The Support of Strangers

As helpful as close friends and relations can be during this difficult time, you might also need or want the comfort and consultation of a more impartial party. Many women find that it is beneficial to see a mental health professional and/or to talk with other women who are going through or have recently gone through a divorce.

Professionals Who Can Help

Ending a marriage and breaking up a family is a wrenching, confusing, and exhausting experience that can pummel the psyche and stun the spirit of the most balanced and upbeat person. Yet, staying cool and collected is vital to making good choices and to sustaining an acceptable quality of life for your family during a divorce. Many women find that consulting with a mental health professional gives them the added support they need to prepare for a divorce and to keep them steady during the divorce.

While time and money are often in short supply, it is invaluable to have a neutral and confidential professional helping you sort out and cope with the mishmash of feelings, thoughts, and demands bearing down on you. Therapy will also help keep emotional baggage from interfering with your decision-making or exacerbating unpleasant or potentially volatile situations with your husband. The cleaner and quicker the divorce proceedings, the better for everyone involved (including children) and the sooner you can begin healing and rebuilding your life.

Your therapist's expert opinion might also be useful in the divorce proceedings, helping you to get a quick and favorable settlement. A therapist can also give you tools for dealing effectively with your spouse, both during and after the divorce, with regard to paying bills, physically separating, and coparenting your children. If you have kids, you and your ex-spouse will need to coordinate parenting time and interact at their school, sports, and other activities—including graduations and weddings—for years to come. A therapist can give you techniques for handling anger and hurt—yours, your spouse's, or your kids—so you can avoid or diffuse confrontations and other damaging behaviors.

For these and other reasons—among them, just feeling better and saving your energy for the battle ahead—I strongly suggest that you consult with a therapist for at least a few sessions, if not regularly throughout and immediately after the divorce. As a matrimonial lawyer, I've seen out-of-control emotions foul up a woman's case time and again. Without an appropriate emotional outlet, you, too, could bend to an unfair settlement out of guilt, emotional exhaustion, or low self-esteem. Or you could sabotage negotiations or refuse a fair settlement out of anger, irrationality, or confusion. Or you could urge your attorney to file frivolous motions to spite your spouse. Not only could this prolong the process and inflate divorce costs, it could also leave you with a less favorable child custody and financial arrangement.

In choosing a therapist or other mental health professional, such as a psychologist or social worker, always check credentials to make sure the person is qualified. It's also a good idea to briefly interview a few different prospects over the phone to get a feel for whether the two of you will click. If you feel uncomfortable with the therapist after a few visits, you can always change to another. But don't expect immediate and complete relief from negative emotions. Therapy is a treatment, not a cure. Only with time and the absence or reduction in your life of the cause of your angst will you heal completely.

Support Groups

Most cities (or counties) have women's divorce groups that meet periodically, usually weekly or monthly, offering group members a forum to share experiences and support one another. Often, some group members form close friendships that go beyond the parameters of the group. But the main benefit of a group is that it provides "strength in numbers," on the premise that women going through divorce need to know they're not alone and they're not "bad" people.

The central purpose of a group is twofold:

1. To help women get through the divorce process
2. To help women recover emotionally as well as practically (self-improvement, career development, single parenting, dating, etc.) after a divorce

Support groups usually welcome women at all stages of the process—from those merely courting the idea to those who are well into the process of rebuilding their lives. Having divorce veterans in a group can be particularly reassuring and helpful to women in the early stages of a divorce or separation.

Many groups are "self-help" and run by divorced women with little or no professional training. While technically these groups do not provide therapy, they can be very therapeutic and serve a valid and beneficial purpose. Other groups are facilitated by a mental health professional and can be a good, cost-effective alternative to individual therapy while also providing the benefit of the "we're-in-this-together" group support.

There are also divorce support groups comprised of both men and women. These groups are fine for socializing—*after* your divorce is final and you're back on your feet emotionally. They're usually ineffective and can even be harmful before and during a divorce, when you are emotionally vulnerable. All too often, members in coed divorce groups get romantically involved, and it very rarely turns out well, can add emotional upset at a time when you need to be focused, and can mess up your divorce case.

TKO!

DIVORCE MISTAKE #4
Confiding too much and to the wrong people.

Getting Your Bucks in a Row

When it comes to money, ignorance is not bliss, especially during a divorce. Being oblivious to or careless about your finances is a surefire way to complicate your divorce case and batter your financial future. In later chapters, we'll go step-by-step through the preparations and processes required to protect yourself from any financial shenanigans your husband might pull and to secure an equitable financial settlement. For now, let's focus on your financial survival during the divorce process.

Interim Cash-Flow Projections

One of the top three concerns of most women is how they will survive financially during the divorce. (The other two major concerns are how they will survive financially after the divorce and child custody.)

It is a valid worry, given that:

- The woman's household income usually drops substantially as soon as the divorce process begins.
- The woman usually retains at least temporary custody of any children and absorbs the majority of child-related expenses during the divorce process.
- The woman's living expenses often increase during this same period, due to the legal costs and expenses associated with the divorce, such as added costs for child care and professional services previously handled by her husband.
- Women, on average, earn 22 percent less than men.

Although those realities can make you feel like burying your head in the sand, you cannot afford to do that. Instead, you should look your finances square in the eye and come up with an interim strategy for surviving until you can secure the divorce settlement you need and deserve. This is not the in-depth financial profile you'll need to prepare for your attorney, which is covered in Chapter 5. What you need to do right now, before you do anything else, is figure out how much money you need to cover your (and your children's) basic living expenses and where that money is going to come from.

Here's a fairly simple method for doing this:

1. Create a schedule of all your monthly living expenses—such as food, gas, utilities, clothing, child care, medical, haircuts, etc.—and all your monthly bills—including mortgage or rent, car loans, credit cards, car insurance, health insurance, etc. Specify the amount of each item and any payment due dates. If you and your spouse divvy up expenses, indicate who normally covers what.

2. Create a list of all your household income sources, including from employment income (including your spouse's), bank accounts (checking, savings, money market), businesses you own or co-own, rental property, dividends, child support from a former spouse, etc.

3. Create a list of any other potential sources of funds that might be available to you, such as from retirement accounts, trust funds, jewelry or other personal valuables you could liquidate, etc. Specify the source, the amount, whether it is owned jointly with your husband, and whether it is legally available to you without his knowledge and permission.

4. Create a best-case scenario in which your husband assumes responsibility for specific debts and/or expenses and contributes a specific amount of support (child and/or spousal) to you.

5. Create a worst-case scenario in which your husband pays none of your household expenses and none of your monthly bills.

6. Evaluate both the best-case and worst-case scenarios to determine whether you'll have enough money to get by until the official financial settlement is determined. If not, how might you obtain additional funds and/or reduce your debt/expenses? Identify any potential emergency financial relief options, such as cashing in a 401(k) or selling a luxury item. Determine whether you'll need your attorney to ask the court to grant you emergency financial relief while the divorce is pending.

However rosy or glum these best-case and worst-case scenarios might be, remember that the settlement you end up with will most likely be somewhere in between the two. Don't let these initial projections discourage or intimidate you. The law is designed to give both parties an equitable settlement; it is up to you and your attorney to make sure that the letter of the law is carried out.

PROACTION: THE BEST FIRST STEP TOWARD MENDING A BROKEN HEART

Carla and Jeff had been married for fifteen years and had two children. Carla was a homemaker and part-time bookkeeper; Jeff worked on Wall Street. Carla was extremely angry with her husband when she found out her husband was cheating on her with a woman half her age. She also felt depressed and rejected. But she did not allow her emotions to get the better of her. Instead, she got the help she needed so that she could focus on making good decisions with her divorce.

Carla saw a therapist and relied on a good support team of close friends and family to help her get through the rough patches. She also prepared well for her divorce by utilizing a financial planner to determine her budget for the future and to analyze the assets and debts of the marriage. She provided her attorney with all the necessary financial documents and a future budget. Consequently, Carla came out of the divorce with a good divorce settlement and a healthy emotional outlook, prepared emotionally and financially to move forward with her life. ∎

Preliminary Financial Precautions

Money is usually the thing most men focus on—and most women neglect—in planning and preparing for a divorce. It is also one of the most common ways in which estranged husbands take revenge on their spouse or look out for themselves at the expense of their spouses (and sometimes their kids).

Listed on the following page are several things you can do to protect your financial interests before filing for divorce or immediately upon learning that your husband might or has filed for divorce or separation.

- Pay off and close as many unsecured joint debts as possible, especially credit cards and lines of credit.
- Close any low-balance and inactive joint accounts.
- Establish a bank account in your name only.
- Get a current copy of your and your spouse's credit reports (all three bureaus). Take action to correct any discrepancies; look for any debts you were unaware of; make note of any negative marks perpetuated by your husband alone.
- Take inventory of and keep a close watch for any unusual withdrawals or changes in any assets—checking and savings accounts, life insurance, inheritance, personal property, etc.
- Check the balances of all debts, particularly credit cards and open lines of credit, and keep close tabs on those balances, so that you can quickly catch and address any excessive or unusual activity.
- Don't create any new debt or make large purchases with your husband.
- Avoid making new personal debt (without your husband), doing so only if absolutely necessary.
- If you currently pay any of your husband's bills, try to get him to pay them himself, being careful not to upset the apple cart. As a word of caution: if you're both on the loan or you live in a community-property state, you are equally liable for his bills until the divorce is final unless your divorce settlement stipulates otherwise.
- Stash cash. Put aside as much money as you can, preferably in an account in your name only and that your spouse knows nothing about.

Studies have shown that although women handle most of the month-to-month budgeting and bill-paying, they tend to think in the short-term when it comes to money. They typically leave the long-term investments, financial planning, and money management to their husbands. While married, women often have a false sense of financial security, when, in reality, they live month to month if not paycheck to paycheck, regardless of the amount of their monthly income or personal paychecks. Consequently, women in all income brackets often find themselves in serious cash-flow trouble when their financial rug is pulled out from under them during a divorce.

Don't be a statistic and don't be caught off-guard, unsure of your financial footing and struggling to support yourself and your children. You will be much better off doing this initial homework for the short-term and then preparing to fight for a settlement that will ensure your secure financial future, as outlined in forthcoming chapters.

TKO!

DIVORCE MISTAKE #5
Not knowing your financial situation.

Chapter 4

Better Your Odds:
Beef Up Your Legal Muscle

"One hires a lawyer as one hires a plumber: because one wants to keep one's hands off the beastly drains."

—Amanda Cross, *The Questions of Max*

THE LAWS GOVERNING DIVORCE and separation are numerous and complex. To complicate matters, the rules vary from state to state and county to county. Entering the divorce ring without sufficient legal clout in your corner is apt to leave you dazed and confused and could lead to a disastrous outcome. Yet, women often fail to get the legal support they need—either because they're too trusting or naive, believing their spouse won't fight dirty, or because they believe that they know enough to fend for themselves without legal counsel. More often, however, it's because they fear they can't afford a lawyer. Legal fees can be expensive, and the more complicated and fiercely contested the divorce, the higher the cost. But in reality, and especially in adversarial divorces, few women can afford not to retain legal counsel, and failing to do so can end up costing far more than retaining appropriate legal council would have.

That does not mean all women need to, or should, run out and hire a high-dollar, cutthroat lawyer. Indeed, my advice is to steer clear of reputed "barracudas," because they tend to excel in confrontation rather than negotiation. When you're deal-ing with a contentious spouse and a messy divorce, you need an attorney who is aggressive, not antagonistic, and who fights smart, not recklessly.

Though most divorces are contested, 90 to 95 percent are settled without having to go to trial—and the majority, whether contested or not, are settled with the help of attorneys. That said, not all women need a lawyer to handle every aspect of the divorce or separation. In some circumstances, you can do some of it yourself and retain an attorney to advise you, ham-mer out any sticky issues, and negotiate the final settlement. I must stress, however, that this approach is *not* advisable in high-risk cases—such as those involving an abusive spouse, a custody battle, or substantial amounts of assets or debts. On the flip side, if the split is simple and amicable, you might be fine with a do-it-yourself (DIY) divorce. Even then, however, I strongly recom-mend consulting with an attorney at least once or twice.

To Do or Not to Do It Yourself

The cost of a divorce, including attorney costs, can range from a few thousand dollars for an uncontested case to five figures for a contested case. So it is no wonder that some people are inter-ested in going the do-it-yourself divorce route. A *pro se* divorce—in which both parties agree 100 percent on every aspect of the divorce and then complete and file all the legal documents themselves (without the aid of an attorney)—can save money and expedite the divorce process. But DIY divorce is advisable for only a small percentage of divorces and separations. In many cases, going it alone without legal representation can be a seri-ous mistake with devastating consequences.

Sometimes, though, self-representation is workable. It is usu-ally safe to do it yourself—or mostly yourself with some consul-tation from a legal aid service and/or an attorney—if you can answer a certain *yes* to *all* of the following conditions:

○ You and your spouse have contributed equally to the household and/or agree on the quantified contribution of each to the household.

○ You and your spouse have no minor children together or agree on all issues pertaining to child custody, child visitation, child rearing, child support, etc. This should include a detailed *parenting plan* outlining all aspects of the child's life, now and in the future.

○ There is no history or threat of abuse, intimidation, or battery (against either spouse or any children in the home).

○ You and your spouse have relatively little marital and personal property and/or agree on the division of all property.

○ You and your spouse have relatively little debt and/or agree on the distribution of all debt.

○ You and your spouse are confidant neither has failed to disclose all assets and debts.

○ You and your spouse mutually agree to divorce or separate.

○ You and your spouse mutually agree to all the details of physically separating.

○ Neither you nor your spouse is on active military service.

○ Neither you nor your spouse has retained an attorney or filed any legal documents relative to the divorce or separation (including temporary orders) with the courts.

○ No bankruptcy is pending or impending.

○ You and your spouse are both capable of supporting yourselves and/or agree to any spousal support arrangement.

○ The settlement provides adequately for the immediate and long-term welfare of any minor children.

○ You and your spouse both feel the settlement is fair and prudent, are mentally and emotionally capable of making that assessment, and were not coerced into agreeing to any terms.

○ You and your spouse have documented all the stipulations of your divorce or separation, you have both signed and dated the document, and it has been notarized.

You will need to complete a substantial amount of complicated paperwork, file it appropriately with the court, and pay the required fees. Although county clerks are usually willing to provide some direction, it is not their job to help you complete your paperwork or to counsel you on matrimonial law and the particulars of your case. If you need that kind of advice or help, you should hire an attorney for at least one consultation or, if your income is low enough, consult with your local legal aid service.

You should also be aware that although the legal system is generally accommodating to people who choose to handle their own divorces, there is still strong resistance to self-help divorces in some areas of the country. If you happen to live in one of those areas, you could encounter unhelpful or even hostile attorneys, judges, and court clerks. In that case, your best bet is to hire an attorney who is willing to assist you in doing as much as possible yourself and to deal with the courts on your behalf.

Every state has its own forms, processes, and fee structures. You can get a list of the forms you'll need and information on processes and fees from your local court clerk's office. Many courts also offer preprinted forms for some, if not all, of the required divorce documents. Alternatively, you can purchase legal forms from a local office supply store or an online store; just make sure you get the right forms for your state and county.

You and your spouse will also likely need to appear before the judge for a divorce hearing, in which case you'll need to be prepared to answer specific questions. In some courts, a divorce can be granted by *affidavit* without both (or sometimes either) spouse appearing in court.

Finding out whether or not you need to appear in court and figuring out which forms you need and how to fill them out and file them can be daunting. To avoid mistakes and to ensure against annoying clerks and judges, I suggest you research your county's requirements and processes before you start the action and that you hire an attorney to at least review your finished paperwork before you submit it. Most will charge a reasonable hourly fee for this service, and paying for a good matrimonial attorney's time and expertise to make sure you're on the right track will be money well spent.

Of course, if things get too complicated, conflict arises, or other unforeseen circumstances throw a wrench in the works, you can always retain an attorney to handle the sticky portion of the case or to take it from there. And if your spouse files any legal documents on his own volition or retains an attorney at any time during the DIY divorce process, you should seek legal assistance pronto.

When DIY Divorce Can Be Dumb, Detrimental, or Dangerous

Getting a divorce or separation without legal representation is unwise under any of the following conditions:

- Either spouse is accused of physical, sexual, or nonphysical abuse (verbal, emotional, psychological) against the partner
- Either spouse is accused of physical, sexual, or nonphysical abuse of a child, child endangerment, or child neglect
- The parental fitness or responsibility of either parent is called into question
- Either spouse is accused of abandonment, gross neglect, or irresponsible behavior that undermines the stability of the home
- Either spouse has a criminal record or is accused of engaging in criminal activity
- Either spouse has a history of or is accused of substance abuse, including alcohol and prescription drugs
- Either spouse has a physical or mental impairment or critical health problem
- Either spouse is an illegal immigrant
- Both or either spouse is financially overextended and/or in the process or on the verge of bankruptcy

- Both or either spouse owns a business (privately held)
- Either spouse has a history of financial irresponsibility or defaulting on court-ordered financial payments, such as child support
- Either spouse has a history of willful unemployment or underemployment
- Either spouse is known or suspected to have hidden assets
- Either spouse is known or suspected to have made debts without the other's knowledge and consent
- Either spouse has moved or threatened to move to another county, state, or country
- Either spouse has threatened to take any minor children
- Either spouse has threatened suicide
- Either spouse has threatened violence against any family member or family friend
- Either spouse has attempted to manipulate, influence, coerce, or terrorize the other spouse into agreeing to any terms and conditions of the divorce (or marriage, for that matter)
- Either spouse has attempted to manipulate, influence, coerce, or terrorize any minor children or to turn the child against the other parent
- Either spouse has threatened not to comply with the stipulations of the final agreement—whether child support, child custody, leaving the family home, paying assigned debts, etc.
- Either spouse is being argumentative, aggressive, combative, intimidating, unkind, or disrespectful to the other spouse
- Either spouse has sought legal counsel and/or already begun the legal divorce process
- A trusted confidante and/or legal advisor has strongly suggested you hire an attorney

The Best One-Two Combination:
Legal Brains + Legal Brawn

When a couple heads down the rocky road to separation or divorce, each must begin the transformation from partner to ex—with separate needs, wants, interests, and lives. That means feeling, thinking, and behaving as an individual rather than as a team. Often, you must force yourself to make choices and act on them independent of your husband long before you actually feel separate from him. A strong support team can help you navigate the emotional side of that road—and a good matrimonial attorney can steer you down the legal side.

In an ideal world, especially one involving children, you and your spouse would sit down together and calmly, compassionately, and considerately decide how to end your marriage; divide up all the bills and property; be respective, if not supportive, of one another; and coparent your children all the way through their college years. In real life, people can and often do get petty and nasty during a breakup. Some, especially those who view divorce as a personal rejection or negative reflection on them, can get aggressive, defensive, selfish, and vindictive. A good attorney offers the best protection against such attacks and the best assurance of securing a fair settlement no matter what your spouse's response.

POW!

SOCIAL ACCEPTANCE

Only 25 percent of U.S. households consist of the traditional family: a married couple and their children. Of the other 75 percent, most include at least one divorced adult. As abnormal as a divorce or separation might feel when you're going through it, in most social circles divorced households now comprise the majority and include millions of decent, "normal" people.

Experienced matrimonial lawyers are familiar with the laws, procedures, court systems, court clerks, judges, other divorce attorneys, and precedent-setting cases in your area. They are also dialed into federal divorce laws and guidelines as well as local government agencies, mental health professionals, and financial analysts that may be called upon in a divorce. A good divorce attorney will have good working relationships with all the important players within your jurisdiction's legal system.

It is almost always in a woman's best interests to at least consult with an attorney—and her own attorney. You must not delude yourself into thinking that your husband's attorney or your family lawyer is going to adequately represent both of you. A single lawyer cannot represent the best interests of more than one person.

If you are still questioning whether you need an attorney, ask yourself what the risks are and what the costs would be of not getting the settlement you want and need. For instance, is there any chance your spouse will seek and might get custody? If so, would that be in your child (or children's) best interests? Is he willing to contribute to their medical, child care, and college expenses? Will the financial terms your spouse is likely to want and could get shortchange you, depriving you of property and income you are entitled to and need to survive after the divorce? Will he refuse to move out of your family home? Will you have to sell it? Is he unwilling or unlikely to agree to an equitable distribution of assets, including pension plans and any businesses he or the two of you own, putting you at a financial disadvantage for years to come? Are you certain he will meet any debts that he should pay and not stick you with them? Is there any chance he will refuse or renege on your bottom-line settlement needs and requests? If he's amenable to a fair settlement now, will he continue to be so if he changes jobs or remarries?

A contentious and unpredictable spouse is not the only reason most people need a good divorce attorney. Just as our lives have become more complex, so, too, have the laws that determine how a shared life is best divided into two separate lives. Some laws are even deliberately designed to discourage divorce or to force a particular outcome, which might not be favorable for one or either party. Another potential problem, though rare, is the possibility that the judge and even court clerks could favor one attorney or one spouse over another, which can make a case more difficult.

A good matrimonial attorney will provide the legal expertise you need to make good decisions and has the legal power to get those decisions implemented in court.

THE HIGH COST OF INADEQUATE LEGAL REPRESENTATION

Rebecca was a dedicated violin teacher and devoted mother engaged in a protracted custody battle with the father of her son in which she was represented by a court-appointed lawyer. About six years into the process, the local child welfare agency found the father to be neglectful because he had rented out his son's bedroom, forcing the child to sleep in the same bedroom with him and his new wife. They had sex in front of the boy; they also allowed him to watch violent movies until late at night. Consequently, the father was limited to an hour of supervised visitation per week.

These events, along with the custody battle, took a toll on the boy. He began misbehaving in school, and after revealing suicidal thoughts, he was hospitalized for several short periods. It was then determined he would have to attend a special school two hours away.

Rebecca and her son spent every summer with her parents across the country. The boy's behavior and emotional well-being improved dramatically during these visits with his loving grandparents. Even his court-appointed legal guardian agreed he did much better with his grandparents. The educational and therapeutic options were also better for him there. At the end of one summer, he did not want to return home.

However, the judge assigned to the case did not want the boy to remain out of state. So when Rebecca appeared in court after the summer without her son, who remained with his grand-parents, the judge was irate. He held Rebecca in contempt of court and sent her to jail, where she remained for three months.

Meanwhile, the boy's grandparents went to their local court, and the judge there granted them custody of the boy. That is when Rebecca hired me. I immediately went before the court and argued that the judge had gone too far by punishing Rebecca so severely simply for leaving her son with his grand-parents, where he was clearly better off. Within hours, Rebecca was freed from jail. Soon after, she joined her son and his grand-parents at their home.

However, the custody case was not yet over and was still being handled by the same judge. A few days after Rebecca's release, he ordered her back to jail. His clerk even left a threaten-ing message on her parents' voice mail! An emergency motion stopped the order, and after a lot of hard work, a new judge was assigned to the case. This judge eventually granted Rebecca custody and allowed her and her son to live with her parents, where her son was thriving.

Had Rebecca known her rights and retained a good lawyer from the beginning, her custody case might have lasted nine months rather than six years. And it would have spared much of the emo-tional turmoil that she and her young son went through. ■

Teaming Up with a Kick-Ass (So Yours Won't Get Kicked) Lawyer

Just to be clear: the objective is *not* to hire an attorney whose MO is to kick your spouse's behind. The objective is to retain a reputable lawyer who will work assertively and skillfully, but also ethically, to protect yours. You want an attorney who is an expert negotiator and problem-solver. Of course, if your spouse or his attorney tries to fight dirty, you also want an attorney who knows when to take off the kid gloves and how to get it on in the courtroom.

Even if you use a mediator (as discussed in Chapter 6), you still need your own attorney. A mediator is a neutral third party whose job it is to help the two spouses come to agreement on the main disputed issues of a divorce or separation. A mediator does not provide legal advice or services to either of the individual parties. So you'll want your own attorney to at least review the mediated settlement and to guide you through the filing and court process. If the mediation comes to a stalemate, your attorney can represent you in negotiating whatever issues mediation was unable to resolve.

In addition to providing you with legal advice and assistance, she will also keep you on the straight and narrow. For example, she'll remind you that hanging on to the crystal vase may not be worth possibly losing the car. She'll strongly suggest that bending to your spouse's pitiful pleas for unrestricted visitation when his habitual drug use would endanger your child (or children) is not looking out for their welfare.

How to Find the Right Attorney for You

Your lawyer will be your legal trainer, legal coach, and legal manager all rolled into one. She'll help prepare you for the fight. She'll advise and guide you through each round. She'll advocate, negotiate, and duke out the details on your behalf. Not all divorce attorneys are created equal, though, and you'll want to make sure you hook up with someone who is up to snuff and suits you. To that end, I suggest the following three-step approach to finding and hiring an attorney:

1. Check around to get the names of a few matrimonial lawyers in your area. Female friends and colleagues as well as women's support groups are good sources.
2. Interview two or three candidates over the phone to determine whether each meets the basic qualifications of a good matrimonial attorney.

3. Have a preliminary consultation with your top choice to determine whether the attorney is right for you and is willing to take your case. If not, have a preliminary consultation with another candidate.

The most common and arguably the best way to find a good matrimonial lawyer is through personal recommendations. Nothing is quite as assuring and revealing as a word-of-mouth endorsement that comes from or through someone you know and trust. This might be family, friends, coworkers, neighbors, or professionals with firsthand knowledge of divorce attorneys in your area, such as a therapist, your children's pediatrician, financial advisor, business attorney, social worker, legal aid volunteer, or a domestic violence center staff member.

Another option is to call your state and/or local bar association for a list of lawyers specializing in matrimonial law in your area. Keep in mind that these are dues-paying membership organizations that simply maintain a referral list of members in good standing. Bar associations are not consumer advocate organizations, and they do not base their referrals on the ability or track record of the lawyers. However, the American Bar Association can tell you whether a particular attorney is a member (and most practicing lawyers are) or has been disciplined or disbarred. That helps rule out the bad eggs but isn't very helpful in identifying the good ones.

A third strategy is to contact your local courthouse to find out which judges hear divorce cases and when upcoming hearings are scheduled. Then go to a few hearings and watch different lawyers in action. If any impress you, the clerk or bailiff should be able to tell you the attorney's name.

Probably the least effective method of finding an attorney is going through the telephone directory and simply picking whoever jumps out at you. If that is your only source, select five or six potential candidates to investigate.

Actually, I encourage you to thoroughly check out any attorney you might be thinking of hiring, including those that you hear about through a personal referral. You should look for certain essential qualifications and then interview two or three candidates to determine which one is the best fit for you.

There has been much discussion about whether it is better for a woman to retain a female or male lawyer. Some people feel a woman is better represented by a male divorce attorney who has a better understanding of how men think and who is unlikely to be accused by opposing counsel of playing the feminist card. Others feel a female attorney is better able to empathize with a woman client and will work harder for her "sister." In my experience and opinion, it doesn't matter whether your attorney is a man or a woman. What matters is that the attorney you choose is well qualified and the right fit for you. A good matrimonial lawyer should meet these basic qualifications:

Specialization in matrimonial law. Your attorney must have current and sufficient experience in handling divorces, custody issues, and the various legal issues associated with marriage and the dissolution of marriages. If you are ending a domestic partnership, make sure the attorney has handled similar cases. If she also practices other types of law, such as criminal, real estate, estate, or business law, this might be helpful to you, too, depending on the issues in your case, but it isn't necessary. Specialization in divorce law is essential.

Track record of successful out-of-court and trial settlements. The best matrimonial lawyer is one who is both a practiced negotiator and a skilled litigator. You want a consummate pro with the demonstrated ability to work toward and recognize a good settlement offer as well as the proven capability to know when not to compromise and how to argue your case in court for the best possible outcome.

Local judicial experience and expertise. Your lawyer should have considerable experience in practicing matrimonial law in your area. She should have a solid working knowledge of state and county laws, the local judicial system, local judges, and other lawyers in your area. She should also be familiar with local government agencies, nonprofit organizations, and other resources associated with matrimonial and family law cases.

Experience handling issues specific to your situation. If you're facing a nasty custody battle, you want an attorney who has successfully represented women with similar cases. The same goes for any other critical aspect of your case—whether it be alimony, palimony, domestic violence, abandonment, complicated property settlements involving businesses or substantial wealth, or whatever. Be leery, though, of attorneys who promise the moon and "no problems"; make sure cockiness is not a substitute for competence.

Established, efficient legal practice. Good lawyers are always in demand, so the fact that an attorney has a busy roster is a good sign. At the same time, however, your attorney should not be so busy that she is unable to answer your calls promptly, meet with you when needed, and work on your case. Your attorney should have a substantial but manageable caseload as well as adequate support staff (secretaries, paralegals, assistants) and at least one partner or a trusted colleague who is available when she is not. Be leery of an attorney who suggests passing you off to an associate and showing up only for court or emergencies. Her offices should be clean and comfortable, in a safe location, and include enclosed spaces for private consultations.

Reasonable rates and billing arrangements. Your lawyer's fees should be about the same as those of lawyers in your area who have the same areas of specialization, level of experience, and size of practice. She should tell you her fees (hourly or flat) up front and whether she requires a retainer and, if so, the amount. She should agree to meet with you for an initial consultation for free or at a nominal charge, to provide regular itemized bills, and to refund any unused portion of the retainer.

You can obtain most of this information by scheduling a short phone interview with the attorney. If that is not possible, you can interview one of her staff members or send an e-mail query. Be prepared to give a general description of your situation in a few short sentences; you can be more specific later, if and when you have an initial consultation. Make sure the attorney is taking new clients.

You can also ask for and check references, and you should check with the local bar association to make sure the lawyer is in good standing. Once you've thoroughly checked out potential attorneys and eliminated any duds, schedule a consultation with the candidate you feel is most likely to provide the legal representation you think you'll need.

The Initial Consultation

The initial consultation to determine whether you want the attorney to represent you and whether she wants to take your case can sometimes be accomplished over the phone. However, a one-on-one office visit is the norm and what I recommend. The main purpose of an initial consultation is for you to give the attorney a clear picture of your case and for her to give you an idea of how she would handle it. It also enables you to get a feel for whether you click with the attorney. A face-to-face meeting is a much better forum for accomplishing these dual purposes than communicating by phone or e-mail.

Most attorneys will do the initial consultation at no charge. Some charge their standard or a discounted hourly rate, which is typically due at the time of the consultation. A preliminary consultation usually lasts an hour, rarely much more than that. You'll have a lot of ground to cover in a relatively short period of time, so you should prepare in advance for the meeting.

The attorney will want a detailed description of your situation—including your specific goals and concerns regarding each key component of the case: child custody and visitation; financial arrangements during and after the divorce; any domestic violence, criminal activity, or drug abuse issues that need to be considered; and any other pertinent information. The description should also specify your main reason (*grounds*) for seeking a divorce or separation (or responding to your spouse's petition naming same). It is helpful to provide this in writing beforehand, keeping it to no more than three pages, so the attorney can review it prior to the meeting. If your spouse has already initiated action and/or if you have a prenuptial agreement, bring that documentation to the meeting, or, better, send photocopies beforehand.

During the meeting, give concise information and answer the attorney's questions honestly, completely, and succinctly. Do not add unnecessary detail or talk about how you feel—with the exception of any fears you might have for your or your children's safety. Bring a list of questions, a notepad, and a pen with you. Listen carefully to the attorney's answers and advice, and jot down information you might need later.

If you're feeling anxious about the consultation, you can bring along a close confidante who is familiar with your situation. Discuss the upcoming consultation in advance, going over important issues you want to cover with the attorney and asking your friend to remind you should you forget anything during the meeting. Her supportive presence alone will help you to stay calm and focused during what is often an intense and emotionally draining meeting.

You should also ask the attorney questions about how she operates and intends to handle your case. Questions to ask during the preliminary consultation include the following.

- Have you handled many cases similar to mine?
- Is there anything about my case that you feel is unusual or potentially challenging?
- Is negotiation or litigation your stronger suit? (Of course, the best response would be "equally adept at both.")
- How would you describe your negotiating style?
- How would you describe your courtroom style?
- What percentage of divorce cases you've represented has been settled out of court?
- Have you represented clients in mediated and/or collaborative divorces? Are you willing to do so?
- What is the standard divorce process in my county?
- Are there any special considerations or potential glitches with the local court system of which I should be aware?
- Do you have basically good working relationships with local judges, court clerks, and divorce attorneys?
- Do you think my settlement goals are reasonable and obtainable? If not, why not and what do you suggest instead?
- What approach and specific actions do you think are most appropriate for my case? Why?
- Do you see any potential problems or sticky issues? If so, what are my options for avoiding or resolving them?
- How will you keep me informed of the progress of my case?
- How long do you estimate the process will take?
- How much do you estimate it will cost?
- Will anyone else in your office be working on my case? If so, who, in what capacity, and at what rate?
- Can you suggest ways in which I might keep my legal fees down? Do you recommend against any of these in my case? If so, why?
- Are you available and interested in taking my case?

If your attorney answers all of these practical questions to your satisfaction, the next question is yours alone to answer: Is the chemistry right? By the time you and your attorney have gone over all the practical issues, you should have a fairly good idea of whether:

- You "click" with your attorney.
- You feel confidant she "gets" and respects you.
- You feel comfortable disclosing intimate details of your life with her.

Though you shouldn't get too chummy with your attorney, the chemistry between you must be conducive to developing the level of trust and communication needed in an effective attorney-client relationship. Your attorney will learn things about you and your life that only your most trusted friends (if anyone else) knows. She will have an up-close-but-professional view of a very personal and painful experience in your life—at a time when you're feeling vulnerable and not in your best form. To feel safe enough to allow that degree of intimacy, you must have a personal connection with your attorney.

Once you've covered all the key issues and are confidant this is the attorney for you, you should discuss fees and payment terms in detail (see below). If you then decide to hire the lawyer, she will ask you to sign a retainer agreement and will give you a statement of your rights and responsibilities as a client. She might also send you off with homework to do in preparation of your first official meeting as attorney-client, which will be on the clock and on your dime.

At the consultation, the attorney should provide you with a strategy for your case and outline your options and rights.

Legal Fees

Most matrimonial lawyers typically charge an hourly rate for their services. The current going rate is $200 to $300 an hour, which can be higher in some areas of the country and higher for high-profile lawyers and cases. Most attorneys charge in fifteen-minute increments. That means you will be charged 25 percent of the hourly rate for work the attorney or her staff do on your case that consumes 1 to 15 minutes of time, 50 percent for 16 to 30 minutes of work, 75 percent for 31 to 45 minutes of work, and the full hourly rate for 46 to 60 minutes of work. So covering several questions and issues in a single phone call that lasts 30 minutes will be burn less money than five phone calls of 5 to 29 minutes each.

Almost all matrimonial lawyers require a retainer. A retainer is similar to a down payment on a house or car, with a percentage of the total cost paid up front in a lump sum and the balance paid in installments. The differences are that it is impossible to know the final cost of a divorce or separation or how long it will take until the process is completed. An experienced attorney can usually come up with a close estimate of her costs once she knows the hot issues of the case and your goals.

The average retainer for a contested divorce case is $3,000 to $5,000 but can be lower for relatively quick and simple cases and more for cases the attorney expects to be complicated and/or prolonged. Again, the costs depend in part on where you live. The attorney's expertise and the size of her practice can also impact the retainer amount. Usually, the retainer amount is pretty much set in stone with little or no room for negotiation, but some attorneys will consider a reduced retainer on a case-by-case basis. It can't hurt to ask. While most retainers are payable up front, some attorneys will agree to a reasonable payment schedule. Again, it can't hurt to ask.

Now, here's the tricky part: Billable hours are *usually* deducted from the retainer until the retainer has been used up (after which the client is billed weekly or monthly for the additional charges) or the case has been closed (after which any balance remaining on the retainer is refunded to the client) . . . but not always. Sometimes the retainer is used like a security deposit to guarantee you'll make all your payments and is paid back only after the case is closed and you've paid all your hourly charges. Sometimes, though more rarely, the retainer is more like a signing fee: is not refundable and hourly charges are not deducted from it. So make sure to clarify whether hourly charges will be deducted from your retainer and whether it is refundable.

You'll also need to know whether all expenses will be applied against the retainer (if any are) and whether some expenses are not included in the hourly rate. For example, you will usually be billed separately for court filing fees, long-distance phone calls, postage, etc.

Once in a while, an attorney will represent a client on a flat-fee basis. That may consist of a single fee that covers the overall process, in which case the work to be performed is itemized; any work that might be required beyond those items would be completed under a separate agreement at additional charge. In rare cases, the attorney will ask for a flat fee for each of the disputed issues; however, this makes it very difficult to estimate and prepare for actual costs, and it is considered unethical in most parts of the country.

Whatever your attorney's standard fee and payment structure, you need to know this information up front—and you need to be honest about your ability to pay. Retaining an attorney can be intimidating, and not having the financial resources to pay for legal representation can be frightening and humiliating. As justifiable and normal as those emotions are, don't let them stop you from getting the legal support you need. Ask your attorney for ways in which you might reduce costs. If you have limited financial resources, your lawyer may be willing to reduce her fees and/or work out a payment plan that is doable for you. She may also be able to ask the court to order your spouse to pay your attorney fees and/or essential expenses, such as for a business valuation or expert witness, as discussed in Chapter 5.

Once you and your attorney have ironed out the services she will provide, how much she will charge for them, and the payment arrangements, she will draw up a retainer agreement for you to sign. Of course, this assumes you have decided to hire her and she has accepted the job. Remember: you are the "boss" of your divorce or separation, and your attorney works for you.

What to Expect from Your Attorney

A good matrimonial lawyer will:

- Explain the legal process, how much it will cost, how long it will take, and any challenges she foresees in your first meeting
- Express a clear understanding of your needs and goals and demonstrate her support of them through her legal suggestions and strategies
- Treat you with respect, consideration, and compassion (Though an attorney's job is to provide legal—not emotional—counsel, you want an attorney who couples logic with empathy.)
- Work to contain your legal costs—but never suggest or initiate money-saving shortcuts that might jeopardize your case or well-being
- Provide you with astute information and advice, but know that you are the final decision-maker in your case
- Communicate with you in a clear, complete, and timely manner, and be available by telephone or e-mail and by appointment when you need to provide her with information or to get information about your case
- Listen to you carefully, answer all your questions, and be sensitive to your needs
- Give you sufficient advance notice of all deadlines, conferences, court dates, negotiation sessions, and court decisions
- Be honest and straightforward in delivering both good and bad news (If the most likely settlement will leave you with insufficient resources to maintain an acceptable standard of living

or not selling the family home you desperately want to keep will undermine your financial well-being, you need to hear the truth so that you can make the best possible decision.)

- Refer you to other professionals and resources to help you through the divorce and postdivorce process—such as financial advisors, family therapists, domestic violence support, business valuators, etc.
- Work well with local judges, county clerks, other lawyers, and other professionals involved in the case (She will be courteous, cooperative, and professional in all of her dealings on your behalf—including those involving your spouse's attorney, for example, by providing information promptly.)
- Be assertive and proactive while showing a willingness and ability to negotiate and problem-solve
- Be discrete (She will not discuss your case with anyone other than the people you have authorized her to discuss it with, nor will she discuss any other client's case with you.)
- Treat you like an individual and your divorce as a unique case—not like a statistic or just another legal procedure she's handled time and again
- Not create unnecessary conflict, delays, and costs by coming off like an uncompromising shark bent solely on winning
- Never ask for a lien on your personal or marital property
- Not be arrogant and/or confrontational
- Never make final decisions without you
- Never ask you to sign anything without ensuring that you understand and agree with it
- Never bullies, chastises, or ridicules you in any way
- Never makes sexual overtures to you or anyone else involved in your case

How to Be a Champion Client
Your lawyer is only as good as you enable and allow her to be. She needs to know where you're coming from and where you

want to go with regard to the divorce or separation. She needs to know your reasons and objectives as well as your boundaries and vulnerabilities. She needs full disclosure of all the facts of the case—including any that might cast you in an unfavorable light. A negotiation session with your husband's attorney or, worse, a court hearing is no time for your lawyer to find out that you have a bankruptcy pending, an alleged substance abuse problem, an extramarital affair going on, or any other such issue that could put her on the ropes with no opportunity to prepare her defense on your behalf.

Your attorney also needs you to trust her legal expertise and to carefully consider her legal advice when making each of your decisions concerning the divorce or separation. The best attorney in the world cannot fight effectively for you with her hands tied behind her back. Your decisions are yours alone to make, but you'll be doing yourself no favors by basing them on anything other than your own common sense coupled with your attorney's expert suggestions. Here are some general guidelines for working effectively with your lawyer:

- Be personable but keep it professional. Seek legal support from your attorney and emotional support from family and friends.
- Be honest and forthcoming with all information relevant to your divorce or separation.
- Clearly communicate your goals and ground rules.
- Speak up! If you don't understand or agree with something, let your attorney know.
- Ask questions, voice your concerns, and express your opinions.
- Make it clear to your lawyer that no significant decisions should be made without you.
- Keep all your appointments and be on time. If an emergency arises, call as soon as possible to reschedule the appointment or to let your attorney know how late you will be.

- Carefully compile and complete all the required paperwork on a timely basis.
- Bring copies of all required documents to your lawyer's office and keep your own copies neatly filed away.
- Jot down any questions or issues you want to discuss with your attorney before the appointment or before calling.
- Pay your bills on time. If you are having financial difficulties, discuss them with your attorney so she can help you address them proactively.

TKO!

DIVORCE MISTAKE #6
Sleeping with your attorney—or with any person involved in your case, such as your marriage counselor, financial advisor, real estate appraiser, etc.

When Your Lawyer Doesn't Measure Up

If you are dissatisfied with your legal representation, you can always fire your lawyer. For instance, if you find your lawyer is disrespectful toward you, makes decisions without you, or fails to notify you of court dates, you should put your lawyer on notice that such behavior is unacceptable. Then, if problems arise again, you should drop your lawyer and hire another one.

As a word of caution, though, changing your lawyer midstream can significantly increase your legal costs. It could also undermine your case, because if it has already gone to court, the judge may not grant an extension of time, which the new attorney would likely need to prepare the case.

To ensure as smooth a transition as possible, it is best to find a new attorney before parting ways with the first one. Your first lawyer must give all documents and other items relating to your case to your new lawyer and must fully cooperate in the transition. If you have problems switching lawyers and cannot resolve them quickly, contact the agency in your state that admits lawyers to practice, such as the state board of bar examiners. All lawyers must be in good standing with the state to practice law, and every state has a grievance procedure that can result in a lawyer's disbarment (loss of license to practice law). While this route should be taken only in serious situations, keep in mind that you do have recourse against an unscrupulous attorney.

When you dismiss an attorney, you still have to pay any fees owed for services provided thus far. You may also lose your retainer (or whatever amount left of it), and you will need to pay a retainer to the new lawyer. Switching lawyers can also annoy judges, especially late in the process, and can delay the court proceedings. So the sooner problems with your attorney are addressed and the most appropriate corrective action taken, the better.

Chapter 5

Your Best Defense: Offense (a.k.a. Preparation)

"The difference between transformation by accident and transformation by a system is like the difference between lightning and a lamp. Both give illumination, but one is dangerous and unreliable, while the other is relatively safe, directed, available."

—Marilyn Ferguson, *The Aquarian Conspiracy*

WOMEN ON THE VERGE or in the throes of divorce or separation tend to assume one of two stances. They either 1) cower in the corner—feeling intimidated, overwhelmed, and defeated before they begin, or 2) charge out swinging wildly—feeling angry, vengeful, and ready to do some damage. Some women swing dizzily between the two. While both approaches are natural and completely understandable, neither will serve you well in a divorce or separation, because they are emotional responses rather than strategic actions. The safest and most effective stance in a divorce is to be proactive, and that requires planning and preparation.

No one is ever completely prepared for a divorce or separation. The emotional, psychological, and lifestyle adjustments can only go so far until after the divorce is over and done with and enough time has passed for the hurt to heal and the dust to settle.

But both the divorce and the transition afterward will go more smoothly and will more likely yield a favorable outcome if you— and your attorney—go into it knowing the score and are prepared to deliver and deflect blows, should push come to shove.

Information Is Power

The more information you have, the better your decisions will be. The more information you provide your attorney, the better she can represent you. You need to know what your rights, risks, and odds are. Your attorney needs to know your strengths and weaknesses, your needs and concerns, and what's going on in your marriage, your family, and your household.

That is why it is important for you to have basic knowledge of divorce in general and the laws of your county and state specifically by talking with trusted confidantes, reading books, researching at the library or on Internet, and consulting with your attorney and other experts. It is equally important for your attorney to know the particulars and any peculiarities of your situation. You may not even know some of those important details at this time—and in a divorce, what you don't know can very well hurt you.

Being well-informed and prepared not only improves your chances of success and reduces the risk of injury but it also saves time, aggravation, and money. Any information you can give your attorney is information he won't have to track down on your dime. Putting it in writing and providing substantiating documents will also reduce the amount of billable time you spend explaining your situation to him and he spends explaining your case in negotiation conferences.

A good matrimonial lawyer will give you the opportunity to gather information for your case and will tell you what information and documentation he needs as the case proceeds. For now, you can give yourself a big leg up by preparing a package of information for your attorney to review in advance of your first working meeting. In fact, your lawyer might have asked for at least some of the following information during the initial consultation in which you hired her.

A Short History of Your Marriage

It might seem ironic that to end your marriage you need to rehash its history for your attorney. It might also seem contradictory, given the rule of sticking to the facts and not venturing into personal waters with your lawyer. However, a marital history is, by definition, a written account of the facts of a marriage or domestic partnership. Knowing how your relationship evolved and failed as well as the various dynamics of your household will be useful to your attorney in developing the "premise" of your case, which will serve as the foundation of your case (more on that later in this chapter). It can also help you to stay focused and strong.

The best way to accomplish this is to draft a short history of your relationship with your spouse, writing down the major facts and events in chronological order. This history should be no more than two typed pages and should include the following:

Courtship: date and circumstances under which you and your spouse met; duration and nature of premarital relationship, including each of your living arrangements during that period; expensive gifts given to one another; major purchases made together; any shared expenses

Prenuptial or postnuptial agreement (if any): whose idea, why, when

Wedding: date, who organized and paid for it (or which portion of it); who attended; any outstanding wedding expenses and who is responsible for paying; what happened to any wedding gifts

Children: names and birth dates of children born to or adopted by you and your spouse during your courtship and/or marriage

Stepchildren: names and birth dates of any children from previous marriages/partnerships living in or routinely visiting your home (how often)

Parenting: who has been the primary caretaker; made major decisions regarding children's health, school, religion, friends, activities, etc.; paid for necessities, life/health insurance, medical bills, child care, activities, etc.

Professional development: any degree, professional license, or vocational certification that you and/or your spouse earned during the marriage; if so, when, type of degree, costs; who covered which household expenses and how (income source, including student loans); who handled which household responsibilities during that period

Financial contributions to household: who worked outside the home, doing what, for what durations; annual income for each year of marriage

Individual contributions to household: who has handled cleaning, home repairs, car repairs, shopping, bill-paying, organizing family/social events, etc., for most of relationship; any recent changes

Decision-making: who initiated any household moves, major purchases, and other major changes in the household and relationship

Real estate: property purchased during the relationship (including your family home); type of dwelling; when purchased; price paid; who paid (or what percentage paid); who owns (what percentage); who handles/pays for maintenance, repairs, improvements; when it was sold and distribution of any profits (if sold) or estimated current value; street address (if still owned)

Businesses owned: by you and/or your spouse; name and type of business

Domestic violence: any spousal or child abuse of any kind; nature of, dates, perpetrator, locations, witnesses, police or other interventions

Intimacy: level of affection between you and your spouse; amount and nature of time spent together; frequency and quality of sexual relations; any extramarital affairs (who, when); any instances of desertion (when, for how long, where did he go)

Marital problems: past and present; nature of, when, frequency, severity (if relevant)

Remediation: efforts to remedy marital problems and save marriage; steps taken, when, and for what duration; who initiated, who paid for, effect of

Improprieties: instances of drug abuse, alcoholism, criminal activity, gambling addiction, sexual perversity, reckless behavior, etc. on the part of either spouse, any family member, or guest of the household; nature of, perpetrator, when

In articulating your contributions to the relationship and marriage, make sure to include any assistance and support you provided your spouse in obtaining an educational degree, license, employment, business, or permanent resident alien card. Do not forget to write about your financial contributions to the marriage and the emotional support you have provided your spouse. Emotional support includes helping your spouse through a difficult period, overcoming addictions or bad habits, and family relations.

Include any other information you feel is relevant to your divorce and might help your lawyer in representing you.

Every person's marriage and divorce situation is different. Don't assume your lawyer has heard it all before. Tell your unique story as best you can. Be specific and succinct.

About You

Your lawyer needs to get a feel for your life prior to the marriage, what assets and abilities you brought to the marriage, how your life might have changed (for better or worse) during the marriage, and your ability to be self-sufficient after the marriage. To that end, prepare a short biography that provides the following:

Name history: maiden name and any other names used (for example, first marriage)

Previous marriages: date of marriage, date of divorce, and primary reasons for divorce

Education: any degrees, special honors, certifications, etc.; when received

Employment: your current profession; positions held (job title, employer, dates of employment) and reasons left; specify the reason for any gaps in employment history (such as having and raising children, health problems, attending school, caring for a sick relative, etc.)

Health: current general status of your health; any past or existing health problems or disabilities, including physical, emotional, and psychological

Financial status: credit standing, ability to manage money and pay debts, net worth, property and other assets acquired/owned prior to marriage

Social: family, friends, colleagues, who can provide support and possibly be used as corroborative witnesses; any way in which your spouse/marriage has interfered with you or your children's family and social relationships, religious practice, and/or personal interests

Achilles' heel: any past, current, or alleged wrongdoing or personal problem that your spouse may try to use against you

About Your Spouse

You should provide your attorney with essentially the same type of biographical information on your soon-to-be ex. In both his and your bios, be factual, truthful, and as objective as possible, and keep each to a few paragraphs (no more than a single page).

Gathering Data and Documents

The onset of the divorce/separation process is the best time to pull together the documents your lawyer will need to evaluate, build, and plead your case. These are the financial and other important personal papers many women stash somewhere and ignore, sometimes not bothering to really look at them. Others are documents you may not even know exist, if you've had a peripheral role in the business aspects of your marriage or if your spouse has been hiding things from you.

Financial Records

Your attorney will require comprehensive information about every detail of your family's finances, past and present. This may be easier said than done if you haven't been intimately involved in all of your family finances. Though most women handle some or all of their family's day-to-day finances, many are unaware of the long-term, big-picture components, such as investments, retirement accounts, trusts, and insurance. Most haven't a clue of the net worth (total of all debts subtracted from total value of all assets) of their marital estate—to which they are legally entitled to an equitable portion in a divorce settlement.

Marriage is, among other things, an economic partnership. As such, you have a right to records affecting the finances of your family—including any accounts and holdings in your husband's name only. It doesn't matter whose name is on (or not on) them. What does matter is that you know the full extent of your financial standing and have the records to back it up.

The following is a list of documents you should try to obtain in the original and get several copies of in preparation for your divorce/separation:

- Bank statements: checking, savings, money market
- Mortgage papers, property deeds, appraisals
- Promissory notes, loan statements
- Installment loan (auto, home equity) papers and statements
- Credit card statements
- Stocks, bonds, mutual fund portfolios, brokerage account statements
- Business records and books, agreements, and contracts
- Tax returns, both personal and business
- Pay stubs and income statements
- Insurance policies (life, health, homeowner/renters, disability, business)
- Employee benefit records
- Social Security, disability, worker's compensation benefit statements
- Pension and retirement plan policies and statements
- Wills, trusts, power-of-attorney documents

- Receipts and warranties for expensive items
- Utilities, child care, and other monthly expenses and record of payment
- Bankruptcy and financial judgment paperwork
- Credit report (current, from all three reporting bureaus)
- Safe-deposit box numbers and inventory of contents
- Prenuptial or postnuptial agreements
- Resumes (yours and your spouse's)
- Loan applications
- Any other financial documents involving you, your spouse, or your children (for example, day care or school tuition bills)

You'll need income statements (pay stubs) and monthly financial statements from the last six months and annually reported financial documents and tax records from the last five years. These documents contain important information about the assets, debts, and income of the marriage. For example, pay stubs will not only disclose income but will also show if money is being taken out for pension, annuity, investment, health, or other company or union benefits. Tax returns report rental income and interest income, which can reveal if your husband owns real estate or investment accounts. The tax returns may also contain schedules listing businesses your husband owns and from which he earns income.

Loan applications are an excellent indicator of the assets of the marriage, because the applicant typically endeavors to portray himself in the best financial position on such documents.

Resumes can provide knowledge of such marital assets as educational degrees, professional licenses, and special skills that were acquired during the marriage. Resumes will also describe former employers where your spouse may have acquired assets such as pensions or annuities.

Credit card statements can expose the dissipation of marital assets on an adulterous affair—for example, showing charges for jewelry, hotels, restaurants, and vacations that are out of the ordinary. In addition, if your spouse has a cash business he has illegally not listed on his tax returns, it is important to obtain credit card statements and expense receipts to show the lifestyle that is afforded by the cash received.

Be resourceful in attempting to obtain the documentation. These documents can be obtained directly but discretely from your husband, the family accountant, lawyer, or your husband's financial planner or business manager. They may be located in the marital residence or in your husband's business office. The Internal Revenue Service will provide you with copies of any tax returns you have signed. Deeds are located in county registrar or city hall offices where the property is located. Information and statements concerning bank accounts, mortgages, loans, investments accounts, credit cards, pensions and other employer benefits may be obtained by contacting the specific institution or employer.

If you cannot obtain certain documentation, your divorce attorney will seek such information during the legal proceedings.

When you start collecting these documents, set up a simple, easy-to-use filing system that you and anyone you designate to access it on your behalf can easily understand. Keep it current and in a safe place where your husband cannot access it, such as a locked cabinet at your work or at the home of a trusted relative or friend.

Other Important Papers

You should also make at least two sets of photocopies of other important family documents, including birth certificates, marriage licenses, driver's licenses, passports, Social Security cards, medical records, health insurance and prescription cards, and any court and legal papers, such as restraining orders, adoption papers, and immigration papers. File one set of copies in the same cabinet with your financial documents. Give one set to a close confidante for safekeeping.

POW!

PHOTO OPPORTUNITY

Make a videotape or take photographs of your valuable and sentimental belongings. Make a copy; keep the original in a secure place (locked cabinet, safety-deposit box) and give the copy to a trusted relative or friend. Making a visual inventory of your valuables will ensure against leaving anything out (rather than counting on your memory) and will be useful in determining the worth of your possessions for the divorce settlement. If your spouse takes, sells, or destroys an item, the video/photos can also be used to prove it existed and to determine the cost of replacing it.

Creating a Budget

If you don't already maintain a record of the money coming in and going out of your household, start doing so now. Keep a written record of all income received and how it is allocated—how much goes to bills, living expenses, child care, savings, retirement plan contributions, etc. Specify the amount, date, and source of all income—for example, your paycheck, your husband's business draw, an annuity, the sale of property. Keep track of who pays which bills, any major purchases (for what, how much, who bought), and the amount each of you consume weekly on personal spending.

Maintain careful records of any money you contribute and have contributed to family expenses, because you will likely have to provide a full disclosure to the court if your husband challenges your figures. A budget will also help you to identify any unaccounted-for funds and estimate your postdivorce financial requirements. Ultimately, it will help your attorney (or the judge, if the case goes to court) determine an equitable financial settlement.

You can log the budget in a handwritten notebook, a spreadsheet on your computer, or an electronic bookkeeping program such as Quicken. However you record this information, make sure to do so in a way that doesn't make your husband suspect you are doing so in preparation of a divorce or separation. This will be especially challenging if your spouse has handled all or most of your family's finances, so be discrete.

TKO!

DIVORCE MISTAKE #7
Not knowing about or not including all assets and all debts of the marital partnership.

Dollar Wise

Divorce puts a strain on any budget, but especially so for women. Now more than ever, you need to economize and carefully manage your money. When preparing and going through a divorce, you should:

- Not go on a spending spree or make any major purchases, such as real estate, cars, furniture, etc.
- Use the money available to you prudently
- Put money aside in your own account
- Discourage your husband from making new debt, not cosign with him (or anyone else) on any new debt, and refuse to allow him to secure a debt with marital property
- Try to pay down and close any joint open and revolving credit accounts (credit cards, home equity lines of credit, etc.)
- Establish at least one credit account in your own name, because it may be difficult to open new credit immediately after the divorce

Keeping a Journal

Start documenting important aspects of your family life that might be relevant to your divorce or separation. Keep track of how each of you spends your time in and out of the house.

Record the division of labor in your household (who does what, when), the time your husband spends with you, and how each of you spend time with your children.

This information will help to determine any imbalance in household responsibilities, parental involvement, and commitment to the partnership. It will also help to quantify your contributions to the marriage, which includes everything you've done as a:

Homemaker: cooking, cleaning, laundry, repairs, shopping, errands, entertaining

Parent: caretaking, home-schooling or helping with homework, bathing and hygiene, school and social activities, doctor's appointments, religious training, skills training, entertaining, disciplining, comforting

Administrator: paying bills, balancing accounts, watching investments, communicating with creditors, bookkeeping, record keeping, initiating and supervising repairs and services

Some women are shocked to learn that their contribution to the marriage must be given a monetary value. In the eyes of the law, the contract of marriage is a financial agreement between two partners, and so each partner's investment of love, time, and care are measured in dollars and cents, just like their financial contributions. In my experience, the divorce cases yielding the best financial terms for women have been in situations in which the woman was knowledgeable about the monetary worth of her role in the marriage. So it is important for you to keep a log of all that you do for your family.

Of course, you should also record any and all forms of abuse (emotional, verbal, physical), detailing the time, place, date, and specific offense of each instance as well as any witnesses and police report numbers. Note your husband's specific words and actions; if you cannot remember them exactly, write down the substance of what he said or did, how he said or did it, and to and in front of whom. If you use his exact words, enclose the statement in quotation marks to differentiate direct quotes from indirect quotes.

You can also use your journal to record any questions, concerns, and fears you wish to discuss with your lawyer.

POW!

ECONOMIC INEQUALITY

According to the United States Census Bureau, recently separated and divorced women are more likely to live in poverty than their male counterparts. Fewer than half of all divorced women receive child and/or spousal support.

Devising a Game Plan

In preparation for your first meeting with your attorney, you should give some thought as to how you want the bout to play out and to turn out. This involves planning the first major steps in the process: initiating legal action, taking any necessary precautions, telling your spouse and others, and physically separating.

Developing a game plan also includes outlining how you want to live after the divorce or separation—and you need to be specific. For example, rather than telling your attorney, "I want to make sure I have enough money to live comfortably," you might say, "I need $3,000 a month to cover my mortgage, utilities, car payment, insurance, child care, groceries, and other living expenses."

To enable your attorney to help you get from where you are now to where you want to be, he also needs to understand exactly where you stand and how and why you got there.

Your Why

Every person in a divorce or separation has a unique position within the situation, and behind that position is a fundamental "why." Together, where you stand in the relationship and how you came to be in that position form the "theory" that determines the primary objective of your case. Just as strengthening the physical "core" of one's body is essential to a prizefighter, so, too, will defining your position and the reasons behind it develop and strengthen the core of your case.

Contemplate what led to the deterioration of your marriage and your breaking point, when you decided enough is enough and chose to fight for your future. Go over the relationship in your mind, aligning your feelings with things that were said and done. Talk it over with people you trust. Jot down specific incidents. Try to come up with the essence of your situation—the nut of why you are divorcing or separating and the justification for the settlement terms you desire.

This is the "theory" of your case—essentially, a way of framing the facts to show your side of the situation in a way that puts you in a favorable light and substantiates your position and your objective. Sometimes, this is very simple: Your husband cheated on or abused you, is a drug addict or has a gambling problem, or abandoned the family, and his behavior has threatened your and your family's emotional, financial, and/or physical security. Other times, it is more complicated, such as your husband has become distant and disinterested in you because you did not change in the ways he wanted—in which case, your theory might be abandonment, in that he removed himself emotionally, if not physically, from the relationship. Perhaps you are the one who has fallen out of love with your spouse, changed to the extent that you are no longer compatible with him, or behaved in an inappropriate way that has damaged your marriage beyond repair. Your role in the disintegration of your marriage may be a part of your theory, too.

You might come up with a few different theories. If so, try to boil them down into one comprehensive theory or prioritize the different theories in order of which pack the most punch. In one or two sentences, write down the theory so that you can clearly articulate it to your attorney.

Your lawyer should then work with you to develop your theory. In doing so, she will consider all of the information and supporting documents you have provided him. She will likely ask you questions and for additional information, and he may request additional information from your spouse's attorney or experts. The theory is the foundation upon which your lawyer will build and present your case. She will use it to argue your case in negotiations and in court. Indeed, the theory is the main tool used to educate and gain the empathy of the judge who will be making crucial decisions about your life.

Your Goals

People get divorced or separated for many different reasons—and yet for the same basic reason: their marriage isn't working and they want to improve their lives. To help make your hope for a better future a reality, your lawyer needs to know specifically what you want your life to be like after the divorce or separation.

Carefully consider what is imperative for your and your family's well-being once you are no longer married. Think about where you want to live, how much money you will require, where the money will come from, whether and how you will earn outside income, and what property you want to keep. If you have children, consider where they will live, who will care for them, where they will go to school, what activities they will pursue, and how much their essentials will cost and where that money will come from. Plan out your ideal parenting (child custody and visitation) arrangement.

Set up a postdivorce financial goal for yourself as well. Determine how much money you will need to pay for your desired lifestyle, which assets you can afford to maintain, which debts you and your spouse will each assume, and your ideal child and/ or spousal support arrangements.

Give some thought to which of these goals are most important to you, whether your spouse is likely to challenge any of them, and which ones you are willing and unwilling to compromise. Be prepared to discuss these goals with your attorney.

A THEORY OF ECONOMIC EQUALITY

Jamie was a working mother and homemaker. Her husband, Rich, had a higher income and contributed more money to the marital household than Jamie. But Jamie ran the household and was the primary caretaker of their two children.

Jamie's case theory was that she was an equal partner in the marriage, because in addition to the income she earned outside the home, she also made significant contributions to the marriage in important nonfinancial ways. Therefore, she was entitled to equal assets of the marriage. All the facts, arguments, and communications of the divorce proceedings were based upon and supported the theory of her case—and resulted in a favorable fifty-fifty split. ■

Interim Assistance

The divorce process usually takes a while, and it can be months or even longer before a settlement is reached, finalized by a judge, and enforced. In the meantime, you are entitled to live your life in security and safety. Sometimes you simply cannot wait until the end of the bout to get the assistance or protection you need. This becomes a serious issue if you have inadequate financial resources or if your spouse is prone to violence or vindictiveness.

You may need money for a variety of reasons, such as to leave an abusive situation and establish a new home, to pay bills if your spouse walks out or refuses to contribute to household expenses, and to pay your attorney fees. Even though the settlement your lawyer negotiates and the court eventually grants might require that your spouse pay support, your legal fees, and specific debts and expenses, you may need money to hold you over until then. In that case, your attorney may be able to get a temporary child support and/or spousal maintenance order.

Depending on your situation, you might need to request one or more of the following emergency orders:

- Temporary financial support
- Temporary child custody
- Protective order—restraining your spouse from abusing, harassing, stalking, and threatening you and/or your children
- Kick-out order—to remove your spouse from the family home
- Restraint of assets—prohibiting your spouse from selling, destroying, giving away, liquidating, or hiding any property, investments, or other assets

These and other emergency relief motions are discussed in greater detail in Chapter 10. For now, make note of which type of assistance you might need early in the divorce process and why, then discuss these with your attorney at your first meeting.

Round One: What, When, and How to Begin

If your husband has already filed for a divorce or separation, the question isn't when to take your first swing but how to fight back. If you and your spouse are no longer living together, the question isn't when and how to physically separate but how to ensure your family's welfare during and after the legal process. In either case, you and your attorney must now determine your next moves.

On the other hand, if you are the one initiating the breakup and have not yet filed for divorce or physically separated from your spouse, you now need to determine how best to do both.

Should you tell your husband first, before you take any legal action? Should you file first and then inform him? Should you sit down with your husband in a well-rehearsed, carefully planned setting and tell him your plans? Should your lawyer send him a letter stating you've hired a lawyer and asking for the name of his attorney? Should you physically separate before you file for divorce, at some designated date while the divorce is in process, or after the divorce is finalized?

Discuss these options with your lawyer. Explain your current situation, making sure to include details regarding your husband's emotional state and potential reactions. Decide together what you should do first and when.

The timing of these actions is important. You want your spouse to be as calm and steady as possible when he gets the news. It is probably best not to announce a divorce just before his mother has major surgery, he gives a big presentation at work, or you leave him with the kids for a week while you go abroad on business. By the same token, make sure you are emotionally ready to handle the situation properly. If you are anxious or afraid, call in your support team and do something positive for yourself to boost your confidence and calm your nerves.

Be considerate, be prepared, and be careful. But don't prolong the inevitable simply to avoid dealing with the unpleasant but necessary steps that must be taken in a divorce or separation. No one involved, including your children, benefits from that, and dragging your feet could trip you up. Your needs in ending the marriage and in not living with your spouse are important considerations, too. Though it's reasonable to wait a few days or weeks to begin the process, you need not and should not put your husband's priorities above your own.

Only you can decide when and how best to end your marriage—and only after consulting with your lawyer. It can help to talk it over with trusted confidantes as well. The most important factor is the level of cooperation—or conflict—you expect from your spouse. The extent to which you and your husband can work together and through your individual attorneys to resolve any disputes will largely determine the steps you need to take and in what order.

In an ideal situation in which both parties are cooperating fully, the first round would go something like this:

1. You talk with your spouse and the two of you agree to divorce or separate, as well as to interim living, financial, and parenting (if you have kids) arrangements while the legal process is under way.
2. You meet with your attorney to go over all the details and prepare all the paperwork.
3. Your attorney files the petition to divorce or separate.
4. Your husband is served the divorce or separation papers and responds promptly and as agreed in your earlier conversation.
5. You and your husband physically separate.

It doesn't always go that smoothly. If you and your attorney are confidant it will, you can certainly give it a go and then adjust course if your spouse hits below the belt by contesting the terms you'd agreed to previously or by countersuing. But it is always wise to discuss such contingencies with your lawyer beforehand, so they don't come out of nowhere and knock you both for a loop.

If you have reason to believe your husband could fight you tooth and nail on every point or on those you cannot risk compromising, you and your attorney should discuss your options and potential outcomes in depth before doing anything. Then, proceed with caution and stay light on your feet, prepare to immediately switch tactics if the need arises. You might also need to get emergency relief orders to prevent anticipated problems or in response to problems that develop once the process begins.

At the other extreme, your husband may be passive rather than aggressive. After being served the divorce or separation papers, he may ignore them and fail to respond. In that case, you may be entitled to a *divorce by default*, provided you've followed the proper procedures in your state and your husband doesn't come forward with a counterclaim in the meantime.

TKO!

DIVORCE MISTAKE #8

Moving out of your family home or leaving your children in your husband's custody temporarily when your objective is to remain in the family home or to be the custodial parent. Any temporary arrangement usually serves as a blueprint for the divorce settlement and has a big impact your case.

Planning the Physical Split

Be prepared to discuss with your attorney your preferences for physically separating from your spouse. Specifics to cover include:

- Who moves out
- When the move-out will occur
- Who will be and not be present during the move-out
- With whom will any child(ren) and pets reside
- Who keeps or takes which property
- Who will pay which bills and living expenses (groceries, clothing, etc.)
- The nature and limitations of your intimacy/relationship with one another

Talk with your attorney about any reservations you might have and any arrangements you think your spouse might dispute. Ask for and carefully consider your lawyer's advice. Put together a viable physical separation plan—and then come up with Plan B, because things don't always go as planned, especially when it comes to splitting up a family.

Contingency Plans

Be prepared for your husband to respond negatively when he learns you are divorcing him and want one of you to move out. Even the most rational and normally lovely people have been known to behave horribly when confronted with the reality of losing their spouse and their home. If it is a shock to your spouse or if he is emotionally sensitive, he may become despondent and sullen, lay a guilt trip on you, plead for you to reconsider—and then turn around and try to get back at you. If your spouse has trouble controlling his temper, he could get angry and lash out at you, verbally if not physically. He may refuse to leave the family home, demand or threaten to take the children or pets, or destroy property. Divorce seems to have a way of bringing out the worst in people, especially men, for some reason.

So before you hit your husband with any of this stuff, develop a contingency plan that includes a safe place where you (and your kids) can go overnight or for a few days if things get heated. Pack a bag with a change of clothing, personal hygiene necessities, copies of important documents, and some cash. Keep the bag hidden or out of the house (for example, in your car), and make sure any medications and child security objects (such as a blanket or doll) are in a place where you can grab them, along with the bag, at a moment's notice.

Be careful. If your spouse becomes violent, threatens violence or to kidnap your children, or behaves in a menacing or mentally unstable way, *leave immediately*. Grab your children and your bag and go. *Never* leave your kids behind. If your spouse tries to stop you and your kids from leaving an unsafe situation or harms any of you in any way, call the police. Get out as quickly and safely as possible.

Otherwise, if you and your children are in no apparent danger and you want physical possession of your family home, do not move out temporarily or leave for an extended period of time. Doing so could make it difficult for you to regain possession of the home in the divorce settlement.

Word Out: Who to Tell, When

At some point, the important people in your and your family's lives will need or want to know that you and your husband are no longer a couple. As a rule of thumb, it is better for those within your inner circle to hear it from you rather than from your spouse or through the grapevine. It is normal to feel awkward, embarrassed, and sad when sharing this information with your relatives, friends, coworkers, neighbors, religious leader, children's teachers, and your children's friends' parents. Telling mutual friends and business associates of both you and your husband is even more uncomfortable and tricky; you need to make sure they won't misjudge and work against you. Take care not to badmouth your husband, particularly to anyone who might get word back to him, and never do it in front of or in hearing range of your children.

Even more delicate will be any communications you have with your in-laws. Your husband should be the one to inform them of the divorce or separation, and you should not attempt to tell them your side of the situation. If you have children, their grandparents and other relatives on your husband's side will need reassurance from you that they will remain in your children's lives—unless, of course, any of your husband's family members pose a safety risk to your kids. Otherwise, be cordial and considerate, but take care not to reveal too much.

As a reminder: you should confide in at least one person early on and surround yourself with a strong support system. Your burden will be easier to bear when shared with people who care about you and understand what you're going through.

Chapter 6

Eye of the Tiger:
Rising to the Challenge

"A moral choice in its basic terms appears to be a choice that favors survival: a choice made in favor of life."

—Ursula K. Le Guin, *Dancing at the Edge of the World*

A DIVORCE CAN GO any one of several ways—ranging from a relatively easy, quick, and inexpensive settlement to a vicious battle that lasts decades and costs tens of thousands of dollars. It depends in large part on whether you and your spouse are in dispute over any aspects of the divorce, and if so, over how many and how vehemently. To some degree, it also depends on whether one or both of you are using the divorce as a way to punish, humiliate, or manipulate the other.

When the husband and wife cannot agree on all of the settlement terms, the divorce is considered *adversarial*. There are different ways to resolve an adversarial divorce, but each requires the assistance of outside help—and for the wife to be tougher than she might normally be. The husband can have an advantage in an adversarial divorce simply because the wife is uncomfortable with being an adversary. Women are often accustomed to being nice and nurturing, rather than aggressive and self-serving. It is also often difficult for women to stand up for themselves and to be strong at a time when they are already emotionally and sometimes physically exhausted from the stress of a failing marriage and impending divorce. But when you're fighting for divorce terms that will determine your well-being and the quality of your family's life for years to come, you can't afford to cower in the corner. When you're up against a mighty foe—even though he might have been the love of your life and your best friend—you simply cannot afford to cower in the corner. Sometimes, you've just got to suck it up, put up your dukes, and let him have it.

Only you, your spouse, your individual attorneys, and time will tell which of the following fighting styles you'll need to settle your divorce.

Lightweight: Cooperative Divorce

In a *cooperative*, or uncontested, divorce, the two spouses are on relatively good terms and mutually agree that the marriage is over and on all of the important issues. What's more, the two parties remain in agreement throughout the divorce proceedings and afterward, when the terms of the agreement are enforced.

If you are among the lucky few whose divorce ends cooperatively, it might go something like this: You and your husband go to a café or bistro and calmly, if sadly, decide to end your marriage without lawyers, courts, mediators, or any outside intervention. Over a cup of coffee or a glass of wine after a good meal, the two of you discuss and scribble down the terms of your breakup on a napkin.

Together, you decide all the major issues, such as where each of you will live, with whom any children will live and how you will coparent them, and how will you divide all your belongings, bills, savings, retirement plans, and other finances. You base these decisions on what you know to be the best interests of your family as well as on a good understanding of what you are entitled to under the law as it applies to you.

A cooperative divorce that actually pans out as planned will definitely be faster, easier, and cheaper than any contested divorce. However, even if you decide a cooperative divorce is the right option for you, I strongly advise you to have at least one consultation with your own matrimonial lawyer—and to read the rest of this book—before sitting down with your husband in a café or wherever to set out the specific terms of your divorce or separation. A good divorce lawyer will tell you which issues you and your husband should discuss and come to agreement on, including things you husband may be unaware of or not think of. She will advise you of your rights and may recommend what she, as *your* attorney, believes are your best options. This professional advice and expert second opinion will be well worth the investment, providing you with guidelines to follow when discussing the terms with your husband.

Whatever terms you and your husband agree upon, make sure to document them, whether in a notebook or on a napkin. I recommend that you then have your attorney draw up the legal settlement (based on your and your husband's informal agreement) and file it on your behalf. While you can draft the papers yourself or hire a paralegal service to do it, you should be very careful when going that route. If the paperwork has not been completed and filed correctly, your case could get hung up in the ropes of the legal system. At the very least, have your attorney review the final agreement before you sign it, so she can make sure you haven't given up any important rights or shortchanged yourself and your children.

The other thing to consider is that many cooperative divorces start out well but then hit an impasse on one or more important issues. In other instances, the two parties fundamentally agree on all the important issues but don't know how to iron out the details and/or complete the necessary paperwork. If that happens, don't panic. You can get some professional help to get you past the deadlock—for example, by hiring a mediator or collaborative attorneys—and still possibly avoid a messy, protracted, and costly divorce.

POW!

SHORT AND SWEET

Some states offer a "shortened divorce," requiring less paperwork and less time than the standard process. To qualify, the marriage must be of short duration, the divorce must be uncontested, the debt and property must be minimal, and the divorcing couple must have no children together.

Welterweight: Mediated Divorce

Mediation is a process by which you and your husband sit down with an objective third party and endeavor to reach agreement on the issues that you are unable to resolve through talking directly with each other. A mediator is a facilitator whose sole job is to guide you and your spouse toward a mutually agreeable compromise. Although a mediator can advise both you and your spouse on the letter of the law and suggest legally viable compromises for the two of you to consider, a mediator cannot provide individual legal advice or legal representation to either of you. No mediator can or should make legal decisions for you, and no mediator should ever coerce or bully you into agreeing to anything.

The purpose of mediation is to assist you and your spouse in carefully considering and trying to reach agreement on disputed issues in a controlled environment in which logic, rather than emotion, prevails. Mediation is not the place to air or resolve marital problems. Just as a mediator cannot provide individual legal counsel, neither is it the mediator's role to provide marriage counseling.

You have the option of putting all of the issues, some of the issues, or only a single issue of the divorce on the mediation table. For example, you might agree to meet with your husband and a mediator to try to work out a child custody and parenting plan but leave the financial settlement to your attorneys. By the same token, you might go into mediation hoping to resolve all issues but come to agreement on only some of them, leaving the remaining issues in dispute to be negotiated by your individual attorneys or decided by a judge.

Each mediation session typically lasts one to two hours. It can take as few as two and as many as ten sessions to reach an agreement or to determine you cannot agree on some or all issues. Once the mediation process has come to a conclusion, the mediator will write up the settlement on which you and your spouse have agreed. A final session will be held to go over the written agreement and to have you both sign it.

Mediation can save time and money—provided that all of the following apply:

○ There is a balance of power between you and your spouse.
○ Negotiating a fair settlement is a priority to both of you.
○ You feel confident that someone with an air of authority and good negotiating skills will be able to get you and your spouse to compromise.
○ You have a small number of tough issues to resolve.

If all else is in order but you have several thorny and complicated issues, a mediator may help you to resolve them, but it may be time-consuming and costly. (Mediators usually charge about the same hourly rate as a matrimonial lawyer.) If the mediation fails, however, and the settlement must be negotiated by your and your spouse's attorneys or decided by a judge, mediation can be a total waste of money.

The advantage of mediation is that a good mediator will try to facilitate a solution that is fair and acceptable to both you and your spouse. A judge, on the other hand, may impose a solution that isn't satisfactory to one or either of you. Once your case goes in front of a judge, you must live with the judge's decision, whereas you are never obligated to accept the terms set by a mediator.

As beneficial as mediation can be, it is not a viable option in certain cases. Mediation only works well when both parties are relatively equal in resources and force of character. Mediation will not work if any of these conditions apply:

- You and your husband do not trust each other.
- Either you or your husband is dominant in personality, finances, or in another manner. (One spouse has great influence over the other, whether through manipulation, spousal battery, or a domineering personality.)

If you and your spouse are an equal match in negotiations and you feel confident mediation might work for you, it is still wise to consult with your own lawyer before you begin mediation so that you know what to ask and look out for. You should also always have your attorney review the mediated divorce agreement before you sign it. Finally, you should definitely hire your own attorney to tackle any issues not resolved through mediation if you feel the mediator is biased in favor of your husband, or if the mediator and/or your spouse are trying to bully you.

This brings up a potential problem with mediation as a whole. The mediator's job is to bring you and your husband together to reach an agreement, not to protect you or to get the best terms for you. What sometimes happens in mediation is that the spouse who is more flexible, more timid, more passive, more vulnerable, and/or more compassionate ends up making more concessions; this is often the wife. Needless to say, this process lends itself to disastrous consequences when the wife is less articulate, less aggressive, less confident, and less familiar with the finances than her husband, is submissive to a dominant husband, or is a victim of domestic violence. Because of this, many women's rights groups, including the National Organization for Women, oppose any mandatory mediation.

Choosing the Right Mediator

Most mediators are either lawyers or therapists. In most cases, it is best to hire a mediator who is a divorce attorney and has training and experience in both mediation and family counseling. Psychologists with extensive divorce mediation training and experience can be helpful when emotional issues are preventing a couple from resolving disputes in their divorce—especially those issues involving children. Whether you choose a lawyer or a therapist as a mediator, make sure to choose an experienced professional with expertise in both the legal and emotional aspects of mediation, and don't be afraid to check references.

As a matrimonial lawyer, I am familiar with mediators—ranging from the good, the bad, and the ugly. One of the best mediators I've come across worked for many years as a matrimonial attorney representing wealthy people in divorces before becoming a mediator. This background has served her mediation clients well, particularly with complex financial settlements involving substantial assets and businesses. She also brings in an experienced psychologist to address nonfinancial issues in the mediation, especially those concerning children. Another excellent mediator I know is both an attorney and a psychologist and has been mediating divorces for more than fifteen years. She is highly skilled in diffusing potentially hostile situations and has had excellent results in mediating cases involving considerable emotional and financial conflict.

One terrific, if slightly unconventional, divorce mediator in my area has coupled her legal background with substantial and ongoing mediation, communication, and yoga training. She takes a holistic approach to mediation, focusing on each person's concerns and fears about the final agreement rather than on their individual positions. She is especially mindful when the marriage includes children, knowing that the spouses must continue to relate to each other after the divorce, at least on matters concerning their kids. Believing that the negotiating process is as important as the agreement itself, this mediator conducts mediation sessions in such a way as to prevent any additional damage to the relationship and with the long-term welfare of both parties and their children as a priority.

On the flip side, I have come across mediators who have made monumental mistakes—such as omitting important assets from the divorce agreement, failing to properly valuate a business, and not uncovering hidden assets. These mistakes typically result in one of the spouses, usually the wife, getting shortchanged, which cannot be fixed once the divorce is finalized.

While an incompetent or careless mediator can make serious mistakes, the worst mediators, in my view, are the ones who are biased or manipulative. Biased mediators can pressure women (or men) into accepting inequitable financial settlements. Before hiring a mediator, you can (and should) ask to review some of his past mediated agreements with your lawyer to check for bias toward either the husbands or wives.

Finally, as in any field, there are some rotten eggs in the pack—like the unscrupulous divorce mediator who, after failing to mediate a divorce agreement between a husband and wife, then tried to represent the husband in a full-blown adversarial litigated divorce. A mediator should never go on to individually represent either party in the same case or a related case.

Middleweight: Collaborative Divorce

For divorcing parties who are unable or unwilling to work out a settlement together or with a mediator but wish to avoid the destructive character assassination usually associated with an adversarial divorce, there is a nonadversarial alternative called *collaborative divorce*. If you and your husband are dedicated to settling your issues and to not injuring one another emotionally or financially, this little-known but fast-growing alternative may work for you. A collaborative divorce is especially beneficial to couples who cannot agree on anything or much other than their mutual desire to minimize the toll the divorce will take on them and their children.

In a collaborative divorce, each spouse hires her and his own collaborative law attorney, both of whom are retained for the sole purpose of negotiating the divorce agreement without going to court. The lawyers each sign an agreement, promising to represent their respective client in negotiating a mutually agreeable settlement. Often, the attorneys will also agree to withdraw from the case should the collaborative process fail. (On the off chance that happens, you would then need to retain a new attorney to litigate the divorce.) In contrast, with a traditional adversarial divorce, both lawyers focus on building a case with the *expectation* of going to court, even though about 95 percent of divorce/separation cases are settled out of court.

Essentially, collaborative divorce brings a nonadversarial, team-oriented approach to divorce that focuses on resolving disputed issues while still providing individual legal representation and protection for each spouse. This typically results in a more productive negotiation process as well as a more favorable settlement for both parties. If the lawyers are skilled negotiators and both you and your husband want to end the marriage as quickly and painlessly as possible, a collaborative divorce can also be considerably less expensive and less emotionally painful than a litigated one.

Like mediation, collaborative divorce reduces the negative aspects of a contested divorce. Unlike mediation, collaborative divorce also provides individual legal representation and looks out for the interests of each spouse. In a successful collaborative divorce, the settlement is likely to be fair and equitable, because there is no third party, such as a mediator or a judge, pressuring either party to settle quickly, to make compromises they are uncomfortable with, or to cave into an unfair settlement.

Because collaborative divorce is a relatively new concept, it might be intimidating to the average matrimonial attorney who does not have training and experience in the collaborative divorce process. It might also feel intimidating to you and/or your spouse if there are trust issues or an imbalance of power between you. But its potential merits make it worth considering if you and your spouse are candidates for it.

The collaborative divorce process consists of you and your lawyer meeting with your spouse and his lawyer to create and negotiate settlement options. Collaborative attorneys receive special training to facilitate these sessions. The lawyers commit to work as a team to resolve all the issues of the case, using constructive settlement strategies rather than adversarial techniques, which tend to be destructive. The lawyers also consent to:

- Fully disclose all assets and finances without formal court-mandated proceedings
- Agree upon and share experts to help determine the value of property, if needed
- Settle custody issues without subjecting you or your children to being evaluated by a court-appointed psychiatrist or other expert
- Focus on creative problem-solving techniques

For a collaborative divorce to work, you and your husband must also commit to negotiating until you settle your disagreements, including all financial and child custodial, parenting, and support conflicts, without going to court or even threatening to do so. Both of you and both of your attorneys must also agree up front that there will be no tolerance for slash-and-burn tactics or a take-the-money-and-run mentality.

Lawyers who use the collaborative divorce process believe that litigating brings out the worst in everyone, because the court process does not take into account the negative emotions that typically accompany a divorce. In fact, it usually aggravates bad feelings between divorcing parties. Collaborative law attorneys are trained to deal effectively with the emotional reactions you and your husband may feel. It is these reactions that frequently impede constructive resolutions during adversarial negotiations. Because the collaborative process levels the playing field and neither party is looking to exploit the weakness of the other, the end result is usually a more equitable settlement without either you or your husband being on the receiving end of the nastiness associated with many adversarial divorces. Since a collaborative divorce enables you and your spouse to share experts and to settle more quickly, it can also save money.

Collaborative divorce considers the whole picture, addressing the needs of the family as a whole and the emotions and welfare of each of the people involved in the divorce, including children. In so doing, collaborative divorce can greatly ease the stress of separating people and property, while also yielding a more beneficial outcome than the typical adversarial litigated divorce. This offers one of the sanest and healthiest ways to divorce, and I think it is the wave of the future.

That said, collaborative divorce is not for everyone. *If your husband is uncooperative, controlling, abusive, or the least bit vindictive, you should not use collaborative divorce to end your marriage.* Likewise, if your objective is to make your husband pay through the nose for leaving you, then collaborative divorce is not for you—and you'd better prepare for a long, costly, and brutal fight.

But if there is a balance of power and a spirit of cooperation between you and your husband and you both want a divorce that is fair and as easy as possible on the entire family, then a collaborative divorce may be for you. Keep in mind, however, that even though you and your husband and your respective lawyers are committed to the collaborative process succeeding, if negotiations reach a dead end, you are not forced to stick with the collaborative model. You can exit the collaborative process at any time and begin a negotiated or litigated adversarial divorce, usually with a different lawyer.

If that happens, the judge to whom your case has been assigned will likely order your lawyers to try to reach a settlement. If the lawyers cannot settle the contested issues within the specified time frame, the judge will set a discovery schedule, whereby you and your husband must disclose to the court financial and other information relating to the issue(s) in dispute and your attorneys are given a final opportunity to settle these issues on your behalf. If you and your husband are still unable to resolve the issues, your case will go to trial. During a trial, the lawyers will present evidence to a judge and maybe even a jury. This evidence may consist of documents, photographs, and testimony relating to the issues in dispute—and some of your family's dirty laundry may be aired in public. In the end, the judge will resolve the issues that you and your husband could not.

TKO!

DIVORCE MISTAKE #9
Continuing divorce negotiations when it is no longer pro-ductive or financially or emotionally worthwhile to do so. If you hit a brick wall and can't find a reasonable way over or around it, litigate and let a judge knock it down.

Heavyweight: Negotiated Adversarial Divorce

When a cooperative, mediated, or collaborative divorce is not feasible or if one of those strategies is attempted but fails, you have no choice but to go with an adversarial divorce or separa-tion. An *adversarial divorce* is one in which each spouse retains a lawyer who is dedicated to representing and protecting the inter-ests of that party—by whatever legal means necessary, including going for the jugular of the other spouse and going to court. However, in the majority of cases, the two lawyers will try to negotiate a divorce agreement outside of court. If they succeed, that is a *negotiated adversarial divorce*.

Although a good matrimonial lawyer will try to negotiate your divorce first, she will be ready, willing, and able to go to court if push comes to shove. And she won't hold punches in defending you and fighting to win your case. If that means beating your spouse to a pulp in negotiations or in court, then so be it. Of course, you can expect your spouse's attorney to be equally aggressive.

Once you and your spouse have each retained an attorney, the two lawyers will begin the negotiation process. This consists of a series of meetings—which can be in person, on the phone, via e-mail, text messages, letters, or any combination of these—until they reach a settlement or determine they cannot. The results of these negotiations are often detailed in formal *settlement letters*.

The rounds of a negotiated adversarial divorce go something like this:

1. The lawyers exchange basic information and formal introductions, if they do not know each other. An experienced lawyer will either be familiar with her opponent or will be able to quickly size him up.
2. The lawyers discuss the initial steps they will take in the case and may even identify the main issues or problems they'll need to address in hammering out a settlement.
3. You and your spouse will each fill out a financial disclosure form, under your respective attorney's direction. The attorneys will then exchange these financial statements as well as any other pertinent financial documents and expert reports.
4. If there are any pressing matters, such as money to pay bills and child-related issues (custody, visitation), one of the attorneys may request court intervention via emergency motion(s).
5. The lawyers begin informal negotiations. Each establishes her client's opening position and wish lists, which

are often inflated. Then the attorneys will engage in the verbal equivalent of staking each other out, circling round to get a sense of her opponent's strengths and weaknesses.

6. The formal negotiations are marked by a steady barrage of steely jabs and lots of nimble footwork. The lawyers argue, posture, and cite the law as if it were a trusted old friend. They suggest compromises and claim impossibilities. They may literally puff out their chests, stare each other down, slam fists on tables, and walk out in real or feigned anger. There may be yelling matches followed by cold silences between contacts.

7. Eventually, the attorneys reach a compromise on one issue and then another and another, until an agreement is hashed out—or one or both of the clients call a halt to negotiations and head to court.

Some negotiations take place in a *four-way conference* that includes the two attorneys and the divorcing spouses. These meetings are usually held in a conference room at one of the lawyer's offices, with you and your attorney sitting on one side of the table and your husband and his lawyer on the opposite side.

You should meet with your attorney in advance of any such conference to go over all the issues that may arise during the meeting as well as your financial and life goals. Be prepared to revise or scale back on some of your goals and to set your priorities. You and your lawyer may also need to come up with a worst-case strategy, clearly defining the extent to which you can compromise on specific issues. It is also a good idea to summarize your husband's position after each negotiation session—and then hold him and his attorney to whatever concessions he made if he tries to backslide later.

A four-way negotiation can be useful in moving your divorce toward a better, faster conclusion. But if not conducted properly, they can backfire. For example, excessive posturing and chest pounding on the part of one or both lawyers can hinder the process of reaching an agreement. Verbal brawling and unnecessary head butting on anyone's part is not only unpleasant but it is also unproductive and can escalate costs and incite a negative response from the opposing side. There are instances in which an attorney deliberately engages in this type of behavior to stall the process, because:

- His client isn't ready or prepared to settle the case.
- The lawyer isn't prepared for the meeting.
- The lawyer just wants to burn up some of the retainer before settling (though disgusting, it does happen occasionally).

Another problem that can arise during a four-way is that too much time is spent haggling over a small detail, such as who gets a certain piece of furniture. Most of the time, this has more to do with emotional issues than with wanting a fair divorce settlement. That's why it's important to work on the emotional aspects with your support team or therapist and focus on the facts of the divorce during negotiations.

There needs to be at least two cool heads in the room at any given time; otherwise, too much time will be spent exchanging blows rather than resolving issues. Sometimes, a four-way will briefly break up, either to ease tensions or for private client-attorney discussions. The two sides will separate and meet in a hallway or another room to discuss strategies, offers on the table, and what is negotiable.

A four-way is usually most productive when it takes place near the end of negotiations, when the major issues have been settled and the divorcing parties are anxious to resolve secondary issues. The best-negotiated adversarial cases are those in which the lawyers are knowledgeable, respect each other's skills, and focus on resolving the issues.

If the negotiations are successful, one of the attorneys will draft the divorce agreement. Each attorney will review the agreement, along with any accompanying divorce documents, with their respective client. Of course, if you have any concerns or questions, you should resolve them with your lawyer before signing. After you and your spouse have both signed the agreement, all that's left is to file the paperwork with the court and for a judge to approve it.

POW!

ARBITRATION

The courts may appoint an *arbitrator* (also called a *referee*) to determine some or all of the disputed issues in a divorce case. The arbitrator is usually an attorney or retired judge. An *arbitration* process is similar to mediation, except that the final decision is made by the arbitrator rather than by the two spouses. In arbitration, each spouse presents her/his respective position, and then the arbitrator makes the final decision. You and your attorney should prepare for an arbitration hearing just as you would prepare for a trial before a judge.

Extreme Competition: Litigated Divorce

When all else fails and two embattled spouses cannot reach agreement on all issues of their divorce or separation, the case must be litigated. A *litigated divorce* is one in which the lawyers representing each of the divorcing spouses present and defend their respective cases in court, and then a judge decides the outcome. Although court-decided divorce settlements are usually fair, the judge's decision may or may not include the settlement requests of either spouse, even those the two spouses might have tentatively agreed upon prior to the court's intervention.

Sometimes, a court summons is the only way to get a recalcitrant spouse to stop behaving like an ostrich with his head in the sand and to wake up to the reality that the marriage is over. Similarly, if your husband and/or his lawyer will not cooperate in a coherent decision-making process, then you will have no alternative but to involve the courts. Indeed, you may want to begin court proceedings when it becomes apparent that, for any reason, the divorce is not moving forward as it should and the impasse is putting your and your family's future in jeopardy.

Once in a blue moon, it is wise to come out of your corner swinging with litigation right from the start—for example, when you know or have good reason to suspect that your husband intends to take you down for the count and show no mercy whatsoever. As a rule of thumb, however, litigation should be employed as a last resort, after all other options have been tried and failed. Although all women in a divorce must be prepared for a knockdown, drag-out fight, it is never wise to provoke one without due cause. For one thing, litigated divorces consume a lot of time and money. Of course, if you are struggling to pay bills and cover living expenses during the process because your husband has stopped contributing to the family finances, your lawyer can petition the court for emergency relief. Even worse than the financial stress that often accompanies a litigated divorce is the emotional toll it takes on everyone involved.

In the best-litigated cases, the lawyers think of the children first and come up with creative solutions to thorny issues and complex financial matters. A good judge, or her court-appointed attorney, will listen to the disputes and provide guidance in how the court views the problems and solutions. The judge's opinion may give you a glimpse of what would happen if the case were to go to trial. Your and your husband's attorneys should use this information as a guide in negotiating on a settlement, if the divorce hasn't been finalized and that is still an option.

The worst-litigated cases are those in which one or both lawyers inflame the situation by filing needless motions and raising ridiculous obstacles and/or in which one or both spouses resort to mudslinging and character assignations with the single-minded objective of walking away with a better settlement.

While you may think this could never happen in your case, you alone do not control the process. The lawyers' tactics and/or the judge's approach can cause an adversarial divorce to spiral out of control. They can also erode any civility between you and your spouse that might have existed. Of course, blatant animosity between the two of you can also fan the flames of contention.

For example, let's say that negotiations begin cordially, but then your spouse refuses to give in to one of your demands and no amount of persuasion or pressure from your lawyer can move him. So, you subtly indicate that if your husband does not relent and give you what you want, or at least make a better offer, you will expose this or that unsavory fact about him and/or his behavior. In response, he makes a similar threat; he might even throw your dirty laundry on the table. Before you know it, the two of you have your fists up and flying, slicing each other to ribbons with insults and injury.

Meanwhile, the judge's primary objective is to get your case settled, finalized, and out of the ring to lighten his caseload. So the judge applies pressure to your lawyers, who apply pressure on each other and on you and your spouse. This pressure from the court usually comes in the form of a settlement deadline. If you don't meet the deadline, the case will begin moving toward trial. Until the judge actually decides the case, however, you usually still have the opportunity to settle out of court.

Even when you and your spouse and your attorneys are on the up-and-up, at some point in a litigated divorce your lawyer will likely submit documents with the court that are critical of your husband and may even spin the truth in your favor and against him. Your husband's lawyer may very well turn around and do the same thing with regard to you. Although this is normal in a litigation situation, it is usually uncomfortable for the parties being made to look bad in the court's eyes.

It is also likely that, when the judge asks your lawyer what it would take to get you to settle, your lawyer will ask for more than you actually want. You should know that this is a negotiating position from which your lawyer intends to negotiate down. You should also be prepared for your husband to become incensed by your outrageous request. Accordingly, your husband's lawyer is apt to do the same thing and may even do it first and worse, which could enrage or terrify you. For instance, although you and your husband have agreed all along that your children will live with you and you will have physical custody of them, once you get to court, he may begin requesting they live with him. To support his request, he may also add allegations that you are not a good mother. Even though you are told these claims are merely a negotiating position, it is likely that you will find it difficult to even read these claims about you on paper. You may be furious or depressed or both. You may feel like lashing back at your husband by revealing damaging things about him or even making exaggerated or false claims against him. Even if you do not retaliate at all, the exchange will likely cause lasting hard feelings between you, which never serves anyone well and is especially difficult when children are involved.

Once the mudslinging and backstabbing begin, it becomes all the more difficult to settle the divorce and put it all behind you. Accusations written in court documents and statements made in court continue to be very hurtful long after the fact.

Some women choose the tough fight of a litigated divorce when they don't have to, and they and their families needlessly suffer the consequences not only during the divorce but afterward. Other women have no other choice but to enter the litigated arena to get a fair financial deal or to protect their children. These women boldly stand up against their husbands and fight courageously to protect themselves and their children.

BREAKING FREE OF A DRUG ADDICT

Clarisse, a forty-something mother of a young child, was estranged from her husband of more than twenty years, Jim, who was a drug addict. Over the years, Jim's addiction worsened, and he would come and go from their home for months and sometimes years at a time. After they had a child, his behavior grew even worse. He graffitied her house, repeatedly took all their money, and even threatened Clarisse's life.

During his last disappearance, Jim was arrested and placed in a drug rehabilitation program, and Clarisse finally hired a divorce lawyer. Jim refused to cooperate, claiming he would agree to the divorce only if she gave him money and joint custody. The case went to court, where it dragged on because her lawyer had failed to file the correct papers, to request a conference with the judge, and to ask the court to set a trial date. That is when Clarisse fired her attorney and hired a new one.

The correct documents were filed immediately to set up a conference with the court. Clarisse and her attorney refined their theory of her case: that she should be allowed to be free of her drug-addicted, violent husband who squandered her hard-earned money and put their child's safety and welfare at substantial risk; that she should not have to pay him support; and that she should be granted sole custody. Though Jim would be allowed to visit his child and maintain a strong relationship with her, he would not have a say in major decisions about the child's education or upbringing as common in shared or joint custody.

During the court hearings, the new attorney presented the theory of Clarisse's case and supported it by detailing the family's history, which demonstrated Clarisse's responsibility and Jim's irresponsibility. Because Jim had spent the family's money for drugs and frivolous purchases, repeatedly threatened Clarisse with violence, damaged and destroyed their property, and failed to provide financial support for his own child, he was not entitled to any of their marital property, including their home and things they had acquired together. Clarisse's lawyer further argued that the case should be concluded quickly due to the damage already inflicted on Clarisse and her child by the delays caused by her previous attorney and Jim's stubbornness.

In preparation for the trial, information was gathered from the child's social worker and police officers, in part by using subpoenas requested by the attorney and ordered by the judge. Clarisse was intimidated by Jim because he had abused her, so the attorney coached Clarisse to help give her the confidence to confront him in the courtroom.

When the trial date arrived, the judge tried to delay the case, but the attorney argued that Clarisse had waited long enough and worked hard to prepare for this date, that she could not wait for another time to face her abusive husband in court, and that the hearing should proceed as scheduled. The judge relented, and Clarisse got her day in court and testified against her abuser.

The judge granted Clarisse a divorce, gave her all the marital property, and awarded her full custody of her child. He ruled that she did not have to pay Jim any money, nor would Jim be allowed to interfere with how she chose to raise her child. As they left the courtroom, Clarisse, who had been very reserved during the entire case, grabbed her attorney's hand and, with tears in her eyes, hugged her and whispered in her ear, "Thank you. You've set me free!" ∎

TKO!

DIVORCE MISTAKE #10

Initiating a divorce but then reconciling or living separately for a while and leaving your divorce action dangling. This enables your spouse to go to court for a final divorce judgment without even telling you. If you file for divorce but decide not to move forward with it for a while or indefinitely, you should request a dismissal of your case.

Chapter 7

Different Stakes in Different States

"The great crises of life are not, I think, necessarily those which are in themselves the hardest to bear, but those for which we are least prepared."

—Mary Adams, *Confessions of a Wife*

IN THE UNITED STATES, most of the laws affecting divorce and separation are established by state legislators and vary from state to state. For example, some states have laws mandating that children's wishes be considered in determining child custody, while other states do not. Even when two or more states have the same or a similar law, the nuances of that law and how it is applied can vary from one state to another. For instance, although several states allow spousal support when one spouse doesn't have the means to cover living expenses, some of those states can disallow the support if the spouse's marital conduct is improper, while others don't consider marital conduct at all in determining spousal support.

There are also federal laws relating to divorce and separation, which apply uniformly to all states. For example, one federal law makes not paying court-ordered child support a felony. Another, the Bradley Amendment, enacted in 1986 to help improve child support compliance, removed the ability of judges to reduce child support payments in the event of the paying parent's unemployment, bankruptcy, or incapacitation.

Another thing to keep in mind is that matrimonial laws are subject to change, so the laws under which, say, your neighbor's divorce was granted several years ago may not apply anymore. Needless to say, the federal and state matrimonial laws are too numerous and complicated to cover in this book. However, a good matrimonial lawyer will know all the pertinent laws and will know how to apply them to your case.

For now, let's take a look at the major variances between a few basic matrimonial laws that are likely to be a factor in your divorce or separation.

What or Who Is to Blame?

The idiom "all is fair in love and war" does not apply to love that ends in war. When a married couple divorces, the law requires that it must be for a legitimate reason recognized by the state in which the couple is divorcing. The specific reasons, or *grounds*, for divorce or separation are mandated by state law and fall into two categories, *fault* and *no fault*. If you live in a state that allows no-fault divorce, you will need to declare what caused the divorce, choosing from a few generic grounds that place blame on neither spouse. If you live in a state or county that has only fault grounds or if your lawyer advises you to declare fault (in states where that is an option), you will need to substantiate who and what caused the divorce, choosing from a long list of more complicated grounds that do lay blame on the other spouse.

Admitting to yourself how and why your marriage failed is difficult. Announcing it in a permanent court record that is subject to the scrutiny of your husband as well as the lawyers, clerks, experts, and judge involved in your case takes guts and careful consideration. You may feel embarrassed or reluctant to publicly describe the behavior that led to the divorce or separation. You may find it difficult to pinpoint your one reason or the primary reasons for splitting up with your husband. You may be concerned that none of the grounds recognized in your state apply to your case.

You may be spared that angst if you live in a strictly no-fault state and do a cooperative divorce with your husband alone and without lawyers, a mediator, an arbitrator, or a judge's intervention. In that case, you would simply declare one of the no-fault divorce grounds recognized in your state. Otherwise, you will have to reveal and describe the wrongdoing of your husband that led you to seek a divorce, at least to your lawyer, and this information will be available to your spouse and his lawyer as well as the court clerks and judge involved in your case.

As with other aspects of your divorce, this process will be much easier if you're properly prepared for it. The history of your marriage and your theory of its demise, both of which you put together during your early meetings with your attorney, will help you and your lawyer define and defend your grounds for divorce. Understanding grounds for divorce and how they apply to your case is critical if you live in a fault state, but it can also be helpful in substantiating the settlement terms you might want in any state, including no-fault jurisdictions.

No-Fault Divorce

A no-fault divorce is one in which the person suing for divorce is not required to declare a grounds that faults the other party with doing something wrong. Instead, the spouse filing the divorce simply declares a reason that essentially states that the marriage simply isn't working, without faulting the other party. The allowable no-fault grounds are specified by state law; the most common are "irreconcilable differences," "incompatibility," "mutual consent," "irretrievable breakdown in marriage," and "living separate and apart" (for a prescribed number of years).

Another hallmark of no-fault is that the respondent cannot stop the petitioner from getting the divorce—in theory, anyway.

In reality, although *unilateral no-fault divorces* are obtainable in many states, the matrimonial laws in a few states make it virtually impossible to divorce someone without that party's consent and agreement to all the terms of the split or without a court order after a trial.

All states currently allow some form of no-fault divorce, but some states make it more difficult, sometimes extremely difficult. Broadly speaking, the more conservative the politics in a region, the more difficult it is to obtain a no-fault divorce in that state, on the contention that no-fault encourages divorce whereas fault discourages it. Some lawmakers and experts argue that no-fault can leave husbands on the short end of the stick with regard to child custody, while others argue that it can put women at a disadvantage in the financial settlement. Ironically, the most difficult state in which to get a no-fault divorce is New York, one of the most liberal states in the country, but also one with a large Catholic population.

Nine states, including New York, currently do not recognize no-fault grounds but will allow divorce without declaring fault if the couple legally separates for a specified period of time. Twenty-two states allow the parties to choose between fault and no-fault, and twenty-three states require a period of legal separation, ranging from 180 days to five years, before a no-fault divorce action can be initiated. In a few states, the period of separation can be reduced if both parties consent to the divorce (in Virginia, this applies only if there are no children). In Ohio, a no-fault divorce will be denied if one party contests the grounds of incompatibility. In Tennessee, a no-fault divorce is allowed only if there are no children. The District of Columbia requires no grounds of fault or no-fault to be declared but requires a six-month legal separation before a divorce action can be taken. Fifteen states have only no-fault divorce and no option of declaring fault—including California, where the first no-fault divorce laws were enacted; three of those fifteen no-fault states require a period of legal separation first.

Legislators in no-fault and in primarily no-fault states believe that divorce is difficult enough on a family without making it worse by publicly pummeling the other party with unsavory accusations against his character or marital conduct. In fact, one of the main reasons lawmakers created no-fault divorce was because so many spouses and their lawyers were using *legal fictions*—exaggerated, fabricated, or manipulatively spun "faults"—to end marriages in which one or both parties were simply unhappy in the marriage or no longer in love. Unfortunately, cutthroat spouses and/or their unscrupulous attorneys sometimes use basically the same techniques in no-fault divorces, essentially engaging in character assassinations in an attempt to get the settlement terms they want. So you can't assume that because you live in a state that has only or predominately no-fault divorces that your husband and his attorney won't attempt to discredit you in an attempt to finagle the financial or custody arrangement they want.

Even when such allegations are true and can be proven, airing one's dirty laundry can create an adversarial atmosphere where there might otherwise be none or worsen an already nasty fight. This can protract the divorce proceedings, bog down the courts, increase the legal costs for both spouses, and take an even bigger emotional toll on the family. For these and other reasons, no-fault divorces have become the norm in most states and lawmakers in fault states are pushing for changes in their matrimonial laws to make no-fault divorces less difficult to obtain.

One potential pitfall of no-fault divorce is that a spouse whose improper marital conduct did cause harm to the other spouse and/or the marriage can end up with the prize winnings, leaving his or her ex in a heap on the floor. For example, a cheating husband can squeeze his wife out of the family home and retirement funds. Preparing for your divorce and hiring a good attorney will protect you from that kind of unfair situation.

In most cases, a no-fault divorce can save both parties time, money, and a lot of unnecessary grief. That said, sometimes going the fault route (in the states where that is an option) may be the best way to get an expedient and fair settlement. Even if your state allows only no-fault divorce, it is wise to discuss your reasons for divorce with your attorney, so that she can use this theory to justify the settlement you desire and deserve.

Fault Divorce

Although all states in America allow divorce, the matrimonial laws in some states are designed to discourage it. Lawmakers in those states believe it is better for families when couples remain married, especially those with children, except in the most detrimental of circumstances. One of the main ways in which states deter divorce is to request that one spouse prove there is "good cause" for the divorce because of the adverse actions of the other party—which is commonly known as a *fault divorce*. Given the results of recent studies and current trends and attitudes, some legislators now consider this view to be outdated.

Notably, many women's rights organizations have also supported the fault requirement or fault option for divorce, because it has historically provided women with more leverage in financial settlements in situations in which they had little or no other bargaining power. However, recent studies and trends indicate that there are more effective and less adversarial ways of ensuring an equitable settlement than assigning fault to the husband (or wife). In fact, the requirement to prove that the party is at fault sometimes ends up being a mudslinging match that causes more harm than good and does nothing to better the wife's odds of getting a fair settlement. Consequently, some women's rights advocates and legislators are now recommending that fault states move toward becoming primarily or exclusively no-fault states.

In the meantime, if you are ending your marriage in a state that discourages no-fault divorce or offers only fault grounds, you and/or your husband will have to describe the manner in which the other is responsible for the break up of your marriage. These fault grounds must be included in the pleadings filed with the court, and you may have to stand up in an open courtroom and justify your grounds for divorce to the judge.

Grounds for divorce are not always contested. Your husband may decide to pick his battles and not contest whether and why you should be granted a divorce. He may agree to whatever ground(s) you specify to conserve his energy and legal expenses for duking it out with you on financial and/or custody issues and/or to move the divorce along. Conversely, he might contest the grounds in an attempt to avoid an adversarial litigated divorce involving a big fight over money or for no other reason than to prevent the divorce altogether. If he succeeds in contesting the divorce and you are unable to prove your grounds in court, you must remain married (though you do not have to live together) and you may not get an equitable share of the martial estate. While such a tactic is distressing, it does offer you some, albeit small, protection: If the court does not grant you a divorce and your husband has supported you during the marriage, then his obligation to support you continues.

On the flip side, if your husband contests your grounds for divorce but his misconduct during the marriage was so egregious as to "shock the conscience" of the court, not only will you get the divorce, you may also get a greater share of the family assets than you might have otherwise.

So it is vitally important for you to define and prove your grounds for divorce. Even if your husband does not contest the divorce, you should clearly articulate and substantiate your grounds for divorce so that your attorney can utilize them as a tool in negotiating your settlement if the need arises. Most good lawyers prefer to declare at least two grounds in the divorce pleadings. Each of the thirty states that have fault divorces, whether as a requirement or an option, specify the grounds that are allowed in that state. Following are descriptions of the most common fault grounds.

Abandonment

If your husband has moved out of the family home or has been gone for an extended period of time, it may be considered abandonment and used as grounds in a fault divorce. Again, each state has its own definition of abandonment, with the required amount of time the spouse must be absent from the home usually ranging from six to twelve months. The spouse must leave without the intention of resuming the marital relationship. If the wife consents to the husband leaving or kicks him out, it is not considered abandonment and is a defense to this ground for divorce.

Adultery

When either party engages in sexual relations with someone other than his or her spouse, it is considered adultery and is grounds for divorce. Because adultery is still considered a crime in many states, it is rare for two spouses to agree to a divorce based on adultery. Consequently, sexual involvement with others is more often used to substantiate a claim of cruel and inhumane treatment.

If one spouse is cheating, it may be a defense to the other party cheating. Other defenses to the adultery ground include condonation of the adultery, forgiveness of the adultery, or procurement (when the husband entraps his wife, for example, by enlisting someone to seduce her).

Confinement

When one's spouse is convicted of a crime and sent to jail, confinement may be used as a ground for divorce. The length of the incarceration and certain other requirements, such as when the imprisonment takes place, vary from state to state. In

New York, for example, confinement can be used as a ground for divorce when the spouse has been in prison for three or more consecutive years. Time served while awaiting a conviction and sentencing also counts toward the necessary time period.

The most difficult part of using these grounds for divorce is having the imprisoned spouse served in prison; the service processor may need to go through a central location rather than deliver it directly to the spouse.

Constructive Abandonment

Constructive abandonment is when one spouse refuses to have sexual relations with the other for a period of time and the other spouse was ready, willing, and able to do so. Many men in fault states use the grounds of constructive abandonment because they don't have any other reason for divorce. It is also considered one of the mildest of the fault grounds for divorce, and so many couples use it to avoid conflict. Often, proving constructive abandonment becomes a he-said, she-said sparring match and a matter of credibility. For example, in defense of a wife using this ground, the husband could counter that they did have sexual relations or that their choice to not have sexual relations was mutual.

Conversion

A conversion ground—also referred to as grounds for divorce based on a "decree of judgment of separation" or an "agreement of separation"—is often used to initiate a divorce after a period of legal separation. The separation may be either required by law as a prerequisite to divorcing in that state or a voluntary decision made by the husband and wife to allow them time to reconcile or to prepare for a divorce. A conversion ground may also be used in a fault state when there are no other legal grounds for divorce. In fault states and in no-fault states requiring a specified period of separation prior to divorce, the ground of conversion may be used if both of these conditions have been met:

1. The parties have lived separate and apart pursuant to a separation agreement or judgment for the specified period of time required in that state.
2. The party seeking the divorce has substantially complied with the terms and condition of the agreement or judgment.

In any case, you usually go through the same steps to legally separate as to get divorced—except that you don't have to prove grounds for separation and you do for divorce. The separation agreement will (or should) set out the details of your separation, including financial and child custody and parenting issues, as they would and probably will be in a divorce. Of course, you are still married—and so you cannot marry anyone else, and you retain all the legal rights and responsibilities conveyed by marriage. A separation agreement also means that both parties have agreed to separate and to all of the terms of the agreement.

A conversion fault is most commonly used in states that do not offer no-fault grounds. In those states, the couple must live separate and apart for a specified period of time while substantially complying with all the terms and conditions of the separation decree, judgment, or agreement. That is also the case when the couple decides to use a no-fault ground in states offering the option of either a fault or no-fault divorce.

Cruel and Inhumane Treatment

Cruel and inhumane treatment (also called *cruelty*) can be claimed, or pleaded, when your husband's behavior intentionally so endangers your physical and/or mental well-being as to make it unreasonable or unsafe for you to live together. Cruelty is the most common ground for divorce, and it is a catch-all for various forms of marital misconduct in addition to harmful behaviors aimed directly at one's spouse. For example, many states include drug and alcohol abuse, confinement to a mental institution, commissions of crimes against nature, a wife getting pregnant before marriage without the husband's knowledge and consent, and either spouse preventing the other from entering the family homes as part of the cruelty ground as well. (A husband cannot claim cruelty if the husband's violence is the reason the wife blocked him from the family home.)

What constitutes cruelty in one state may not in another. In fact, the requirement can vary from one court to another within a state. In some places, for example, you must show that your husband has been guilty of *serious misconduct* on a repeated basis—that is, he has done something to cause you severe emotional and/or physical harm more than once or twice over the course of your marriage.

The longer you have been married, the more evidence you must present to prove that you have been repeatedly mistreated in this way for a long time. Most lawyers agree that you need to be able to give a detailed description of at least three specific incidents of cruel and inhumane treatment within the last five years. It helps, but is not necessary, if you have police reports, witnesses, photos, and/or an order of protection. Your therapist can be an excellent witness of the symptoms and stress you have suffered.

Although there are no statutory defenses to this ground for divorce, some defenses to cruelty have been successfully argued in case law. For example, a wife may claim as a defense to her husband's ground of cruelty that her refusal to admit him to the marital residence (the allegedly cruel behavior on her part) was provoked by his violent behavior.

TWO GROUNDS ARE BETTER THAN ONE

After suffering years of degradation and loneliness at the hands of a cruel and distant husband, Marianne filed for divorce in her no-fault home state of New York. She explained her situation to her attorney, providing him with numerous examples of the ways in which her husband, Peter, had mistreated her throughout their marriage. These included his complete lack of sexual contact or even affection toward Marianne, and a litany of emotional, psychological, and verbal abuse. Despite overwhelming evidence of spousal battery, Marianne's attorney decided not to plead cruel and inhumane treatment, based on his assumption that doing so would incite Peter to retaliate and his fear that it might hurt her case. Instead, he pled only constructive abandonment . . . and not very effectively. Because Peter contested the divorce, the case went to trial. Marianne's attorney was unsuccessful in proving constructive abandonment, and the case was dismissed. So, after spending a considerable amount of time, money, and emotional anguish on a litigated case, Marianne was still stuck in a loveless, hurtful marriage. In desperation, she hired another attorney and began the divorce process all over again. Her new lawyer asked insightful questions, took detailed notes of all the instances of neglect and mistreatment, and built a strong case for divorce on the grounds of both constructive abandonment and cruel and inhumane treatment. When Peter realized that Marianne and her new lawyer were not about to back down and were prepared to dress him down with damning evidence in court, he consented to the divorce. Had she been properly represented by a fearless lawyer the first time, it probably would have spared her the hardship of going to trial and freed her from a miserable marriage much sooner. ∎

Property Distribution Laws

In every divorce, all of the material property acquired by the couple during the marriage must be divided. This includes all income, real estate, vehicles, pensions, any investments and businesses, and any possessions purchased for mutual use or benefit. Each state has its own set of laws governing one of two methods of dividing up marital property: community property or equitable distribution.

TKO!

DIVORCE MISTAKE #11

Not clearly and completely defining all of the reasons that led you to divorce and withholding crucial information about your husband's misconduct to avoid his wrath, embarrassment, or despair. You're divorcing him; you're not responsible for his feelings. You should be more concerned with giving your attorney the information she needs to establish the theory of your case. Whether you're getting a fault or no-fault divorce, your lawyer needs to understand your grounds to build and defend your case.

Community Property

In a community property state, all of the income earned and assets obtained during the marriage are usually divided right down the middle when a couple divorces. In most, but not all cases, any personal property the individual spouses brought to the marriage and any inheritances bequeathed before or during the marriage remain the sole and separate property of that person. However, any increase in the value of property realized during the marriage may be considered community property, as may separate property that becomes commingled with community property. So if the real market value of the home you owned prior to your marriage increases by $80,000 during the course of your marriage, your husband may be entitled to $40,000, half of that gained equity—but not always.

There are only seven community property states. Initially, all seven had a *fixed equal-division rule* whereby all marital property was divided fifty-fifty between the husband and wife. Today, only California, Louisiana, and New Mexico still follow that rule. Idaho and Nevada require an equal division of community property unless there is a "compelling reason" that warrants an unequal division. While Arizona, Texas, and Washington continue to follow the spirit of an equal split, community property statutes in those states leave the final say on the division of property to the courts.

If you live in a community property state, it is important to know exactly what "equal" means in your jurisdiction. For example, if you are disabled or have been raising small children and have been unable to work, you might be entitled to more than 50 percent of the marital estate (and not equally responsible for all of the community debts). You should also keep in mind that the property division will be based on the net value of the marital estate—that is, the fair market value of all community property less the total amount of all community debts.

POW!

WHEN COMMUNITY SPELLS TROUBLE

In the absence of a prenuptial agreement, a wife who earns more than her husband in a community state may have to give him half of the marital estate—even if he cheated on her or was a bum who sat on his duff while she worked hers to the bone. On the other (and more common) side of the coin, community property laws can make it difficult to put a dollar value on a wife's nonmonetary contributions to the marriage, such as maintaining the family home, supporting the husband's career or business, and caring for children. In either case, a good matrimonial lawyer can help better your odds by arguing for a more equitable, rather than an even fifty-fifty, split.

Equitable Distribution

Under the *equitable distribution* system of dividing up a marital estate, which is also called "common law" and "marital property law," the courts view a marriage as an economic partnership to which both spouses contributed in individual and valuable ways. As in a community property state, all of the property acquired during the marriage—with the exception of inheritance, gifts, and personal injury awards—are considered marital assets. Likewise, any property owned prior to the marriage is considered the separate property of that spouse. However, in an equitable distribution state, the marital property is divided equitably, but not necessarily in two equal halves. In some equitable distribution states, a spouse may also retain equity gained in property acquired prior to the marriage.

A few states mandate that a fifty-fifty split be used as a *starting point*, from which any adjustments are based on the *relevant factors* of the case. This method is even sometimes used in states that do not have a case law requiring a fifty-fifty starting point. Some courts recommend that couples and their lawyers work toward a fifty-fifty *ending point*.

The factors that go into determining equitable distribution vary from jurisdiction to jurisdiction, and the value assigned to each factor is also variable. The courts generally consider such factors as:

- The outside income of each spouse
- Each spouse's contribution to the household
- Each spouse's contribution to parenting any children
- The age and health of each spouse
- The type and extent of the couple's marital property
- The type and extent of the separate property of each spouse
- The length of the marriage
- The number of children and their ages and health
- The professional licenses and credentials of each spouse
- Any businesses, professional practices, and investments owned individually or jointly by the two spouses

Remember, marriage is an economic partnership. You have a right to full disclosure of all assets and debts of the marriage and to at least 50 percent of the marital estate. To get a good property settlement, make sure to identify all of your contributions to the marriage, financial and otherwise (homemaking, parenting, helping husband with career, etc.).

Mandatory Versus Voluntary Intervention

Many states require or recommend mediation or counseling, or both, before a divorce can be granted. Some require mediation and/or counseling only under specified circumstances, such as when a couple is engaged in a custody battle. Other states leave mediation and counseling entirely up to the couple.

When mediation or counseling is court-ordered, the court usually appoints the mediator or therapist as well. The mediation or counseling fees are typically paid by one or both spouses, depending on each person's ability to pay and the situation. In some cases, the judge may order the husband (or the wife) to pay the full cost of the mediation or therapy.

When these types of interventions are not required, and are either recommended by the court or completely voluntary, you might still want to consider divorce mediation or family counseling. If you think it might help your case or your family, discuss the possibility with your attorney and your close supporters to get a better feel for whether outside intervention might prevent you from going to court and lessen the stress and/or expense of the divorce—or if it is more likely to just prolong the process. If you do decide to volunteer for this type of outside intervention, make sure to review any agreement before you sign it. You might also want to have your attorney present during any mediation sessions.

Child-Related Issues

The matrimonial laws governing issues related to children are numerous, complex, and variable from jurisdiction to jurisdiction. That said, certain issues are addressed in one of two or a few basic ways, and each individual state then adds its own caveats and conditions to these general rules.

Child Custody

The major child custody laws and rules that vary are:

- Which factors are considered and not considered in determining custody (though some states have no set guidelines)
- Whether the Uniform Child Custody Act is used in determining custody, and if so, which version (year) of the act is currently in use in that state
- Whether both sole and joint custody are options and whether either is favored and, if so, under which circumstances
- Whether the familiarity of the primary caregiver is a factor in determining the "best interest" of the child
- Whether the child's wishes are considered in determining custody, and if so, whether the child must be a certain age to exercise this right
- Whether a parenting plan must be filed with the court (required by only a few states)
- Whether grandparents are guaranteed visitation rights (applicable in less than ten states)

Child Support

The major child support laws and rules that vary are:

- Whether and which guidelines or other method of calculation is used to determine the child support amount
- Which factors are considered or not considered in determining the support amount
- The duration for which support will be paid
- Whether back support can be garnished
- Whether and under which conditions child support can be waived by mutual consent of both parents
- The method(s) by which support can be collected
- The recourse(s) available for collecting delinquent support payments

Spousal Support Laws

The major spousal support/alimony laws and rules that vary from state to state are:

- Whether either spouse is eligible for alimony or maintenance
- Which factors are and are not considered in determining support eligibility
- Whether lump sum, periodic, and rehabilitative support are awarded
- Whether permanent alimony is awarded and under what conditions (such as a long marriage)
- Whether marital misconduct is a consideration in determining eligibility

Residency Requirements

All states require that one or both spouses maintain a permanent residence in the state in which the divorce/separation is filed. Most states also specify that one or both couples reside in the state for a specified period of time, which varies from six weeks to twelve months. If you've recently moved or plan to move before filing, check with your attorney or with your local divorce court to determine your state's residency requirements.

TKO!

DIVORCE MISTAKE #12
Assuming that your settlement must conform to the terms a judge would order if your case went to trial or to a prescribed formula that does not consider the unique factors in your case. Though some matrimonial laws are strictly enforced, many allow flexibility to accommodate individual circumstances.

Chapter 8

Ringside Casualties: Protecting Children

"A mother's love for her child is like nothing else in the world. It knows no law, no pity, it dares all things and crushes down remorselessly all that stands in its path."

—Agatha Christie, *The Hound of Death*

ONE OF THE MOST damning and hurtful terms associated with divorce is "broken home." Having parents who can't get along and who then split up is hard enough on kids without society making it worse by labeling their families "broken"—which is just another way of saying "not normal." Children of divorce need their home lives to remain as intact and "normal" as possible, with the only substantial changes being that dad and mom don't live together anymore . . . and perhaps (ideally) that their sparring with one another has ceased or lessened. Just because a couple's marriage falls apart doesn't mean their children's whole world has to fall apart, too. That said, divorce usually does break the hearts of children, so they need extra attention for a while. But hearts do mend with time, love, and support—if, and this is a really big *if*, the parents behave properly during and after the divorce.

Many children of divorce grow up in happy, healthy single-parent or blended-family homes and then go on to become responsible, productive, secure, and content adults. It is not divorce in itself that harms children; it is too much conflict between parents, too little time with and attention from one or both parents, and too little money to properly care for them that can shatter children's lives and scar them for life.

The paradox of this is that women sometimes fail to address these as three separate issues and then sabotage their children's well-being by using one issue as leverage in bargaining another. For example, some women fight aggressively for custody but then settle for insufficient child support and an unequal share of the marital estate to avoid additional conflict with their spouse, thereby shortchanging their children's financial welfare. Some women go easy on all issues, agreeing to terms that are not at all in the best interests of the children, in the false hope that "playing nice" will prevent the father from disappearing from his children's lives and somehow enable him be a better dad when they're with him. Then there are women who want to make their husbands pay through the noses for the right to spend time with their children—those who thrive on conflict and are out to get and to gouge their husband. But those sorts of money-grubbing, conflict-crazed alley cats are few and far between. The vast majority of women try very hard to minimize the conflict and trauma of divorce, especially when children are involved, and are simply trying to do what's right for their families. Unfortunately, in the process, many of them compromise too much on the money side of the divorce agreement and then struggle to support their children.

Some men try to use the children as patsies, fighting for custody not because they really want it or think it's in the kids' best interests but to get a better financial settlement or to salve their bruised ego. These same men are usually incapable of keeping up a visitation schedule with their children postdivorce, much less handling the responsibilities of having custody. Likewise, men who don't seek custody sometimes fail to make or keep a schedule, so there is no consistency for the child and no ability to plan for the child's or mother's life.

Children of divorce—as with children whose parents stay married—need both emotional security and financial security. In fact, matrimonial laws are designed to ensure that all aspects of a divorce settlement relating to children are made with the children's best interest in mind. Your lawyer is also bound by law to represent your children's best interest, even if it is inconsistent with yours. (Of course, the same is true of your spouse's lawyer.)

POW!

CONFLICT HURTS, COOPERATION HEALS

Experts view conflict between the parents as the primary cause of emotional duress and conduct disorders in children of divorce. Children who adjust well to divorce have these three things in their favor:

1. Good relationships with each of their parents before the split
2. Parents who focus on the kids' needs during and after the divorce
3. Parents who communicate and cooperate with one another in coparenting their children

Child Custody

A *custody agreement* (negotiated by the parents and approved by a judge) or *custody judgment* (decided by a judge) spells out the rights of each parent to any minor children from the marriage. This written agreement—which may be settled before, during, or after the divorce is granted—will specify:

- With whom the children will live all of the time, most of the time, or a specified period (such as half) of the time

- Whether both parents will have equal responsibility or which of the parents will have sole responsibility for making all major decisions regarding the children's welfare, including education, child care, discipline, health care, religion, place of residence, curfew, associations with other people, sports, activities, etc.
- A parenting plan or visitation agreement that spells out when the children will be with each parent and each parent's responsibilities during the time the children are with the other parent (The agreement may also specify any restrictions or conditions regarding the parent's behavior while the children are in his or her care.)

Custody Options

Historically, custody was awarded to one parent, who had both sole physical custody as well as sole decision-making authority, and the other parent had limited visitation rights and no decision-making authority. Today, a custody agreement (or court order) might consist of any of the following configurations:

- Sole physical custody with sole decision-making authority
- Sole physical custody with joint decision-making authority
- Joint physical custody with sole decision-making authority
- Joint physical custody with joint decision-making authority

Most courts and child development experts agree that joint custody with joint decision-making authority is the preferred arrangement for most families with fit parents and minimal conflict between the parents. Consequently, most courts award joint custody whenever it is practical and in the best interests of the children. Some states, such as New York, will not order joint custody, but the parties may agree to it.

If one parent has a history of or poses a real danger of child abuse or child endangerment, the other parent should have sole physical custody as well as sole decision-making authority of minor children. If you are in that arena, I urge you to fight like a brave-heart for sole custody of your children.

Another instance in which joint custody and/or joint decision-making authority may not be the best option is when the two parents disagree on many important child-rearing issues and are likely to be in conflict on these issues postdivorce. In that case, the court may grant one parent either sole physical custody with sole decision-making authority or joint physical custody with sole decision-making authority.

When one parent is awarded sole decision-making authority, the other parent is legally obligated to abide by the parenting rules and decisions of the custodial parent.

Sole Custody

An award of sole custody to one parent does not necessarily terminate all rights of the other parent to the child. In such cases, the noncustodial parent retains visitation rights with the child unless there has been a judicial determination that such visitation would be or has been harmful to the child. The court will require the custodial parent to allow a reasonable schedule of visitation, including some summer and school vacation time, specified holidays, and regular contact by phone, unless the custodial parent can show that there has been or will be serious harm to the child caused by visitation with the noncustodial parent.

If a change in circumstances warrants a custody modification, the noncustodial parent may also seek a change of custody in his or her favor at any time while the child is a minor. By the same token, a custodial parent may seek a change in visitation rights if the child is harmed or endangered while in the noncustodial parent's care.

The most common defense to a plaintiff's request for sole custody is that the defendant has always been the child's primary caregiver. In that case, you (as the plaintiff) would need to convince the court that either you were the primary caregiver or that you and your husband were equal caregivers.

Joint Custody

In a joint custody arrangement, the two parents share physical custody and typically also share decision-making authority of their children. In sharing physical custody, the child lives with each parent part of the time. The custody agreement usually specifies how the child's time will be divided between the parents' individual residences—for example, one week with the mother and one with the father—but sometimes the agreement simply states that the parents will share physical custody, leaving the parents to work out a more flexible physical custody schedule between them.

Some parents split the week so that the child spends three and a half days at each parent's home. Other parents alternate weeks or months. In some joint custody arrangements, the child lives "primarily" with one parent and spends every or every other weekend, all or half of all summer and holiday school breaks, and/or one weekday with the other parent.

Most child psychologists now believe that it is usually best for children to live primarily with one parent about 70 percent of the time and with the other parent about 30 percent of the time. Split (or shared) custody, in which the child spends half the time with one parent and half the time with the other, is usually not recommended during a child's formative (birth through preteen years), unless the parents live in the same neighborhood, because younger children tend to need more consistency in their routines and environment than a fifty-fifty parenting schedule allows.

In rare situations, rather than the child going back and forth between the parents' homes, the child stays in the same home and the parent who lives there leaves while the other parent stays with the child for the duration of that parent's custodial time.

Joint custody is based on the understanding that both parents:

- Are committed to having a healthy relationship with their children
- Agree to assume equal responsibility for and to provide equal care for their children
- Are willing and able to comply with the custodial arrangement in an atmosphere of civilized, respectful exchange
- Are concerned with and focused on the physical, emotional, and psychological well-being of their children
- Not only allow but also foster the continuity in the child's relations with the other parent
- Respect each other's parenting abilities and value the contribution each makes to the child's life
- Are not at war with one another
- Are willing and able to communicate well with each other about their child and agree to keep each other appraised of the child's development and activities
- Are capable of handling the myriad details and rituals in a child's life, including but not limited to mealtimes, homework, chores, discipline, after-school activities, and preparation for bedtime

It is helpful and usually less stressful when the parents' homes are in close proximity to one another. No more than an hour's drive apart is recommended, but joint physical custody has worked successfully in situations where the parents have lived longer distances from each other.

A joint custody agreement should include a *parenting plan* that identifies which decisions affecting the child's life will be made jointly by the parents; this typically includes educational, medical, and religious issues. The parenting plan should also specify how the two parents will divide their child's time during holidays, vacations, and special events (such as birthdays) as well as how they will divvy up their responsibilities (both payment of and participation in) for the child's education, sports, and extra-curricular activities, such as music lessons. Many matrimonial lawyers can provide you with a parenting plan worksheet that will help to ensure you cover all the bases.

Because custody has such a profound impact on children, you may want to discuss or review any custody agreement with a good child therapist as well as a sensitive and knowledgeable attorney before finalizing it.

Custody Battles

If you and your husband do not have the kind of relationship that enables you to establish a joint custody arrangement and if you cannot agree to one of you having sole custody, you should see whether your lawyers, a mediator, or parent coordinators can help you to work out the issue. If they cannot, you will have to prepare for court, where a judge will determine the custody arrangement.

Going to court should be the last resort for resolving any issue in a divorce, but if there is one issue best resolved outside the courtroom, it is child custody. Having a judge decide with whom your child will live and how much involvement you and your husband will each have in your child's life is unnerving. As hard as that might be on you—and it will be very hard—a nasty and prolonged custody battle can be devastating for kids. No caring and conscientious parent feels comfortable leaving the welfare of her children in the hands of a stranger. And no child walks away unscathed when his parents fight over him and the child is the prize.

That said, if you and your spouse cannot agree on child custody—and sometimes, it is definitely *not* in the child's best interest for a parent to agree to joint custody or to cede sole custody to the other parent—you must prepare for a court custody battle. In any custody battle, you should do everything in your power to resolve the conflict as quickly as possible and to shield your children from exposure to and involvement in the conflict.

Knowing what to expect and which vulnerable spots to look out for will help you to stay focused on the best interest of your child and on ending the battle as quickly and painlessly as possible.

How the Courts Decide Custody

If the parents do not agree on custody, the court must decide whether to award sole custody to one parent or joint custody to both parents. Most courts base this decision on what is in the best interest of the child, which encompasses the child's educational, developmental, emotional, psychological, social, physical, and material well-being. This usually involves evaluating the relative fitness of each parent to function as a parent—that is, to provide for the emotional and physical needs of the child—on a consistent basis.

The main factors typically used to gauge parental fitness are:

- Whether the parent has been the child's primary caregiver
- How much involvement the parent has had in the child's daily life and on a consistent basis
- The nature and quality of the child's relationship with the parent

Factors that carry negative weight in determining a person's fitness as a parent include:

- A diagnosis of mental illness
- Substance abuse (unless there has been successful participation in a treatment program and the parent has been clean and sober for a period of time)

- Child abuse, child endangerment
- Sexual abuse of children
- Undesirable lifestyle
- Abandonment of child/family
- Imprisonment
- Domestic violence against the other parent

At one time, the courts did not consider domestic violence against a spouse when making a child custody determination. However, due to modifications to domestic relations laws in some states, most courts now consider the effects of domestic violence on children in making decisions about custody and visitation. Under the current revised law, for the courts to consider instances of domestic violence, the victim must be able to:

1. Identify specific instances of abuse, citing the date, time, and nature of each incident.
2. Prove each alleged incident of abuse with a *preponderance of evidence.*

If you are a victim of domestic violence, you should document each incident, via police and/or therapist's reports, so that this documentation can be presented to the court.

Factors that do not (or should not) affect a custody determination include:

- **The parent's gender.** In the past, some jurisdictions or judges had an unspoken presumption in favor of giving custody to either the mother or the father, but that is generally no longer the case.
- **The parent's economic status.** The courts can equalize the parent's economic status through maintenance and child support awards.

- **The parent's discrete sexual activity.** However, in states where homosexuality or related sexual acts are illegal, the courts may rule against custody of a parent who is homosexual, bisexual, transsexual, or transgendered.

A loose presumption in favor of the child's primary caretaker does come into play. The courts may decide not to grant custody to a parent who works excessive and/or irregular hours and to grant sole physical custody to the parent who has more time to spend with the child on a consistent basis. By the same token, however, a parent who does not work full-time outside the home but is unwilling or unable to devote substantial time to the children may also have a weaker claim to custody. When parents work outside the home, the court must also be satisfied that there will be adequate child care arrangements.

Another factor that may be considered in granting custody is whether the parent-child relationships are especially poor or especially good. When the issue of a negative relationship between parent and child is raised, the court will want to determine that the child has not been deliberately brainwashed or alienated against that parent.

Several, but not all, states also consider the children's wishes in determining custody. While not determinative, a child's preference to reside primarily or solely with one parent should be considered by the court. The weight a child's wishes and/or preference will be given depends upon the child's age, maturity, and freedom from parental coercion.

Stability of environment is another factor that courts deem important, and they are reluctant to remove a child from a familiar environment. There is also a strong preference to keep siblings together. In fact, most courts will deny arrangements that separate siblings in the absence of compelling circumstances.

Where religion is a factor in a custody dispute, the court may initially take the posture of noninterference, due to the constitutional protection of religious freedom. However, courts may inquire into a child's actual ties to a particular religion and/or whether certain religious practices threaten the health or welfare of a child.

Ultimately, each custody case is determined on the totality of the circumstances unique to the couple and their children. This usually includes not only the information provided by each parent and their corroborative witnesses but also the recommendations and opinions of outside experts.

POW!

DETERMINING CUSTODY IN NONTRADITIONAL FAMILIES

When an unmarried couple with children splits up, the best-interests standard will normally apply, provided each parent's identity as the biological or adoptive parent of the child is not an issue. If one party is not a biological or adoptive parent, the issue of custody becomes more complicated. It is unlikely the biological or adoptive parent will be deprived of the custody of her child in favor of a domestic partner, unless there is proof she has neglected or abandoned the child. Nor are the courts likely to rule in favor of joint custody, unless there are extraordinary circumstances warranting such an arrangement.

And in This Corner . . . an Attorney for the Kids

In most states, the court will appoint a *law guardian* to represent the interest of minor children in a custody battle. The guardian is usually assisted by social workers with experience and training in helping families of divorce. The law guardian will interview each parent with the child; if the child is old enough, the guardian may also interview the child alone. In some cases, the guardian may serve as a sort of mediator in helping the couple work out custody issues. Ultimately, however, the law guardian will speak in court on behalf of your child and advocate for your child's wishes. If the case goes to trial, the law guardian will have the opportunity to present witnesses and to conduct cross-examinations, like all other attorneys involved in the case.

You should endeavor to cooperate with your child's law guardian in every way possible. It is wise to provide the law guardian with the names and telephone numbers of people who can provide information about your child and support your position for custody. Such third parties may include caregivers, family members, teachers, therapists, religious leaders, neighbors, and friends. You can also provide the law guardian with school reports, psychological reports, letters, and affidavits (sworn statements) from third-party experts involved with your child.

When Child Abuse or Neglect Is Alleged

If a custody case includes charges or suspicions of child neglect or abuse (including sexual), the court will order the local government agency charged with protecting children to investigate such charges. The allegations of abuse may come from the other parent; the child; the child's therapist, teacher, doctor, or other family member; or from an expert involved in the case.

The government agency has the authority to send a social worker to visit your home, interview the child and the parents, issue a report, and be represented by an attorney on your child's behalf in court. To protect your and your child's interests, it is important for you to cooperate with the social worker and for your attorney to review these reports and communicate with the government's attorney.

Child Custody Evaluations

In custody cases, the court may order a psychological evaluation of one parent, both parents, or the whole family if the mental health of either parent and/or a child is in question. The issue of whether a parent is mentally stable may be raised by the other parent, the child's law guardian, a child protective agency, the family's therapist, the judge, or another expert directly involved in the case.

In some states, a similar evaluation may be ordered when a divorcing couple is simply unable to resolve the issue of custody and the mental stability of neither parent is being questioned. For example, in California, a "730 evaluation" may be ordered upon the request or recommendation of either party's attorney, a family member, a therapist, the child's law guardian, or the local child protective services agency. The purpose of the 730 evaluation is not to substantiate or negate a claim of mental instability. Rather, it is to assess the nature and stability of the child's relationship with each parent.

In both child custody and mental health evaluations, a court-appointed evaluator interviews each parent and often the children and usually also conducts psychological testing as well. The evaluator is a neutral party, usually a licensed psychologist, social worker, or therapist. The evaluator's findings and recommendations are then presented in a written report to the court.

Judges rely heavily on these reports and recommendations. However, your attorney or your husband's attorney can challenge them by cross-examining the psychologist during the custody hearings and/or by bringing in additional psychological experts to testify.

Similarly, if a parent is accused or suspected of alcohol or drug abuse, the judge may order drug testing as well as treatment for substance abuse.

The late Justice Thurgood Marshall introduced the practice of using expert testimony in custody cases on the premise that it would provide empirical data on matters of importance in determining custody that were outside the legal realm, such as child development, mental health, child abuse, and substance abuse. This enables judges to make more informed legal decisions regarding custody and visitation. Unfortunately, some evaluators have either disregarded the empirical data or spun it to serve their purpose in arriving at conclusions having no scientific validity. This has left many parents who've received negative reports in such evaluations with no recourse other than to either rebut the findings or hire their own expert.

Historically, the courts have widely accepted the recommendations of forensic evaluators, and there are many horror stories of parents who've lost custody based on recommendations of an inept or biased evaluator. Recently, however, the pendulum has begun to swing the other way. Both the legal and mental health communities now recognize the need to reform the role and the impact of forensic evaluators in custody cases. In the future, you can expect to see more litigants rigorously challenging the forensic reports and more court's discounting the recommendation of experts. However, in many custody cases a forensic psychological evaluation (report) is helpful or even necessary.

Working with Your Lawyer in a Custody Battle

Your lawyer should educate the judge, all attorneys, and any experts involved in the custody dispute on the theory of your case. She will also need to substantiate with facts why it is in your child's best interest for you, and not your husband, to have custody—or for the two of you to have joint custody, if that is your belief and your husband seeks sole custody.

This will require that you document the following information:

- The general nature and closeness of your relationship with your child
- The general nature and closeness of your husband's relationship with your child
- An itemized list of your usual (daily, weekly, monthly, yearly) parenting tasks and activities

- An itemized list of your husband's usual parenting tasks and activities
- Your involvement with your child's family, friends, health care, school, religious upbringing, social activities, special occasions (such as birthdays)
- Your husband's involvement with your child's family, friends, health care, school, religious upbringing, social activities, special occasions (such as birthdays)
- Skills you have taught your child
- Any special needs of your child that you have provided for
- The nature and date of recent incidents providing evidence of your spouse's deficiencies as a parent
- The nature and date of recent incidents providing evidence of your parenting skills
- The nature and date of recent incidents that provide evidence of your spouse's detrimental influence or effect on your child (such as drug abuse, sexual misconduct in the child's presence, etc.)
- A list of any behavior or actions on your part that your spouse may raise to challenge your fitness as a parent
- The names of reliable people with firsthand knowledge of your and/or your spouse's parental abilities and contributions, to be used as corroborative witnesses, if needed, and a short description of the incident/behavior about which they might testify

It is important for you to let your lawyer know everything about you and your spouse that is relevant to the custody of your child, including anything that may cast you in a negative light. Otherwise, your attorney may be taken off guard when the incident is raised in court and won't be able to effectively represent you.

When anticipating or engaging in a custody battle, it is also wise to keep a detailed diary of your child's interactions with you and your spouse, recording any incidents—whether positive and negative—that may be raised in court.

In complex custody cases, it is common to have at least four attorneys involved: an attorney for each parent, the law guardian for the child or children, and an attorney for the government agency. There may also be various therapists, social workers, and psychologists involved, whose reports and expert opinions the court may hear and consider. Your lawyer should carefully review all of the documentation involved in your case and then share this information with you, all of which adds up in terms of time and legal fees. Sometimes, just scheduling a court date when everyone involved will be available can gobble up your lawyer's time. Consequently, addressing substantial custody issues is very time-consuming and expensive.

The Rights of Children

The following "Bill of Rights for Children Whose Parents Are Divorced or Separated" was drafted by Justice James Brands of Dutchess County Family Court, New York, and Justice Ira Harkavy of Supreme Court, Kings County, New York. Most other states have or recommend similar guidelines.

- The right not to be asked to "choose sides" between their parents
- The right not to be told the details of bitter or nasty legal proceedings going on between their parents
- The right not to be told "bad things" about the other parent's personality or character
- The right to privacy when talking to either parent on the telephone
- The right not to be cross-examined by one parent after spending time with the other parent
- The right not to be asked to be a messenger from one parent to the other

- The right not to be asked by one parent to tell the other parent untruths
- The right not to be used as a confidant regarding the legal proceedings between the parents
- The right to express feelings, whatever those feelings may be
- The right to choose not to express certain feelings
- The right to be protected from parental warfare
- The right not to be made to feel guilty for loving both parents

Residential/Visitation Schedule

A schedule outlining when the child (or children) will spend time with each parent is included in the custody agreement or judgment. In a joint custody situation, it will specify each party's routine *parenting time* with the child—the period of time (days, weeks, months) the child will reside with the mother and with the father. In a sole-custody situation, it will specify the visitation time allowed the nonresidential parent. In both cases, the custody agreement/judgment also specifies how the child will spend holidays, vacations (school breaks), and other special events with each parent.

Other arrangements outlined in the parenting/visitation schedule include rules and conditions regarding:

- Where and when (time of day) the parents will exchange the child
- How the child will be transported between parents and who will provide and pay for such transportation
- The manner in which any future scheduling conflicts will be resolved
- The child's safety while in each parent's care
- Child care arrangements while the child is in each parent's care
- Each parent's access to the child's school and athletic events and other activities while the child is in the other parent's care

- Each parent's responsibility regarding the child's clothing and personal property
- Whether and how a parent may communicate with the child while the child is with the other parent
- How the parents will communicate with one another regarding parenting/visitation issues
- How emergency and routine health care issues will be handled while the child is in each parent's care
- Which parenting decisions may and may not be made by each parent while the child is in her/his care, including school attendance, haircuts, wardrobe, diet, bedtime, discipline, social activities, etc.
- Missed parenting time/visitation; whether and how it can be made up

Visitation Considerations

When sole custody is granted to one parent, visitation is one of the few rights the noncustodial parent retains. Most courts now characterize the ongoing parent-child relationship as being a joint right of both the noncustodial parent and the child. Because there is a presumption that such visitation is in the best interest of the child, visitation is provided as part of the initial custody determination, unless it has been demonstrated in court and the judge had declared that such visitation would be harmful to the child.

The visitation rights of the noncustodial parent will be denied only if there is substantial evidence that such visitation would be harmful to the child or if the noncustodial parent has in some way forfeited his (or her) right to visitation. A child's wishes regarding visitation may also be considered and weighed based upon the child's age and maturity, but it will not be determinative.

The best-interest standard is also applied to determine the nature of the visitation, its frequency and duration, where visitation takes place, and whether it will be supervised or subject to any other conditions.

The court generally encourages frequent and regular visitation when the parents live in the same area and when it does not interfere with a child's school schedule. When the parents live some distance away from each other, liberal visitation is usually provided for school holidays and summer vacations.

The question of the need for supervised visitation generally arises only when the noncustodial parent has threatened to kidnap the children, has a drug or alcohol problem, or has a history of violence or threats of violence toward the custodial parent or the children.

If a custodial parent has valid reason to believe that visitation with the noncustodial parent has become harmful or potentially harmful to the child, she can ask the court to modify or revoke the visitation. A custodial parent's willful and unauthorized deprivation of a noncustodial parent's visitation rights has been viewed by the courts as inconsistent with a child's best interest and may be the basis for awarding custody to the noncustodial parent. Another rare consequence of this interference may be the suspension of the noncustodial parent's obligation to pay maintenance and child support, including any arrears during the period that visitation was denied. Remember, visitation is a right of both the child and the noncustodial parent.

Age and Safety Considerations

The parenting time and visitation needs of children depend, to some degree, on the child's age and abilities. By the best-interest measure, the appropriate amount and the nature of the time spent with each parent varies greatly between that of a nursing infant and that of an active teenager. For example, babies and preschoolers generally require more continuity in their daily schedules and a familiar environment, whereas teenagers usually require more flexibility in parenting/visitation schedules to accommodate their school and social activities. Similarly, it is usually not advisable for a young child to travel a great distance or alone (for example, by plane or taxi) to the other parent's home, while it might be fine for older children.

A parent's ability to properly care for a child who has a health problem or disorder, such as autism, diabetes, or Down syndrome, must also be taken into consideration when determining which parenting or visitation schedule is appropriate for the child.

When it comes to divvying up parenting time, one size does not fit all. The age and ability of each child as well as the parenting skills of each parent must be carefully considered, and the arrangement must be flexible enough to accommodate changes in the child's parenting needs over time.

IN AN INFANT'S BEST INTEREST

Lisa and Andy were parents of a one-year-old son and had lived separate and apart from each other for several months when Andy brought a custody action against Lisa. He wanted Lisa to stop breastfeeding their son and to give him overnight visits, on the theory that the breastfeeding was making their son too dependent on his mother and excluding Andy from his son's life.

Lisa, who had been the child's primary caretaker from his birth, had agreed to allow Andy frequent visitation. However, she felt her son needed her at night, and she did not want to stop breastfeeding at that point, because she felt that it was the healthiest option for him, both physically and emotionally.

Lisa's lawyer researched the issue and gathered convincing evidence on the significant benefits of breastfeeding from the La Leche League, books by prominent pediatricians such as Dr. William Sears, and articles published by the U.S. Surgeon General and the American Medical Association. From these sources, she also documented support of the attachment theory of parenting, which asserts that maintaining close and consistent contact with a parent is advantageous to an infant's development. The attorney then identified experts who might testify to the virtues of breastfeeding and attachment parenting.

Lisa's lawyer felt strongly that the law needed to be updated to better protect the rights of divorced and separated mothers to breastfeed their babies and to limit overnight visits during a child's infancy. The case in question could have served as a precedent for initiating such a law. However, the attorney's greater concern was the welfare of her client and her client's child. A custody battle is expensive and stressful for all involved, even a baby, and the risk of going to trial is enormous, because it is difficult to predict what a judge will decide. So Lisa's lawyer focused on working with Andy's lawyer to settle the case out of court, in part by facilitating communications between the mother and father. She presented the evidence on the benefits of breastfeeding and attachment parenting to the opposing attorney. Lisa and Andy went to counseling sessions to discuss parenting issues.

Their efforts culminated in a schedule of frequent visitations between Andy and the child, with a gradual extension of hours over time, culminating in overnight visits. With the support of her La Leche group, Lisa continued to breastfeed even after the overnight visits began. ■

Child Care, School, and Medical Authorizations

When a parent has sole custody, provisions must be made for the custodial parent to enable the noncustodial parent to authorize the child's medical care, school field trips, participation in sports, and other eventualities while the child is in the noncustodial parent's care. The noncustodial parent must also provide the child's school, child care provider, coaches, Boy or Girl Scout leader, etc., with documentation that allows the other parent to, or restricts him from, visiting or picking up the child at the facility or event.

When parents share joint custody, it is also helpful for the custody agreement/judgment to spell out who shall have which rights, responsibilities, and any restrictions with regard to their child's child care, school, sports, and other activities. This will help to avoid conflict and confusion later if, for example, both parents want to be their child's coach or neither wants to pay for swimming lessons. The custody agreement/judgment might also specify that the parent caring for the child will transport the child to scheduled school, sport, and social activities and that the other parent may or may not participate in said events while the child is in the care of the other parent.

Special Occasions and Vacations

The custody agreement/judgment should specify whether and when the child will spend holidays, school breaks, and special occasions, such as birthdays, with each parent. For example, the child may spend his birthday with one parent one year and with the other parent the next; the first half of summer with one parent and the second half with the other parent; Mother's Day with the mom and Father's Day with the dad; the week of Christmas through Christmas Eve with one parent and Christmas day through New Year's Eve with the other parent; and rotate Thanksgiving and spring break between the parents.

The parenting time or visitation arrangement might also specify that the parents will be flexible in modifying the regular parenting time or visitation schedule to accommodate special occasions, such as a family reunion, a child's school graduation, the illness or death of a family member, and family outings and vacations.

The Child's Relationship with Extended Family

Matrimonial laws in some states allow for the visitation rights of grandparents under certain circumstances. In New York, for example, grandparents may be granted visitation rights to their grandchildren if the child's parents are divorced or if one of the child's parents is deceased. Grandparent visitation rights are never automatic, however; the grandparent(s) must apply to the court for visitation rights.

In that case, the court must first conclude that such visitation would be in the best interests of the child. Animosity between the child's parents and the grandparents is not determinative, nor is the child's desire to visit or not visit the grandparent, but these factors are usually considered. Grandparent visitation may be restricted or denied if the child has been adopted and the court has determined that such visitation would interfere with the child's relationships in the new family.

Many states do not recognize grandparent visitation rights. No state provides legal provisions for visitation rights of family members other than grandparents, including the child's aunts, uncles, and adult siblings. Nor does state law allow for the visitation rights of any foster parents, legal guardians, step-parents, family friends, or caregivers who have close relationships with the child.

The custody agreement/judgment can, and should, specify any family members or friends with whom the child should have no or restricted contact due to safety concerns. For example, if the mother's new boyfriend is an alcoholic or the father's brother has a history of child molestation, the other parent can (and should) request, and the judge will likely provide, that the child be prohibited from being in that person's presence under any circumstances or under any of the following conditions:

- Without the supervision of a responsible adult
- When the friend or relative in question is engaging in specific inappropriate behavior (such as using drugs)
- For overnight
- In a vehicle driven by that person

Relocating

A custodial parent may relocate to another state only by court order or upon the agreement of the other parent. Some states allow a custodial parent to relocate with his or her child under certain circumstances and without the other parent's consent.

They may even permit relocation in joint custody situations if accommodations are made to maintain the relationship between the child and the parent who is not relocating. But generally, the courts do not like unilateral moves by one parent.

Courts look at the seriousness of the economic, financial, educational, and/or familial reasons for relocating as well as the effect the move might have on the relationship between the children and the noncustodial parent. Other considerations include the child's age and abilities, the noncustodial parent's parental involvement and parenting skills, and the distance the move will put between the custodial and noncustodial parents' homes.

The courts determine a parent's ability to relocate on a case-by-case basis, and how they rule on this issue can vary greatly within the jurisdiction. A court may allow a custodial parent to relocate across the country from the noncustodial parent in one case—provided the move was justified and was not to deny the noncustodial parent visitation rights—but deny relocation within the same state in other cases, because the reasons for the relocation were not serious enough.

New employment by the custodial parent or the custodial parent's spouse may be sufficient reason to relocate the children. The custodial parent must demonstrate that serious efforts were made to find employment in or near the present location. Other reasons include marriage to a spouse who lives in another state and/or having extended family in the new location.

Child Support

Under the Child Support Standards Act (1989), both parents must contribute to the financial needs of a child. This law applies to all divorce or separation cases involving minor children, regardless of whether:

- The parents were ever married to each other
- Either parent is unemployed

- One parent earns significantly less than the other parent
- The parents have joint custody or one parent has sole custody
- The children live primarily with one parent, split their time more or less evenly between both parents, or live exclusively with one parent
- The noncustodial parent has limited or no visitation rights

When it comes to determining whether and how much child support a parent should pay to the other parent, the courts only concerns are that:

- The child is adequately provided for
- Each parent makes an appropriate financial contribution to the child's support

By federal law, the custodial parent with whom the child lives full-time or most of the time—whether by the two parents' mutual agreement or by court order—has a right to child support from the noncustodial parent. In most joint-custody cases, a custodial parent who does not have financial resources to adequately provide for the child is entitled to child support from the other parent, even if the child lives part-time with each parent.

If you are seeking child support along with a divorce, you should go to the appropriate court in your county; in some states, this is the Supreme Court. If you are seeking only child support (for example, from your child's father to whom you've never been married), then you should go to the family court in your county.

How Child Support Is Calculated
Courts determine the amount of child support to be paid using a relatively simple formula based on a percentage of the

noncustodial parent's income. These *child support guidelines* vary from state to state, and they are strictly enforced. In New York, the formula used to calculate a parent's *basic child support obligation* is as follows:

- Each parent's net income is determined (gross income, less Social Security and local tax only; federal and state taxes are not deducted).
- Any taxes, alimony payments to a previous spouse, and child support payments to children from another marriage/relationship are deducted from the respective parent's income.
- The net incomes of the two parents are combined. If their combined income exceeds $80,000, any amount over $80,000 may or may not be considered, at the discretion of the court.
- The combined income (or the amount over $80,000 determined by the courts) is multiplied by 17 percent (0.17) for one child, 25 percent (0.25) for two children, 29 percent (0.29) for three children, 31 percent (0.31) for four children, and 35 percent (0.35) for five or more children.
- The percentage of the noncustodial parent's portion of the parents' combined income is calculated. This percentage is the amount of the noncustodial parent's income that must be paid as child support to the custodial parent. For instance, if the noncustodial parent's income is 60 percent of the combined parental income, then his or her basic child support obligation is calculated based on 60 percent of his or her income. Whoever is the primary custodial parent receives child support; if custody is split fifty-fifty, then the higher-income parent pays child support to the other parent.

Keep in mind that these are general guidelines and that the basic child support obligation may be more or less, depending on the circumstances of the case.

For example, if one parent's income is substantially greater than the other's or if the mother has not worked or worked part-time so as to be the primary caretaker of the children and household, a greater amount of child support may be in order. Certainly, if the parents' combined income exceeds the maximum allowable amount, the parent seeking child support from the other parent should advocate for the formula to be applied to the full annual income level. To determine an appropriate child support amount, the court may also consider the unique educational, medical, or assisted-care needs of the child, the exceptional financial needs of the parent(s), and/or a disability or other factor that inhibits a parent's earning potential. In some cases, it is reasonable to expect the noncustodial parent to contribute adequately to the child's support so as to continue the lifestyle to which the child has become accustomed. It is very important that the court be made aware of these types of special needs or circumstances early on.

If one parent wants to pay less than or to be paid more than the basic child support obligation indicated by the standard guidelines for that state and they cannot agree on the amount, the matter must be decided in court. Although the state-sanctioned child support formula will serve as the basis in the majority of cases, each situation is unique and there is no hard-and-fast rule for calculating child support. If the judge finds that using the standard formula would result in an unjust or inappropriate result, the judge has the discretion to adjust the award upward or downward based upon certain statutory factors, including gross disparity in income between custodial and noncustodial parent, the standard of living the child would have enjoyed, and tax consequences to the parties.

If child support payments would put either parent below the poverty line, then the court will reduce or increase the amount of child support required. However, by federal law, the court cannot order a parent to pay less then $25 per month, regardless of the parents' income.

Negotiating a Child Support Arrangement
with Your Husband

If you and your husband can come to mutual agreement on a child support arrangement that ensures your child (or children) will be properly provided for over time without going to court, more power to you. In that case, you still have the option of using your state's child support formula or guidelines, which are usually available through your local court and may even be posted on their Web site. As an alternative, you and your spouse may agree to *opt out* of the child support formula altogether.

You can also bypass the basic child support formula if your case does go to court. In either event, opting out of the state's standard guidelines requires a legally executed agreement that includes a provision stating that both parties have been fully advised of the Child Support Standards Act.

Before entering into such an agreement, however, I strongly advise you to consult with an attorney who is familiar and experienced with the specific provisions of the law in this area. If you are considering accepting less child support than the law permits, you and your lawyer should first make certain that:

- There is a valid reason for you to do so
- You know your husband's actual income
- The child support payment is sufficient to adequately provide for your children
- You get something of value in return for agreeing to less child support

Husbands can, and sometimes do, deliberately fail to fully disclose income. Under certain circumstances, such as when the husband is self-employed, it can be difficult to uncover income, but there is usually some recourse. For example, the court has the authority to order your husband to produce a sworn financial statement as well as corroborative documentation, such as pay stubs, business records, and receipts. If the court finds that your husband has voluntarily reduced income or assets so as to reduce the child support obligation, the judge may order him to pay support based on his earning capacity (known as *imputed income*) rather than his reported income.

TKO!

DIVORCE MISTAKE #13
Settling for less child support than you need and to which you are entitled. This is usually the result of failing to pin down your husband's actual gross income or deciding to *opt out* of the standard child support formula in a misguided or misinformed attempt to fight fair, or both. It is important to remember that income is not just earnings and wages; it also includes interest and dividend income, benefits (such as worker's compensation, disability, Social Security, and veteran's, but *not* public, assistance benefits), pensions, fellowships, and annuity payments. It may also include one-time payments, such as lottery winnings, life insurance policies, gifts, and inheritances.

However child support is determined in your case, just make sure that all income is accounted for and that your children aren't shortchanged for any preventable reason.

Duration of Support

Child support is required until the age of twenty-one. By agreement between the parents and/or their lawyers, child support can be extended until age twenty-two if the child is in college.

Emancipation of the child terminates child support. Emancipation occurs if the child is employed full-time, gets married, or enters into the armed forces. If the child is discharged from the military before reaching age twenty-one, then child support resumes. Child support does not resume if a minor child who becomes emancipated for any other reasons moves back into the family home before turning twenty-one.

Method of Disbursement

Most courts provide for three methods of child support disbursement:

Through the court. The payee makes payments to the court's *child support collection unit,* which then distributes the money (via a court-issued check or automatic deposit) to the custodial parent. The child support collection unit usually seeks enforcement against a delinquent parent by seizing tax refunds, bank accounts, or employment checks. Such departments can usually have a delinquent payee's driver's license suspended and take possession of his/her auto on behalf of the custodial parent. This method is the most secure way to obtain support, but it can also be the most bureaucratic and slow.

Automatic payroll deduction. This method can be used if the payee agrees or the custodial parent requests and the judge orders the other parent to authorize an automatic payroll deduction through the parent's employer. The child support money will go directly from the employer to you. You do not have to depend on your ex to make payments on time or take action if there are missed or late payments. This method works great if the parent is not self-employed and doesn't quit or change jobs without reinstating the payroll deduction.

Direct to custodial parent. The payee may give a check, money order, or cash to the custodial parent. This method is advisable only if your ex is reliable and has a history of meeting his financial obligations or if he is self-employed and you do not want to go through the child support collection unit.

Other Shared Expenses in Raising Children

In addition to basic child support—which is intended to cover the basic living expenses of minor children, such as food, housing, and clothing—the parents may also be required to share certain additional expenses involved in raising children.

The court may order that the noncustodial parent (or a parent having joint custody and with whom the child lives 50 percent of the time or less) share the following child-rearing expenses:

Health insurance. The court may order one spouse to purchase or maintain employer-provided health and/or life insurance for the couple's children.

Uninsured health care. The noncustodial parent is often required by the court to pay a prorated portion of any present or future uninsured medical expenses of the children (it is discretionary but often considered). This can encompass medical care, dental care, corrective lenses (glasses, contacts), orthodontia (braces), physical therapy, and psychological counseling.

Child care. If the custodial parent works, the noncustodial parent must pay a prorated share of child care (or after-school care) costs. If the custodial parent is seeking work or participating in qualifying educational activities (that is, leading to employment), it is also within the court's discretion to apportion reasonable child care costs to the noncustodial parent. Keep cash receipts or canceled checks as evidence of payment to the child care provider; you can also have the child care provider testify in court.

The noncustodial (or other joint-custody) parent may also be required to pay for a prorated share of the children's present or future private, special needs, and/or postsecondary educational expenses as well as enrichment activities, such as summer camp, sports programs, and lessons. This determination will be based upon the unique circumstances of the case and the best interests of the children.

A KINDER, GENTLER, SMARTER, BETTER WAY TO CHILD CUSTODY AND SUPPORT

Jim and Angela had two young children, ages three and five, when their marriage started falling apart. They fought often and vehemently, sometimes in front of their children, upsetting them greatly. Realizing that the situation was having a negative impact on their children, the couple went to counseling. Although the therapy helped them to resolve their disputes more calmly, it did not save their marriage.

They decided to split up but remained in therapy to help make the transition to separate households as smooth as possible for their children. With their children's welfare foremost on their minds, Angela and Jim sat down together and worked out a joint custody arrangement with a nearly fifty-fifty time-sharing schedule. They also decided to live a few blocks away from each other so the children would be able to see friends, attend the same schools, go to their favorite places to play, and know the other parent was close by and available. Their coparenting arrangement enabled the children to spend the maximum amount of time with each parent with the minimal amount of shuffling back and forth. When the time came to tell the children, they did so together.

Jim and Angela each retained an attorney with a reputation for negotiating amicably and not engaging in unnecessary litigation. Because they had ironed out most of the custody arrangement on their own, the only major issue to be resolved was child support. Though both parents worked, Jim had a greater income. They resolved this by agreeing Jim would pay Angela a monthly child support amount equal to the difference between what he would pay Angela if she were to have sole physical custody and what Angela would pay Jim if he were to have sole physical custody. Using the standard child support formula, based on his annual salary of $75,000, Jim would pay $1,375 per month support; based on her $50,000 salary, Angela would pay $916 per month. So Jim agreed to pay the difference of $459 per month in child support. Since Jim's income was about 30 percent higher than Angela's, he also agreed to pay an additional one-third of the children's costs for nonreimbursed medical and dental care, child care, extracurricular activities, and educational tuition.

The couple settled the other aspects of their divorce amicably, and neither they nor their children had to enter a courtroom. ∎

POW!

FUTURE OFFSPRING: A NEW FRONTIER IN FAMILY LAW

Advances in reproductive technology are presenting controversial legal challenges for couples who freeze their embryos for future implantation, then later divorce. Should the frozen embryos be considered property and their ownership be decided no differently than a house, car, or pet might be in a divorce settlement? Should they be treated as children with their best-interest "custody" determined by agreement or court order? Should either spouse be allowed to use these embryos to have a child without the other one's permission? Should the noncustodial parent of such future high-tech offspring be required to provide support and be allowed visitation? Should the fertility clinic maintain ownership, having the right to sell or donate the embryos or to destroy them? Divorced spouses often do not agree on what should be done with their frozen embryos. Few states have legislation in place to deal with these issues, and the prevailing politics in that jurisdiction usually dictate the court's rulings on these cases. As the field of reproductive technology grows, these and other issues as well as the litigation and laws that arise from them will become more common. Until then, if you are considering assisted reproductive technology, take the time to research and carefully consider both the medical and legal aspects of such an arrangement. A consultation with an attorney is also recommended.

Chapter 9

Getting Your Dues: Money Matters

"What you focus on is what you get."

—Lois P. Frankel, *Nice Girls Don't Get Rich*

WOMEN TEND TO PICK their battles in a divorce or separation, and of all the battles they might face, the one they're least likely to fight fiercely for is their financial security. Although wives often handle the routine bill-paying, account balancing, and budgeting for their families, many don't know the net worth of their marital estate, let alone what portion of it they're entitled to when the marriage ends. In the confusion and stress of a divorce, some women underestimate the financial resources they'll need to survive and to provide for their children in the short-term as well as for the long haul. Even women who are financial powerhouses can turn into timid church mice during the money rounds of a divorce.

The bottom line: Unless you are independently wealthy (and won't have to give your husband a big chunk of that wealth), you cannot afford to be a pushover when it comes to financial matters in a divorce or separation.

You will need money to provide for yourself and for your children, if you have them, during and after the divorce. That money has to come from somewhere, and if you're like most women, your income alone won't cut it. You will probably also need child support and possibly spousal support from your husband as well as your fair share of the money and property that the two of you own together.

The laws and guidelines for determining who qualifies for child support and how much are fairly straightforward, though there are potential glitches (such as imputed income) and complications (such as divvying up child-rearing expenses beyond basic support), as covered in Chapter 8. Far more challenging is determining and getting whatever spousal support and financial settlement to which you are entitled.

The financial settlement of a divorce or separation has two major components:

1. Division of marital property
2. Assignment of marital debts

Deciding how to divvy up everything that you and your husband own and owe can be one of the most grueling and contentious parts of a divorce. Spousal support is an even more volatile issue. Going to trial and having a judge make those decisions for you isn't any better and, in some cases, is worse. Whether you and your husband slug it out on your own or in a courtroom, the better prepared you are for the financial settlement process, the better your chances are of getting a square deal.

Your first orders of business should be to determine the value of your marital estate and the value of your contribution to the marriage. As difficult as it might be to break down a relationship created out of love into money and things and to then insist on an equitable division of the material remnants of your marriage, it is imperative to do so. If you shortchange yourself now, it could put you in a financial bind that could take years, even the rest of your life, to recover from.

Quantifying Your Contribution to the Marriage

In preparing for the divorce proceedings and developing the theory of your case, identify all of the ways in which you have contributed to the marriage. The next step is for you and your lawyer to put a dollar value on each of those contributions—which includes:

- Any money, investments, real estate, inheritance, and valuable possessions you brought to the marriage (and, if you live in an equitable distribution state, have shared with your husband), even if they've since been liquidated
- All of the income you've earned and other forms of compensation you've received (such as health insurance, profit sharing, stocks, pensions, disability benefits) during the marriage
- Any valuable items you've given to your husband as gifts
- All of the major purchases you've made to "feather the nest" and to otherwise benefit your family, such as vacations
- All of the intangible (nonmaterial) things you've done to benefit your family—raising children, maintaining the family home, entertaining your husband's colleagues, helping out with the family business, giving up your job to relocate for your husband's career, enabling your husband to obtain a degree or vocational training, caring for your spouse's children from a previous marriage or his elderly parents, etc.

Think back and account for contributions you've made throughout the marriage. Don't overlook material and monetary gifts you gave to your spouse or contributed to the household, including those that benefited you as well as your spouse or family. For example, if you had a 401(k) prior to getting married that you cashed out during your marriage to buy a car or to use as a down payment on a house, make sure to let your attorney know (or to factor them in if you're trying to negotiate a financial settlement without an attorney).

Don't hold any punches by ignoring or undervaluing the "intangible" contributions you've made to your family, your spouse, and your home. There is no more valuable or more difficult job on earth than raising children. Maintaining a household takes considerable skill and effort. And there is a whole lot of truth to the expression, "Behind every successful man is a supportive woman." While it may have seemed that your efforts to be a good wife and mother often went unnoticed during your marriage, in a divorce it all counts. Everything you've done to benefit your spouse and your children has a monetary value. But it's up to you and your lawyer to identify and quantify those contributions when presenting and substantiating the theory of your case.

The Net Worth of Your Economic Partnership

In a divorce, the *marital estate*—all of the property owned and debt owed by the couple—must be disclosed, assigned a dollar value, and divvied up between the two parties. Generally, the more property and debt you have, the more complicated this is to do and the more important it is to have a good matrimonial lawyer in your corner. Even if you and your husband have few valuable possessions, little money, and minimal debt, it is important to divide it all up fairly and to have an attorney review any financial settlement before you sign it.

It also helps to do your homework so that you have a firm grasp of your financial situation before you negotiate or agree to anything. This includes:

- Preparing a budget of your postdivorce financial needs
- Cataloging your property
- Conducting cost-benefit analyses to determine whether it is cost-effective for you to receive each asset and assume each debt on your "wish list." For example, can you really afford to keep the house?
- Preparing a net worth statement of your marital estate

The *net worth* of a marriage, as in any economic entity, is the difference between the total value of all assets (money and property owned) and the total value of all liabilities (debts and monies owed) by the two parties. All courts require that each spouse fully disclose the assets and debts of the marriage in a *statement of net worth*. You will also need to provide certain substantiating documentation—such as paycheck stubs, tax returns, bank account statements—at some point. The courts require this information not only for the purpose of dividing the marital estate but also to determine child support and spousal support issues. If you do not comply with this mandatory disclosure, you may be subject to court-ordered penalties or sanctions, legal fees, or a more favorable ruling for your husband.

Ironically, it is not unusual for a husband to report a substantially lower income and/or fewer assets than he actually has. If you are not well-informed of your family's finances, including your husband's income and any investments or business he may own, now is the time to get up to speed—and quickly. Before you agree to any aspect of a financial settlement, you need to know the whole picture and uncover any assets or imputed income.

The first step in determining the net worth of your marriage is figuring out what you have and what it's worth.

Inventory of Property

The *marital property* that must be divided between the husband and wife in a divorce encompasses all of the assets owned by you and your husband. Under equitable distribution laws and most community property laws, everything acquired by either you or your husband during the marriage is considered marital property and is subject to division, with the exception (in most states) of inheritance, gifts to one spouse (and not the other), and personal injury awards.

Each spouse's *separate property*—typically whatever you brought to the marriage—is usually not subject to division (though it can be in some community property states). Personal injury awards, inheritance, and gifts to one spouse but not to or from the other may also be considered separate property.

To prepare for the financial settlement portion of your divorce, you will need to take an inventory of both the marital and separate property of you and your husband. During negotiations, your lawyer and your husband's lawyer will try to agree on what is marital and what is separate property as well as the value of each item. They will then attempt to divide everything equitably, which is usually more or less evenly. Alternatively, they may each propose a general settlement package that does not classify each item as either separate or marital property. Either way, if no agreement on the division of assets and debts is reached, the financial settlement will ultimately be up to the judge to decide what is marital and what is separate property, and then to divide the property between you and your husband. Your lawyer, armed with the information you've supplied her and the theory of your case, will then try to convince the court to give you the most favorable award possible.

Identifying, classifying, and valuing the assets and debts of a marriage is one of the most tedious, and can be one of the most contentious, issues in equitable distribution states. While it can be straightforward in some cases, it can be very complex in others. A useful way to catalogue property is a technique to which I've ascribed the easy-to-remember acronym **ICE-T:** Identification, Classification, Evaluation, and Tax implication. Here's how it works:

Identification. Make a list of each asset and each debt that you and/or your husband have, regardless of whose name the property or loan may be in.

Classification. Distinguish marital property from separate property.

Evaluation. Determine the monetary value of each property. Create a "wish list" of the assets you would receive and the debts you would assume in an ideal financial settlement, ranking the items you are least willing and most willing to relinquish.

Tax implication. Consider how receiving each asset and assuming each debt on your "wish list" in a settlement will impact your tax liability.

You should also do a preliminary cost-benefit analysis of at least your high-priority items. That way, when an offer is put on the table, you will be better able to determine how close or far it is from being equitable. In complex property settlements, it is not uncommon to adjust your numbers and priorities frequently.

Marital Property

Marital property is defined as "things of value arising out of the marital relationship." Technically, anything the courts recognize as property in an equitable distribution state can qualify as marital property under the right circumstances, and as such, be subject to equitable division. An asset or debt is usually deemed marital property if either you or your husband or both of you obtained it between the date of your marriage and the date the divorce (or legal separation) was filed in court. It may also qualify as marital property if you acquired it after the divorce proceedings began and marital assets were used to buy the property. The court typically gives little credence to the name on the titled asset or debt. Generally, marital property includes:

- Money—checking, savings, money market, safety-deposit boxes, cash on-hand
- Income derived from employment—wages, salaries, bonuses, profit sharing

- Income not considered an asset
- Real property—your home, vacation homes, time-shares, investment property
- Vehicles—cars, trucks, boats, motor homes, jet skis, motorcycles
- Retirement plans—pensions, 401(k), IRAs
- Stocks, bonds, securities, annuities
- Insurance policies with cash-surrender value
- Businesses and professional practices in which either spouse has an ownership interest
- Household furnishings—furniture, appliances, TVs, stereos, home computers
- Valuables—jewelry, antiques, art, furs, collectibles
- Gambling and lottery winnings
- Wedding gifts, gifts to both parties, gifts to one another
- Items having sentimental value—photographs, mementos, family heirlooms, pets
- Degrees, professional licenses, certifications, promotions, association memberships, any credential acquired during the marriage that enhances earning potential (equitable distribution states only)

In cases where a business is considered a marital asset and one spouse is going to retain all of the interest in that business following a divorce, the other spouse is entitled to either a monetary or a property award in exchange for the other spouse's corporate interest. In a matrimonial case, a forensic accountant usually determines the value of the business.

Separate Property
Things that do not fall into the category of marital property are considered separate property under equitable distribution law. The types of separate property that are excluded from

equitable distribution and remain with the spouse who possesses them or whose name is on the title are:

- Items you or your husband possessed before you were married, such as jewelry, securities, and real property
- Items given to you or your husband (not to both) during the marriage as an inheritance, a gift from someone other than the other spouse, or an award compensating you for personal injury damages
- Any item for which you and your husband have a written, notarized agreement stating that the property is separate and belongs to one spouse or the other

TKO!

DIVORCE MISTAKE #14
Believing what's his isn't yours. If you owned 50 percent of a business, you wouldn't expect to receive a smaller share of the profits simply because you kept things running smoothly "behind the scenes" while your partner was out drumming up new business. Marriage is an economic partnership, and as such, you are entitled to your fair share of all its assets—including your husband's fancy new degree or wildly successful business.

Conversion of Separate Property to Marital Property

There are three ways in which separate property can legally become marital property and thus qualify for equitable distribution:

1. If separate property increases in value and the increase is a result of you or your husband's direct or indirect contributions during the marriage, the increase in value may become marital property.

2. If the separate property has been commingled with marital property during the marriage, the sum of the property becomes marital property.
3. If the separate property is sold or transferred during the marriage, the proceeds of the sale or transfer may be considered marital property.

For instance, if you received a separate cash gift from an uncle but deposited it into the family bank account, it may then convert from separate property to marital property. Likewise, if you or your husband bought or sold some of the securities from an account you brought with you to the marriage and the value of the account then increased during the marriage, the increased value may be considered marital property.

Similarly, if you owned a house before the marriage, and marital assets were put into the house and the house increased in value during the marriage, the increase in value may be considered marital property. This may be the case whether the investment was in material improvements to the house; in marital money used to pay the mortgage, insurance, or taxes; or nothing more than your or your husband's labor in fixing up or maintaining the home.

If your husband owned a home prior to the marriage, sold it during the marriage, and bought another home with the proceeds of the sale of the first one, this new home may be marital property and may be distributed between you and your husband.

The same holds true for any business that you or your husband may have owned separately before getting married. If the business or professional practice increased in value, and you, your husband, or both of you worked there while married, the increased value of the business may be marital property. Indeed, even if only your husband worked in the business while you cared for the home and family, thereby freeing his time to focus on the business, you actively contributed to the increased value of the business and so it qualifies as marital property.

When the increase in the value of separate property is due to *passive appreciation*, the increase is not considered marital property. Passive appreciation is when the increase in value is due to market forces and not to the actions of either spouse. Passive appreciation is common to stocks, bonds, and real estate. So, if you had a securities account before you were married and it increased in value for no reason other than that the market went up and not because of investment decisions by either you or your husband, the entire value of the account remains your separate property.

Valuation of Property

Once you've identified all marital and separate property, the next step is to evaluate, or determine the monetary value of, each of those items, so that the pool of marital assets can be divided. This process is known as *valuation*. Often, determining and then proving the value of an item, such as a business, requires hiring a professional evaluator and, if the case goes to trial, his or her expert testimony.

The Importance of the Valuation Date

In a valuation, each marital asset is typically categorized as being either *active* or *passive*, and its *valuation date* is specified.

Active assets are those in which an increase or decrease in value is due to the conduct of the spouse having title to that asset—for example, a business or practice in which that spouse has direct involvement. The valuation date of an active asset is typically the day the divorce or separation is filed. The courts view this as the date the economic partnership ends and, accordingly, the point at which the noninvolved spouse is no longer a contributor to, and so is not entitled to a share of, any increase in the value of that asset from that day forward.

Passive assets are those for which any increase or decrease in value is due to market conditions or the efforts of third parties, not to the direct actions of either spouse. An example of a passive asset is real estate. The valuation date of passive assets is usually the first day of the trial (or the date the two parties agree upon, if there is no trial). This ensures that the spouse in whose name the asset is titled does not receive all of a windfall if the asset increases in value during the divorce proceedings. However, recent case law has allowed equitable distribution windfalls on a case-by-case basis.

Keep in mind that the active/passive approach to setting the valuation date is a guideline and not an immutable rule.

Valuing Marital Property

Following are some general guidelines for determining the value of marital property for the purposes of equitable distribution. A forensic evaluator is often required to determine and/or to substantiate in court the value of many of these assets.

Income

You should determine the value of all salaries, wages, gambling winnings, tips, bonuses, profit sharing, and royalties earned by you and your spouse. The tax returns, income statements, paycheck stubs, account statements, and other documentation you pull together for your attorney will provide most of this data.

Also make a list and determine the value of any "perks"—such as expense accounts, freebies (such as laptops and cars), allowances (i.e., child care, Internet service, special clothing), and use of company vehicles, apartments, services, and amenities (i.e., fitness center membership).

Real Property

For a few hundred dollars, you can hire a licensed real estate appraiser to estimate the fair market value of your property—

and provide a detailed report of her *appraisal*—by comparing the condition and features of your home (size, age, location, improvements, amenities) with those of recently sold comparable homes in your area. If you can't afford an appraisal, you can request a *sales analysis* from a real estate broker, who will suggest a competitive market price for your home after comparing it with similar properties. Though not as comprehensive and precise as an appraisal, a sales analysis is usually free—and can be used to price the property if you expect to sell it soon. Another option is for you to check out similar properties currently for sale in your area—which is useful only if you and your husband agree on the value you come up with, because this yields only a ballpark figure that probably won't hold up in court.

Vehicles

The value of a car, truck, boat, motor home, motorcycle, or other vehicle used for personal (not commercial use) is usually the going resale price for a similar vehicle in your area less whatever money is owed for that vehicle. The most commonly used guideline for valuing cars, pickups, SUVs, and vans is the Kelley Blue Book, which all used-vehicle dealerships and automotive loan lenders have on hand. Your insurance agent may also be able to tell you the market value of your vehicle.

Household Furnishings

This includes furniture, fixtures, appliances, recreational items, home electronics, musical instruments, music and book collections, decorative items, kitchenware, linens, gardening tools and equipment, home maintenance tools and equipment, etc. Generally, the distribution of such property is resolved between the two parties through negotiation or a lottery-type process. If the spouses dispute the value and/or who should receive specific property, their attorneys or the court may intervene by having an appraiser determine the value of each item in question. The value of such property is usually the *fair market value*—that is, the price at which a like item would be expected to sell, when neither the buyer nor the seller is under any compulsion to buy or sell and both have reasonable knowledge of the relevant facts.

Beware of what I call the "espresso maker syndrome." This is when a divorcing couple goes to blows over who gets the espresso maker (or plasma TV, or Italian leather couch, or whatever), running up thousands of dollars in unnecessary legal fees arguing over a $150 machine and holding up a financial settlement worth hundreds of thousands or millions of dollars. Such disputes also often have an emotional, rather than a financial, basis—an inability to let go of the relationship or a desire to exact revenge. While it is reasonable to want to hold on to something to which you place great sentimental value, it makes no sense whatsoever to haggle over something that, in terms of both monetary and personal value, is just not worth messing up your financial settlement. Let go and compromise on the small stuff, and save your energy and money for more important stuff, such as getting the family home, spousal support, or a share of your husband's business so that you can support yourself and your family.

Valuables and Collectibles
This may include artwork, antiques, cameras, fine china, jewelry, precious metal (gold bars, silver coins), and various collections (fine books, pewter, guns, records, crystal, pottery, etc.). You may want or need an appraisal of such items by a professional specializing in that field, and the court may require such an appraisal if you go to trial or the value of the declared item is in dispute.

Pensions and Retirement Funds
Pensions, 401(k), 403(b), IRA (individual retirement account), Keogh, money-purchase, annuities, and other retirement

funds that are acquired during the marriage are marital property. You are also eligible to collect on the spousal portion of your husband's Social Security benefit—if you've been married for at least ten years and are not yet eligible to collect your Social Security benefits. The only type of retirement plan that is separate property is a disability pension. The retirement fund may be provided by you or your husband or by either of your current employers or unions. The fund is typically invested and held with a financial institution or a broker, but the courts have been known to recognize even a nonvested retirement fund as marital property.

In a divorce, when either spouse has a pension, a Qualified Domestic Relations Order (QDRO) is usually required. A QDRO is a set of documents that instructs the pension administrator on how to address your and your husband's pensions in accordance with your settlement or divorce decree. The QDRO must be submitted to the judge for signature along with the divorce judgment. The pension administrator must approve it before it is submitted to the court. A pension valuator is usually retained to determine the value of a pension.

Increased Earning Capacity from Education or Training

For the purposes of equitable distribution of assets, some states consider the value of college and university degrees (associates, bachelors, masters, doctorate, medical, law) as well as certain vocational, technical, trade, and professional certifications or training programs (accounting, carpentry, culinary, fire fighter, law enforcement, plumbing, real estate, etc.) obtained by either spouse during the marriage. The increased earning capacity of a degree/certification is based on the average annual salary in your area for people having that same credential.

A forensic accountant should be retained to determine the increased earning capacity conveyed by a degree/certification and which portions of that benefit are separate property versus marital property. This is determined by calculating the difference between the increased earning capacity projected for the total number of years the spouse is expected to reap the benefit of the degree/certification and the percentage of the total benefit amount that is available during the years of marriage.

You may be entitled to a share of only the marital property portion of your husband's increased earning capacity conveyed by a degree/certification.

Increased Earning Capacity from Professional Licenses

This asset encompasses any license required to earn a living in a specific profession or trade, such as medicine, law, accounting, insurance, teaching, real estate, plumbing, electrical engineering, and many others. As with degrees and certifications, the value of a license is in the enhanced earnings capacity it conveys, and a forensic accountant is required to determine which portion of that benefit is marital property and subject to division between the two spouses. In valuating licenses, however, the earnings capacity is based on actual earnings and projected earnings, rather than on statistical earnings for the profession in question.

If your husband is earning substantially less than the average income in your area for people having the same license and years of experience, the court may find that he is not putting his license to "best use." In that event, the court would ask the forensic accountant to determine your husband's potential earning capacity if he were putting his license to its best use.

Again, you are entitled to a share of only the marital property portion of the licensing benefit—that is, the amount available during the marriage. The courts may also consider the value of a professional license when determining the amount of spousal support being granted. In that event, the court may reduce either the maintenance or property division award, because the same income stream is being used to determine two distinct judgments.

Increased Earnings Capacity from Professional Distinctions and Honors

Professional honors, promotions, and other things that lead to increased earning capacity have been valued in the same way as professional licenses to the extent that they provide a provable enhanced earning capacity and the spouse not in possession of the honor contributed to its attainment.

POW!

SHARING THE (SELF-MADE) WEALTH

Courts in at least two states have ruled that the skills or career path of an artisan, actor, professional athlete, investment banker, or any person whose expertise has enabled him to become an exceptional wage earner should be valued as marital property. Even if such as career does not require an academic degree, professional license, or specialized training, the individual's increased earning capacity resulting from a lucrative career that arose during a marriage is subject to equitable distribution.

Businesses

A business that is owned in full or part by either spouse—whether it is a sole proprietorship, a small business, or a large corporation—is considered marital property. There are many methods of valuating a business, and the courts usually do not specify which method to use. It is prudent and often necessary to hire a business valuator with experience in the type of business in question. In most cases, the value of a business will be based on its fair market value. Factors that are traditionally considered in arriving at a fair market value include:

- The nature and size of the business
- The economic outlook of the business and of the industry at large

- The financial history and current condition of the business
- The earning capacity of the business
- The value of any tangible assets and intangible assets (referred to as *goodwill value*)
- The book value of stock or the sizes of the stock block being valuated
- Any dividend-paying capacity

Other accepted methods of business valuation include asset valuation, capitalization of earnings, net excess, and adjusted book value.

The *asset valuation*, or *liquidation*, method calculates the asset and then subtracts the debt and other liabilities to arrive at the price that may be realized if the business were to be sold at this time. This is generally useful when the business has substantial assets that can be sold or liquidated, such as real estate.

The *capitalization of earnings* method is best for valuing products and service-related businesses. With this approach, past earnings of your husband's business would be used to estimate its future earnings, which are converted to a present value for determining your share of the value of the business. The pretax earnings (net income, less personal expenses) are capitalized—that is, multiplied by a factor that considers risk, past performance, future history, and the nature of the business.

The *net excess*, or *excess-earning*, method considers both tangible and intangible assets (reputation of business, brand recognition) in calculating the fair market value of a business. The normal costs of doing business, unusual expenses, taxes, and reasonable compensation are deducted from net income to arrive at the net excess earnings. This figure is averaged and capitalized to determine the intangible (goodwill) value of the business, which is then added to the net income. This method of valuation is useful in any business in which the company's reputation is a component of its success.

The *adjusted book value* method can be used when a business has income-producing assets, such as securities, that are not imperative to the operation of the business. The book value is assets minus liabilities, which is then adjusted for depreciation and the market value of any inventory.

The personal income your husband derives from his business is a significant factor in determining the business's worth and, ultimately, your share of it. Business income can often be determined simply by reviewing tax returns and W-2 and/or 1099 statements. However, it is sometimes difficult to decipher a business owner's true income, and your husband certainly wouldn't be the first to unintentionally or deliberately deflate his income. Issues such as unreported cash, inflated tax deductions, legitimate tax deductions from which personal benefit is derived, reimbursement for personal expenses, and fringe benefits must not be ignored in ascertaining the value of your husband's business.

Professional Practices

Various professional practices, such as law, medical, dental, and accounting practices, are marital property subject to equitable distribution if they were established during the marriage. The appreciation in the value of a practice that was started before the marriage may also be marital property, if the appreciation is a result of your or your husband's contributions to the practice, directly or indirectly, during the marriage.

As with a business, you will need a forensic accountant to value the practice. Generally, a professional practice has two separate components: tangible and intangible assets. Tangible assets include essentially anything that can be sold and therefore converted into money, such as office furnishings and equipment. Intangible assets include client lists and goodwill. Goodwill toward the practice is tied to the practice's achievements, name, reputation, employees, and location, which generate an economic benefit to the owner. The greatest value of a professional practice is often in tangible assets. In contrast, the greater value in a business is typically its tangible assets.

In a divorce settlement, the worth of a practice is usually based on its fair market value, book value, or liquidated value. The fair market value is basically the going rate in your area for a practice of that type. The *book value* is the value specified on the practice's financial statement, if it has one. However, the book value may be misleading, because financial statements often only estimate factors such as depreciation and frequently ignore appreciation of underlying assets. A liquidation model of valuation appraises the value of all tangible assets and liabilities to determine a value available to the owners if they were to sell the practice; it does not consider intangible assets.

When both a professional practice and a professional license (or degree) benefit are involved in a divorce settlement, it can be confusing and complicated. It is important to remember, though, that the value of the practice is distinct from the value of the enhanced earning potential of the license. So, even though both come from the same income source, they are two separate assets and each may be subject to property division and spousal support considerations. However, some courts will reduce either the asset benefit or spousal support, since both come from the same income stream.

Investments

If you or your husband has an economic interest in an ongoing business, such as a corporation or partnership, it is considered a marital asset if the interest was acquired during the marriage. This is usually in the form of corporate stock, securities, bonds, or a partnership interest in the company. You or your husband would have a *partnership interest* in a business that either of you founded (or cofounded) during the marriage. You could also own an *equity interest* in a business in which you have invested money (or another form of asset, such as your expertise) during the marriage. Stocks, bonds, and securities may have been included in employment compensation either of you received from an employer or purchased individually or jointly by you and your spouse during the marriage.

Because these types of assets usually increase and decrease in value according to market conditions, they are usually valued on the date of trial. The valuation standard usually applied to these assets is fair market value. How fair market value is determined depends on whether the company is privately held or publicly traded.

A *publicly traded* business is one that is registered under the Securities Act, which means the company has more than $3 million in total assets or more than 500 shareholders. A privately held company is one in which ownership of the company is restricted to the people who founded the company, inherited the company, or were granted shares by the founders. The stock in a privately held company is held by a small number of individuals, and the stock is not registered under the Securities Act.

When a stock is traded on an established securities market, such as the New York Stock Exchange, the value of the stock can easily be determined. The fair market value will be the amount at which each share of that particular stock is currently being traded (bought and sold), provided it is under normal market conditions. The stock's quoted price will likely *not* be deemed the fair market value if an unusually small number of shares were traded on the valuation day or if abnormal conditions affected the stock exchange quote. Under those circumstances, another method of valuation will be used, as dictated by the United States Treasury Department, as follows:

1. When the stock's highest and lowest selling price on day of valuation can be determined, the *mean method* of valuation is use. The highest and lowest prices are added

together, and this sum is divided by two to arrive at the mean, or average, price.

2. When the highest and lowest selling prices for the date of valuation are unavailable, the closing price of the stock on the date of valuation and the closing price on the last trading day before the valuation (or a date before or after the valuation day, within a reasonable time period) are averaged.

3. When no selling price is available for either the date of valuation or within a reasonable period before or after the valuation date, the fair market value is the mean (average) between the bid and asking price on the date of valuation.

When shares of stock are not registered under the Securities Act, such as with a privately held company, valuation is based on various factors. These typically include the type of business, the growth and stability of the company, the economic outlook of the company, the current financial condition of the business, any prior sales of stocks in the company, and goodwill established by the company to its customer base.

An interest in a stock option plan provided by your or your husband's employer may be marital property and subject to equitable distribution if the plan began during the marriage. However, it also depends on whether the option is contingent upon your or your husband's continued employment with the company after the divorce. If the stock options were granted for compensation for past services, they are subject to property division. However, if stock options were awarded as an incentive for future services, they are usually not considered marital property.

The options statement and stock options plan booklet issued by the plan administrator will explain how the company will treat options under various circumstances, such as divorce. These documents will also specify the number and type of options, exercise price, expiration dates, and the circumstances under which the company issued the options. If you do not have these documents on hand, you can request them from your or your husband's company.

There are two main types of stock options: investment and nonqualified. The primary distinction is that an investment stock option can only be exercised or transferred by an employee, while a nonqualified stock option may be assigned to a nonemployee, though the income will still be taxed to the employee.

Tax Issues to Consider

Before you agree to the terms in a divorce property settlement, you should first consider all of the tax implications associated with the proposed distribution of property. For example, spousal support is taxable income for the recipient and a tax deduction for the payee, unless otherwise noted in the divorce agreement.

Most of the marital property either spouse receives in an equitable distribution agreement is not taxable.

When assets are transferred from one spouse to another pursuant to a divorce agreement or court order, the transfer is not taxable. However, in choosing which assets to advocate for, you should consider the after-tax worth of the asset. For example, $10,000 of cash in the bank is worth more than $10,000 in an IRA account, because tax will have to be paid on the IRA but not on the cash. Similarly, you should deduct from the value of a house any capital gains taxes that will need to be paid.

RX FOR A FAIR SHARE OF FUTURE EARNINGS

Heather married Samuel shortly before he began medical school. They both worked, but Heather worked more hours and took care of the household so Samuel could study. Samuel's income covered tuition and other educational costs; Heather's income paid most of their shared living expenses.

Medical school proved to be harder on the marriage than it was for Samuel. By the time he had completed med school and when he was nearly done with his residency, the marriage was over. They had no savings or debt; they lived in a rented apartment; they had no children together; and Heather had no retirement account from her employment. Their sole asset consisted of Samuel's medical degree. Both parties agreed to hire a forensic accountant to value the medical degree, and they split the cost of the appraisal, which valued the medical degree at nearly a million dollars.

Heather's lawyer argued that due to her substantial contributions to the marriage and the lack of other assets, Heather was entitled to half the value of the degree. Samuel agreed, but he did not have $500,000 or enough separate property to pay her. What he did have was increased earnings capacity over time. The couple and their respective attorneys negotiated an agreement whereby Samuel would pay Heather in monthly installments until she had received her share of the value of the degree. The agreement was written to specify that the payments were equitable distribution of marital property. Consequently, because the benefit was not spousal support, Heather didn't have to pay taxes on it and Samuel didn't get a tax deduction for the payments. ∎

Fight or Settle? Weighing Costs Versus Benefits

After you have accounted for all of your marital assets and liabilities—identified, classified, valued, and considered any tax implications—you should give careful thought to which items are vital and important to you and which you're willing to compromise or let go of. Talk over this "wish list" with your lawyer. You might also want to consult with a close confidante (preferably, someone with a financial background), a financial planner, and/or your accountant.

A word of advice: be realistic. When splitting one household into two and going from two incomes to one, which is the case in most modern divorces, you can expect your expenses to go up and your quality of life to go down to some degree. Simply put, you may not walk away from the divorce with all of your possessions intact, with sufficient means to immediately replace the ones you don't have, and the money to live as well as you might be accustomed. Of course, that does not mean you should walk away with any less than you are entitled to and need to meet your and your family's basic living expenses.

Above all, make sure you can afford to assume responsibility for all of the assets you're asking for and any debts that come along with them. If you get the house but don't have sufficient income to keep up with the mortgage, taxes, insurance, utilities, and maintenance, the cost exceeds the benefit.

Do a cost-benefit analysis for every marital asset on your wish list, carefully weighing the economic gain against the economic cost. Don't let the potential emotional gain or loss enter into the equation. Step back and look at the big picture—analyze how the sum total of all the assets and all the liabilities on your wish list will affect your cash flow, credit status, net worth, and standard of living in both the short and long term. Then revise your wish list according to what is in your best economic interests.

Only when you're clear on what you need, want, and can do without should you enter into financial negotiations with your husband and his attorney. When negotiating, keep in mind that you might be able to use certain material items as leverage in negotiating for something you need more. For example, if you and your spouse have both called dibs on the vacation condo in Tahoe, and he really wants it and you could live without it and really need more cash to live on, you might concede to hand over your equity interest in the condo in exchange for larger or longer cash support payments.

How much you will need to negotiate—and whether you and your spouse will reach agreement without going to court—

depends, in large part, on how far apart your wish list is from your husband's and on how realistic each is. It also depends on how much time, legal fees, and energy you're both willing to expend on fighting over your property and spousal support, if that is an issue on the table.

If and when you and your husband do come to agreement on all money and property matters, either one of your attorneys will draw up the final settlement documentation. Each of you will have the opportunity to review the agreement and modify it (negotiate the modification) before signing it. Once both parties have signed off on a mutually agreeable financial settlement, it will be submitted to the court with the divorce documents for the judge to approve and sign.

If you lock horns in negotiations and call it quits, the property settlement will be decided in court. All of the preparation you've put into the divorce up to that point will come in handy in a trial: the history of your marriage, your postdivorce budget and cash-flow projections, your quantified contributions to the marriage, your property inventory, your wish list (based on a cost-benefit analysis), the theories of your case, and all of the documents and other evidence you've gathered to substantiate your case. Though the decision rests in the judge's hands, you will have done everything possible to better your odds of an equitable financial settlement.

Most courts consider the following factors when determining the equitable distribution of marital property:

- The income and property of each party at the time the marriage commenced and at the time the divorce/separation action commenced
- The duration of the marriage and the age and health of both parties
- The need of a custodial parent to occupy or own the marital residence and to use or own its household effects

- The loss of inheritance and pension rights upon dissolution of the marriage as of the date of dissolution
- Any award of spousal support, alimony, or maintenance
- Any equitable claim to, interest in, or direct or indirect contribution made to the acquisition of marital property by the party not having title, including joint efforts or expenditures, contributions, and services as a spouse, parent, wage earner, and homemaker to the career or career potential of the other party
- The liquid or nonliquid character of all marital property
- The probable future financial circumstances of each party
- The impossibility of evaluating any component asset or any interest in a business, corporation, or profession and the economic desirability of retaining such asset or interest intact and free from any claim or interference by the other party
- The tax consequences to each party
- The wasteful dissipation of assets by either spouse
- Any transfer or encumbrance made in contemplation of a matrimonial action without fair consideration
- Any other factor that the court shall expressly find to be just and proper

The court will also take into account the unique qualities of your relationship and the circumstances of your marriage. The judge will take the information she has been given, consider the arguments made by the spouses' respective lawyers, and then will use her best judgment to distribute all assets and debts as fairly as possible.

The court will then order the actual physical distribution of the property. Depending upon the nature and value of the marital assets involved and the respective financial position of each spouse, the disbursement may consist of a one-time settlement payment or payments made over a period of years upon the sale or disposition of various assets.

SUPERWOMAN GETS A WELL-DESERVED BREAK

Beverly and Asher were married twelve years, had two young children, and owned their home. Asher met Beverly in college after immigrating to the United States. Beverly and Asher earned identical degrees in social work. Then Beverly went to work full-time, while Asher went on to earn a higher degree and eventually to start his own psychotherapy practice. Asher's business was not very profitable and became less so as the marriage grew strained and drew to a close.

During the divorce negotiations, a forensic accountant confirmed that Asher's business was not worth much. Consequently, his lawyer claimed Asher had insufficient income to help support Beverly and their children. Beverly's attorney argued that Beverly had made enormous contributions to the family and to Asher's career, both financially and otherwise. She was the primary caretaker of the children, the homemaker, and the only steady wage earner of the two.

Beverly later testified in court that Asher had explicitly asked her to put her career goals on hold to enable him to pursue his. He'd promised that if Beverly supported the family while he got his degree and built his practice, later he would support them all so she could return to school to obtain the advanced degree needed to further her career.

Instead, Asher's attorney claimed Asher had no financial obligation to Beverly. To add insult to injury, Asher also asked for joint custody, half the value of the apartment, and 50 percent of Beverly's pension.

The case did not settle and went to trial. My theory of the case was that Beverly had been a superwoman—earning an income, running the household, raising the kids, and supporting her husband's career. The judge recognized Beverly's significant contributions and awarded her 100 percent of the apartment, all of her pension, and sole custody. Asher was ordered to pay child support based on his prior earnings, because, the court observed, he appeared to have intentionally run his business into the ground. He was also ordered to contribute to the children's day care, medical, dental, uninsured health care, educational, and extracurricular activity expenses as well as to pay alimony and Beverly's attorney's fees. ■

Debt and Credit Issues

Marital debts are assigned to the two parties in much the same way as assets are divided. You can sometimes convince the court to assign a greater share of the marital debt to your spouse by arguing that he has higher income to pay the debt. You could also advocate that if your debt is due to your spouse not complying with court orders or agreements for support, he should be responsible for the debt.

If you are divorcing in an equitable distribution state, you should request that your husband be held solely responsible for any debt that is not a marital expense.

To help protect your credit, establish separate credit by opening a new credit card in only your name before the divorce is finalized. You should also obtain a copy of your credit report from all three credit bureaus before the divorce action commences and before it is finalized. If you find any errors or reports of bad credit that are your husband's sole responsibility and not yours, you or your accountant should write a letter to the credit reporting companies requesting that these items be corrected or removed from your credit reports. You will also need to provide documentation verifying that the debt has been paid or is not your responsibility to pay.

If you fall behind on any payments during the divorce, you can sometimes avoid a credit problem by writing a letter to the creditor, explaining why you are delinquent in paying, citing your previous history of on-time payment (if applicable), and asking for their assistance in working out a payment arrangement for the future.

Spousal Support

Spousal support, *spousal maintenance*, and *alimony* are all different terms for the same thing: money paid as support to one spouse by the other after a divorce. (This is not to be confused with child support, which is a separate issue.) Spousal support usually consists of interval payments over a specified period of time—for example, monthly payments of $1,000 for ten years or weekly payments of $300 for six months. Sometimes, it is paid in a one-time "lump sum." There is no set formula for determining whether either spouse qualifies for spousal support or how much, how often, and for how long an entitled spouse is to be paid. Each state has its own laws governing spousal support.

The most common factors considered are:

- The length of the marriage
- Each spouse's age and health
- Whether both spouses earned outside income
- The monetary contributions of each spouse to the marriage
- The future earning capacity of each spouse

The court may also consider one or more of these factors:

- The family's lifestyle during the marriage
- The nonmonetary contributions to the marriage of the spouse seeking maintenance
- Whether the spouse seeking maintenance earned less money than the other in order to run the household and care for children
- Any loss of lifetime earning capacity on the part of the spouse seeking maintenance that is a result of having foregone or delayed education, employment, or career opportunities to run the household and raise children
- The ability of the spouse seeking maintenance to "start over" and begin supporting herself (or himself)

The weight given each of these factors may depend on where you get divorced. As a matter of public policy nationwide, however, there is a strong interest in spouses becoming financially independent as soon as possible following a divorce. This means courts are less inclined to award a lot of spousal support for a long time. The major flaw with this predisposition is that courts often do not recognize what it takes for a previously financially dependent spouse to achieve real financial independence. They do not understand how difficult it can be to support yourself when your "job" has been to work, without pay, to support your husband and family. You may need to go to school or get training first and then might have to start your new career in a low-paying, entry-level position. This is especially true if you've had little or no income-producing work experience. If you are in that position, you will probably need to hire a good matrimonial lawyer who will fight hard for you in court.

In any event, few spouses offer maintenance out of the goodness of their hearts, and many judges won't take it upon themselves to order support if neither spouse offers or requests it. So if you need and feel you are entitled to spousal support, speak up now or forever hold your peace. Work with your attorney to develop a convincing theory and to gather evidence to convince your husband or the judge that a maintenance award is in order. Because as difficult as it can be to get alimony in a divorce settlement, it is virtually impossible after the deed is done.

TKO!

DIVORCE MISTAKE #15
Failing to ensure support. If you are granted child and/or spousal support, make sure to protect yourself against your husband's potential inability to pay by insisting that he take out life and/or disability insurance with you as the beneficiary. That is your only reassurance of continued financial support in the event of your ex's death or disabling illness or injury.

Chapter 10

Pro Divorce: A Blow-by-Blow Playback

> "What I'm doing in this car flying down these scream-
> ing highways is getting my tail to Juarez so I can legally
> rid myself of the crummy son-of-a-bitch who promised
> me a tomorrow like a yummy fruitcake and delivered
> instead wilted lettuce, rotted cucumber, and a garbage
> of a life."

—Anne Richardson Rolphe

FEW PEOPLE ENTER INTO a marriage expecting it to end.
When it does, even fewer expect it to end well. Actually, most
people don't know what to expect and assume they have little
control in a divorce, especially over the legal proceedings. Ironically, the legal process is the most predictable part of a divorce,
and you have much more control over it than you may realize.
Indeed, the more in control you are, the smoother the legal proceedings will go and the better the outcome will be.

Remember, about 95 percent of divorces are settled without
a trial. That leaves the majority falling somewhere in between,
with varying degrees of posturing and pummeling exchanged
between the spouses and their respective lawyers before they
work out their differences and put down their gloves, at least
in terms of the divorce settlement. Whether that results in a

quick and easy decision or a nasty drawn-out bout depends to a large degree on how well you and your spouse can each control your emotions so that you'll make prudent decisions, rather than emotional ones, and thus facilitate, rather than complicate, the legal proceedings. Though that is easier said than done, it's doable—and advisable.

The legal requirements and wrangling involved in a litigated divorce are considerably more extensive than those of a divorce that is settled out of court. Chapter 6 describes the basic legal procedures and documents involved in collaborative, mediated, and arbitrated divorce/separation settlements.

The typical rounds of a litigated divorce are, in sequential order:

1. Commencing the action
2. Pleadings
3. Emergency relief motions
4. Financial disclosure
5. Discovery
6. Settlement negotiations
7. Note of issue
8. Trial
9. Final disposition

If you and your husband settle out of court—whether through negotiations (between attorneys), a collaborative divorce, mediation, or arbitration—you will be able to bypass at least the trial phase. Other proceedings covered in this chapter won't apply to your case either. For example, if you and your spouse agree on everything right up front, you can usually go straight from commencing the action to note of issue and then to final disposition. You may not need an emergency relief motion and can skip that phase, or your marital estate may include no assets warranting a valuation during the disclosure/discovery phase.

In any divorce or legal separation, a considerable amount of time and energy goes into completing all of the steps, preparing all of the documentation, and following all of the rules required by the court in question and for the case in question. A missed step or a mistake could mean having to do the paperwork or process all over again, increasing your legal costs and delaying your divorce. A legal faux pas could also hang up or complicate your case, not to mention irritate the court clerk or judge. So it is important for your lawyer to know and to follow all of the court's rules—and for you to have a basic understanding of the legal process.

Knowing what to expect and having a knowledgeable attorney will help you to get the upper hand during the proceedings and a favorable settlement when the final round ends.

TKO!

DIVORCE MISTAKE #16

Disregarding court orders. It's not wise to defy the judge. The penalties can be harsh: disallowing your evidence or testimony in defense of a contested issue because you failed to provide discovery; defaulting the disputed issue or the entire case in favor of your spouse because you failed to show up at a deposition; and awarding legal fees to your ex because he came through with the discovery you failed to provide. If you need more time to prepare for a hearing or provide evidence, have your lawyer ask the court for a reasonable extension in writing—and then follow through.

Commencing the Action

A *matrimonial action* legally begins when either spouse files a *petition* for divorce or legal separation with the court. Some states also require that a summons be filed with the petition.

A summons or petition informing your husband you have filed for divorce or separation, the grounds for divorce, and the relief requested. The summons also requests his response and the name and contact information of his attorney.

A petition (or notice) to the court outlining the basic facts of the civil suit.

The petition usually states:

- The names and addresses of the person filing the summons (the *plaintiff*) and the person upon whom the suit is being filed (the *defendant*)
- That the defendant has a certain period of time (usually twenty days) to respond to the summons
- The general reason (ground) for the action
- The main items the plaintiff is requesting in the final action— for example, child custody, child support, specific property, and legal fees

You must file a summons with the court even if you and your husband both want the divorce and have already mutually agreed (informally) to all terms of the divorce. If yours will be a no-fault divorce, you would also file other uncontested divorce documents. Some courts require that you take additional steps before or along with filing the summons and/or petition. In New York State, for instance, you must first go to the courthouse and purchase an index number, which the court uses to keep track of the case. Some jurisdictions may also require you to file certain other documents along with your summons and petition, such as a statement of income and expenses, a parenting plan, and a notice about using mediation services (if such information is not included in the petition). You will also be required to pay a filing fee to the court.

You can file a summons and/or petition with the court without your husband's prior knowledge. Whether or not your husband is aware of your intentions beforehand, the law requires that you notify him in writing that you are divorcing or legally separating from him. This is usually accomplished by having the summons and/or petition *served* (provided) to your husband, and most courts require that every reasonable attempt to serve the defendant be made.

The plaintiff's attorney usually prepares the summons and/or petition, creating several duplicate original copies, each of which must be signed by the plaintiff and notarized. The plaintiff's attorney gives an original copy to her client, files an original copy with the court, and has an original copy served to the defendant. The defendant's copy is usually hand-delivered by a *server*, a third-party authorized by the court to perform this *personal service*, as it is called. Some courts and some circumstances allow for the summons and/or petition to be mailed to the defendant's lawyer; this is referred to simply as *service*. The plaintiff never serves the summons and petition directly to the defendant.

Upon successfully serving the defendant, the process server returns an *affidavit of service* to the plaintiff's lawyer. This is a short statement whereby the server swears that he or she either properly served the legal document to the person it was meant for or that the process server was unable to serve the papers (for example, the defendant refused them or was no longer living or working at that address). The affidavit of service is filed with the court at the same time as the summons and complaint or soon after.

Spouse's Response to Summons and/or Petition

Your husband's attorney will typically respond to your summons or petition with a formal letter (or form) called a *notice of appearance*. If your husband decides not to hire his own attorney and chooses, instead, to represent himself (acting *pro se*) in the divorce, he may respond directly to the summons with his own *notice of appearance*. If your husband fails to respond after you've made sufficient effort and waited a sufficient period of time, you may be able to get a divorce by default. A *default divorce* is possible when the defendant refuses to participate in the divorce process—meaning, he does not hire a lawyer, respond to court papers, show up in court, etc. In that case, your lawyer would submit an Affidavit of Service along with the required paperwork for an uncontested divorce. The court will usually grant the divorce (or separation), because not responding to the action conveys the same meaning as not contesting the divorce. If you've asked for assets and/or financial support from your husband, the court may give your husband another chance to respond by scheduling a hearing at which both you and your husband (and your respective attorneys) will be expected, but not required, to appear.

Every divorce or separation action is either contested or uncontested. An *uncontested divorce* may be granted in one of two circumstances:

1. The defendant has defaulted on the divorce proceedings
2. The two spouses agree to divorce or separate and to all the settlement terms, and they're just filing the necessary paperwork with the court to make it official

If your husband responds to your summons and/or petition but disputes any of the relief you are seeking, it is a *contested divorce*. Every item you're asking for in your action is considered *relief*: custody, child support, spousal support, and any assets. In fault states, relief also refers to the grounds for divorce. If the defendant contests the grounds and the court rules for the defendant (does not approve the grounds), the divorce may be denied. If the court approves the grounds, the subsequent judgment for divorce would be the "relief" the plaintiff was seeking.

Pleadings

Once the case has commenced, the plaintiff and defendant enter and exchange their pleadings. Unlike a summons, which contains very general statements, the plaintiff's *pleadings* (may be called a *complaint* or *par of the petition* in some states) details the family's income and possessions, what specific items she wants (for example, sole legal custody with primary physical custody of your children, $1,500 a month in child support, etc.), and her position on what happened in the marriage (in fault states). The defendant's pleadings, called an *answer*, may include his *defense* (justification for denying) against any relief (items) requested by and (grounds) claimed by the plaintiff.

Pleadings are usually prepared by the spouses' lawyers. You and your husband must each sign your individual pleadings under *oath* (or *verified*)—that is, notarized. The pleadings is then filed with the court and exchanged with the other party.

Your husband may respond to your verified complaint by serving you with a *verified answer* (the defendant's *pleadings*), in which he either admits or denies the allegations in your complaint. His verified answer may also *set forth* (state) any defense he has to your allegations. A *defense* is an explanation and/or evidence that is intended to invalidate the plaintiff's alleged grounds for divorce. In addition, your husband may choose to *bring* (make) a *counterclaim* for divorce, whereby he petitions the court to grant him (and not you) a divorce and states his requested relief and his grounds (in fault states) for the action. In response to any defense and/or counterclaim made by your husband, you should file with the court and serve your husband with a *verified reply*. In your verified reply, you would admit or deny the allegations in your husband's counterclaim; you might also include your defense against such claims.

Emergency Relief Motion

After the matrimonial action has been filed and while it is still pending in court, you and your children are entitled to live your daily lives in relative security, free of any serious threats to your financial, physical, and emotional well-being. If that security is in any way threatened, your lawyer can file certain motions to alleviate or diminish that risk. This is called a *pendente lite* (action pending) motion.

A pendent lite motion may be for any one or more of the following temporary and immediate forms of relief:

- Child custody (legal and/or physical, sole or joint)
- Child support
- Insurance coverage for you and/or your children
- Spousal maintenance
- Allowing or disallowing minor children to be taken or moved to another state or country
- Restraint of assets (prohibiting your spouse from selling property, liquidating assets, depleting marital monies, transferring for the purpose of hiding assets, etc.)
- Financial disclosure or penalties for willfully failing to disclose financial information
- Requiring an abusive spouse to move out
- Protection from harassment and domestic violence
- Payment of your legal fees
- Payment of expert witnesses (although you must first prove to the court that such experts are needed)

A divorce or legal separation can take months, even years, to settle and finalize. In the meantime, your circumstances can change dramatically. During that time, your husband may stop paying certain bills or significantly reduce his financial contribution to your family. The two of you may be unable to agree on child custody and visitation issues or on which one of you should stay in the family home. Under the stress of a divorce, your husband may become uncharacteristically verbally, emotionally, or physically abusive. So, even if you don't need emergency relief at the start of the divorce, you may need it at some point during the divorce proceedings.

At any time after the summons or petition has been filed and before the judge finalizes the divorce, your lawyer can file an *application* with the court for whatever emergency relief is legally available in your jurisdiction and applicable to your case. A judge will review the application, which is filed as an *order to show cause*. Your attorney then serves the emergency relief motion on your husband or his attorney, if he has one.

A date is scheduled for the parties and the lawyers to go to court, called the *return date*. The defendant (or his attorney) files a response to the order to show cause, called an *affidavit in opposition*. The defendant may also include a *cross-motion for emergency relief*. A hearing is then held, often on the aforementioned return date, in which the court may hear arguments from both lawyers about whether the court should grant or deny the request for *pendente lite* relief. The judge may rule on the motion then but may want time to consider the matter further and to make a written decision. This can take one to three months or even longer.

If the court rules in your favor and your husband does not comply with the order, the court may try to force compliance by holding him in contempt and either fining him or throwing him in jail, or both. Such trips to the county jail are usually brief—unless the noncompliance involves a criminal act, such as breaking a protective order and committing physical assault or other act of violence, in which case the defendant would also have to answer to a higher court and may do substantial time in the "big house."

On the subject of protective orders, the process for requesting and the criteria for qualifying for such an order vary from one jurisdiction to the next. Generally, you are required to convince the judge or another court-appointed authority that your husband has recently caused or has threatened to cause injury to you or your family or damage to your property. An order of protection may prohibit your husband from coming within a specified distance of the family home, your place of employment, and other locations you frequent, such as your parent's home and your children's schools. It may also prohibit your husband from contacting you by phone, e-mail, text messaging, pager, and any other form of communication. It may even include restrictions on your husband's access to your children, if the judge deems it appropriate.

It is essential for you to keep in mind that a protective order does not and cannot provide you with absolute protection against your husband. It merely serves as a potential deterrent to a violent or volatile husband, who may, instead, become so incensed by the order that he strikes out at you in defiance or retaliation. If you need a protective order, do not hesitate in getting one. But take other preventative and precautionary measures as well—such as changing your locks, never agreeing to meet your spouse in a private place to "discuss" things, and enlisting your family, neighbors, coworkers, and neighborhood safety officers to help keep a watch over you, your children, and your property. Report any and every violation to the proper authorities, and call for emergency police assistance if your spouse threatens you, your kids, or your property in any way.

Financial Disclosure

After the initial pleadings have been served and filed and usually before your first court date, you and your husband will have to make full financial disclosure, unless the two of you have formally agreed to waive this requirement. *Financial disclosure* is a written report of all of your and your husband's separate and joint assets and liabilities. This includes, but is not limited to, all money, real estate, personal property, businesses, partnerships, investments, retirement accounts, life insurance, etc.

Each of you must file a separate financial disclosure document with the court, which they must also provide to each other. Many courts require financial disclosure via a sworn *statement of net worth* or the equivalent required by that jurisdiction. A net worth statement provides a detailed accounting of all of your assets, debts, accounts, income, and expenses, which you must swear is accurate and complete (by signing and notarizing). The court may also require both parties to provide the other with substantiating documents, such as tax returns, paycheck stubs, account statements, canceled checks, and asset valuations.

In creating your statement of net worth (or the equivalent document used in your jurisdiction), you and your lawyer will be able to draw much of the information from the extensive preparation you did before the summons or petition was filed. Of course, you may need to update some of this information and will probably need to gather other information and documentation as well. Make sure to check and double-check your figures and to be consistent in documenting income and expenses on either a monthly or annual basis, as any mistake or inconsistency can throw off your numbers.

The purpose of full financial disclosure is to give the court a complete picture of your and your husband's financial situation. In other words, where's the money? Where is it coming from and where is it going? What is the nature of the assets, where are they now, who is using or benefiting from them, and how much are they worth? What is the nature and amount of liabilities, and who's paying them? How much does each spouse earn and how much money does each need to live on and to support the children? The judge needs to know this information as well as other details regarding your and your husband's finances to decide how to divide up assets, assign debts, decide on the amount of child support, establish how the parents will cover the children's extra expenses (such as uninsured medical expenses, day care, activities, and college), and determine whether and how much alimony should be paid by whom and to whom.

Depending upon the complexity of your and your husband's finances and on the level of cooperation and forthrightness between the two of you and your attorneys, financial disclosure may be simple or extensive and may continue for a few weeks or several months. If either party or the judge suspects that the financial disclosure is not exactly accurate and/or complete, the matter will need to be examined more closely in a procedural step generally referred to as *discovery*.

Discovery

The discovery part of a divorce consists of those legal actions used to obtain any additional information or documentation that may be needed to make a judicial (meaning, both legal and prudent) decision about any of the issues of the matrimonial action. Discovery may also be required when the accuracy, completeness, and/or legitimacy of any evidence in the case is challenged by either party (or their attorneys) or the court. The acquisition (*discovery*) and/or evaluation (*investigation*) of such evidence may be required to resolve either custody or financial issues, or both. The need for such actions may arise at any time during the divorce proceedings—from the time the summons or petition is filed until the case goes before the judge for final disposition.

The discovery and investigative phase of a divorce or legal separation may include any or all of the following legal tactics:

- Interrogatories (written questions submitted by one party to the other, which must be answered in writing within a specified period of time)
- Request for documents
- Request for release of information
- Request to admit evidence
- Request for identity of expert witness
- Request for a custody evaluation (conducted by forensic psychologist or psychiatrist)
- Request for medical or mental health evaluation to determine the fitness of a parent in a custody trial

- Request for appraisal of real estate or other property
- Request for valuation of a business, professional practice, or degree
- Court subpoena of either party, corroborative witnesses, or expert witnesses to provide documentation in court
- Depositions of either party or third parties to answer questions under oath at the attorney's office issuing the notice; to take the deposition with a court reporter present

Interrogatories

You and your lawyer may also find that in trying to understand the family finances and assets, you have certain questions that are not being answered by the documents. In a court case, formal, written questions to you or your husband are called *interrogatories*. The person being questioned must respond to the interrogatories in writing, usually through her or his lawyer.

Request for Documents

Either spouse's attorney can request that the other party provide a *copy* of a financial or other document pertinent to the case to both the spouse requesting the document and to the court. Either spouse may also request to see an *original* document if they suspect the copy provided has been altered. The judge overseeing the case may make similar requests of either spouse.

If you cannot access documents that are under your husband's control or are not confident the documents he's provided are complete and authentic, your lawyer can send a *discovery, inspection, and copying* to your husband's attorney. Your husband is then required to provide you with the requested copies of missing documents or with the opportunity to look at original documents within a specified period of time, usually twenty to thirty days. This might include stock certificates, bank records, income tax returns from previous years, land/property titles, loan applications, or any document relevant to financial issues in the case.

Request to Admit Evidence

The attorney of either spouse may submit to the court and/ or the opposing attorney (depending on the state) a *request for admission* of certain facts or expert opinions that are pertinent to any disputed issues in the case. As with interrogatories and requests for documents, the other party's response must be provided within the specified period of time—for example, that a particular account is separate property or piece of real estate.

Request for Identity of Expert Witness

If either you or your husband has submitted a report or opinion of an "expert" on a matter relevant to the divorce—such as regarding the value of your home, your husband's business, or the psychological well-being of your child—the other party or the judge can make a *request for identity of expert witness.* A lawyer (or judge) uses this mechanism not only to learn who the expert witness is but also to discover the expert's credentials, such as education, licenses, and experience. This type of order also asks for a summary of the grounds and reasons for the expert opinion.

The lawyer or judge will often then use the information obtained through this request to find out more about the expert, such as how often and for whom the expert has testified in the past.

Request for Valuation of Property

Either party or the judge may request a third-party *valuation* of a marital asset. A *valuation*, or *appraisal*, is when an expert gives an informed opinion about the monetary value of something, such as a house, land, car, artwork, business, pension, luxury item, or anything else that has value. This opinion is usually based on an established method of analysis for valuing that item that dictates which factors are considered and how each factor is weighted.

A small business is usually evaluated by an accountant or a business valuator. Pensions are typically evaluated by an actuary. Real property is typically evaluated by a real estate appraiser with experience in appraising residential or commercial properties, whichever is being evaluated in the divorce.

If you and your husband agree to sell an item with an uncertain value, you do not need an appraisal. As long as you are putting the item on the open market (making it available to anyone who wants to buy it), you will presumably get the highest market price for it, which for the purposes of property division is usually considered its *true value*. Of course, if there is no viable market for something because it is unique or if you want to sell an item for less than its true value for nonfinancial reasons (for example, to your child), things become more complicated and you may need to hire an expert appraiser after all.

Such experts commonly require *retainers* (money up front), which you and/or your husband will have to pay. If you do not have the financial resources to pay for an evaluation, your lawyer can ask the court to order your husband to pay the expert's retainer.

Depositions

Another tool sometimes used to request and obtain information in a divorce case is called a *deposition*, or an *examination before trial* (EBT). As with interrogatories, if the court grants your lawyer's request for a deposition or EBT, your husband will have to verbally answer direct questions from your lawyer.

Usually, if your husband is to be *deposed* (questioned) at an EBT, at some point your husband's lawyer will also probably exercise his right to depose you. Of course, your lawyer should be present while you are being questioned. Before the EBT, your lawyer should fully prepare you for the deposition by reviewing all of the potential questions and facts in the case. During the EBT, your lawyer will also listen carefully to each question you are asked by your husband's lawyer and tell you whether or not you should answer it.

The EBT will usually be held in the office of either your or your spouse's attorney. The answers will be given under oath, so you must tell the truth. The session will also be recorded, usually by a court reporter, who will sit in the room and type the questions and answers on a special stenographic machine. The court reporter will then prepare a written transcript of the EBT. Some jurisdictions allow for the session to be recorded with an audio recording device rather than a court reporter. A stenographer must then transcribe the audio recording. Although an audio recording is usually much less expensive than a court reporter, it may not be as accurate. If the recording is not clear—for example, because two people are talking at the same time and the transcriber cannot figure out who is speaking—the transcriber is not able to speak up and ask for the questioner or answerer to repeat what was said, as a court reporter can.

CALLING OUT A CHEESY PARTNER

Madelena and Stephen were partners in marriage and in business for many years. They were co-owners of a wholesale cheese company, in which they bought cheese from suppliers and resold it to grocery stores and restaurants. From the time they started the company, the couple worked on the business together. Both had equal access to all business records, accounts, vendors, and customers. During the last three years of the marriage, Stephen took over complete control of the business. He would not permit Madelena to have contact with any suppliers or customers, he hid the business records, and he closed the bank account where they had always done business. By the time Madelena hired a lawyer, she had no idea how much money the business was bringing in or where it was going. Stephen was also giving her less and less money for personal and household expenses.

Her attorney immediately commenced divorce proceedings on Madelena's behalf. She also simultaneously requested *pendente lite* motions ordering Stephen to pay for an accountant to evaluate the worth of the business, an immediate review of the business records, and for Stephen to pay temporary support to Madelena and for her attorney's fees.

During several stages of court proceedings that followed, Stephen failed to disclose all of the business's income. It became clear that to determine the business's true net income, they would need information from the business's suppliers and customers. The court issued subpoenas (court orders) directing the suppliers and customers to provide the necessary documentation or else they would have to appear in court with the information or be held in contempt. The information they furnished demonstrated how much cheese Stephen was actually buying and selling. Based on the true net income of the business, Madelena received an equitable distribution of the business, spousal support, and her attorney's fees. ∎

Settlement Negotiations

The negotiations phase of a divorce or separation usually involves a succession of meetings between the two parties and their attorneys, which are commonly called *settlement conferences*. It typically also involves meetings between the two attorneys and the judge, which may or may not require the direct participation of the parties. Settlement conferences and court conferences may be scheduled at any time during the divorce proceedings, until the final disposition is handed out.

Court Appearances

You may be required to appear in court (make an *appearance*) for a variety of reasons—for example, for a motion conference. Your attorney should tell you when your appearance in court is required or advised. She should also detail what will happen during the court proceedings and, if necessary, go over the testimony you may be required to give and the questions you may be required to answer.

When it is likely that you will be called upon to speak during the proceeding, you and your lawyer will usually sit together in the *well*, the tables in front of the judge's bench. Otherwise, you can sit in the audience while your attorney represents you from the well.

You may be tempted not to attend court hearings in which your appearance is not mandatory or necessary. After all, time in court is time away from your responsibilities, and court proceedings can be stressful or even tedious. But I strongly advise you to make a point of appearing in court at every conference in which your case is on the court's calendar. Your regular and prompt appearance at all court proceedings associated with your case provides several advantages:

- It keeps you fully informed of the proceedings and progress of your case.
- It enables you to see your lawyer in action to make sure you're getting what you're paying for.
- It enables you to immediately respond to unexpected questions or claims raised during the conference that only you can answer, thereby helping to keep your case on track.
- It indicates to the judge, as well as to your lawyer, that you are very interested in and involved with your case and that its outcome is important to you.
- It reminds the judge that her decisions on your case will affect you, a real person, as well as your children.

When the court schedules an appearance, the opposing parties and their attorneys are notified of its purpose and date in advance. The notification may also specify the block of time for which the case has been scheduled, for example, between 9:00 A.M. and noon or between 1:00 and 4:00 P.M. However, it is usually impossible to determine exactly when on that day or within that block of time your case will begin or how long it may last. With that in mind, you should do everything possible to clear your slate for the entire day that your case conference or appearance is scheduled to be heard in court, including any child care arrangements.

Ten Tips for Your Day in Court

You will impress the judge, facilitate your case, and improve your odds of a positive outcome if you abide by the following courtroom etiquette:

- Show up, and be on time, for all court hearings involving your case—whether or not you will be required to testify.
- Never bring your children to court, as they may be disruptive and the proceedings may be traumatic for them.
- When answering questions and testifying, be succinct, be specific, and stick to the facts. Advance preparation with your lawyer will help with this.
- When asked to speak, speak clearly (no mumbling) and use an appropriate speed (not too fast or slow), volume (don't shout or whisper), tone (not shrill or terse).
- Speak only if asked to; don't speak out of turn or call out from the audience.
- When it's your turn to speak, don't swear, mudsling, or name-call.
- Pay close attention to what is being said and take notes if need be.
- Keep your cool and act like a sensible adult. Don't act angry, arrogant, defensive, demanding, defiant, helpless, vindictive, or whiney.
- Dress appropriately—no sexy or grubby attire, extravagant jewelry, or gaudy makeup. Business attire—and a business demeanor—will indicate to the judge (or jury) that you mean business.

Court Conferences

A litigated divorce case typically involves court conferences in which there is a discussion between the two lawyers and the judge or the judge's court attorney. Court *conferences* may be held in the courtroom or occasionally in the judge's private chambers or a conference room of the courthouse. Sometimes you and your attorney are required to attend the court conference; other times, only the attorneys need appear.

During a conference, the judge might also schedule additional conferences, hearings, deadlines for requested information, and other relevant legal proceedings. So when you go to court you should always bring your calendar and know your schedule for about the next six to nine months. When your case reaches the conference stage, your ability to appear in court is crucial.

Before each conference, you should give your lawyer a list of any dates over the upcoming six to nine months when you are not available to appear in court, along with the reason you are unavailable. This list should be relatively short, and the reasons for your unavailability should be valid. Usually accepted reasons to miss court include a child's statewide school entrance or achievement exams, a wedding or other religious ceremony of a close relative or friend, or a long sought-after or an impossible to reschedule medical appointment, or special employment events. Do not make any travel plans that cannot be altered at the last minute during your divorce. The court may not be sympathetic to your claim that you bought tickets and cannot get your money back. You want to always leave the court with the impression that your case is the most important thing in your life; giving lame excuses for why you cannot be present will not convey that message.

The judge will hold these conferences for a variety of reasons. The most common types of court conferences held during the period of time leading up to the trial and the primary reasons for them are the following:

Preliminary conference—to make sure the case is moving along on a schedule.

Compliance conference—to address discovery issues.

Pretrial conference—to decide which, if any, issues are settled and which are to be tried.

Preliminary Conference

A *preliminary conference* is usually held in the courthouse, either in a courtroom or in a nearby conference room, a jury room not in use at that time, or a robing room (where the judge puts on her robe, often right next to her courtroom.) This meeting, which sometimes goes by the term *advance case review*, may instead be held in the judge's *chambers* (private office), which may be in the courtroom or another building. In attendance at the conference will be the judge, the lawyers for the opposing parties, and sometimes one or both of the divorcing spouses. The judge's law assistant and/or a court attorney may also be present.

The purpose of the preliminary conference is to *set forth* (establish) the issues in dispute. During this meeting, the judge will also set up a schedule for the exchange of financial information, depositions, and any motions that the lawyers plan to make. The judge will also set a date for the next conference or all subsequent conferences, depending on the judge's procedures.

Compliance Conference

This is usually the next court meeting to follow a preliminary conference. At the compliance conference the judge's law assistant will usually meet with the attorneys to find out if they are having any problems with financial disclosure or other discovery matters. The conference may serve to help the parties focus on what issues the parties still need to resolve. Dates will be set to monitor the remainder of the discovery process. Then, once the discovery process is completed, court dates will be set for a pretrial conference. If the trial date has not already been set, a tentative trial date may also be agreed upon during the compliance conference.

Pretrial Conference

The pretrial conference is often held in the judge's chambers, and both attorneys must be present. You and your husband may be required to be present for all or part of the conference. During this very important conference, each attorney will make his or her case and advocate the position of his or her respective client on the main issues that remain unresolved in the case. The judge will then offer her input by telling the lawyers what she thinks about the issues. She often will suggest a solution or middle ground that she thinks might be reasonable given the facts and circumstances of the case.

TKO!

DIVORCE MISTAKE #17

Delay tactics. One of the most common ways in which a party in a divorce attempts to impede the process is to fire a lawyer and hire a new one. If you've got good reason to change attorneys, the judge will usually grant you an *adjournment* (a new court date) to give your new lawyer time to get up to speed on your case. But, if the court views you as having deliberately or repeatedly delayed the case, whether by switching lawyers or some other tactic, you may not get an adjournment—much less the judge's favor—and you and your lawyer may not be adequately prepared to fight and win the case.

During or immediately after the pretrial conference, your lawyer should speak with you about what happened during the meeting and any recommendation the judge made during the pretrial conference. If you and your lawyer agree with the judge's solution to all the unresolved conflicts in your case, you can give your lawyer authority to *settle* (close) your case on the terms suggested by the judge, along with the other terms upon which the lawyers have already agreed.

The pretrial conference may take as little as half an hour or most of the day, depending upon numerous circumstances, such as the complexity of your case, the reasonableness or lack of it on the part of your husband's lawyer, and the judge's schedule on that particular day. Just in case, make sure you are available for the entire day so you can focus on concluding your case and getting on with your life.

Settlement Conferences

Not all conferences must involve the judge. At any time during your case, right up to the day of trial, there may be occasions when either your lawyer or your husband's lawyer feels it is appropriate to deal directly with each other (and the opposing spouses) to try to settle your case, or at least specific issues in your case, before it goes to trial. This is called a *settlement negotiation*.

Settlement negotiations may take a variety of forms, including:

- A series of calls, e-mails, and/or letters between attorneys
- A one-on-one conference between the two attorneys, with or without the opposing parties in attendance
- A conference with the attorneys and the judge or the court attorney present, with or without the opposing parties in attendance

Before going to a settlement conference or agreeing to any settlement negotiated by your lawyer, you and your lawyer should fully discuss the terms, conditions, and ramifications of the agreement. It is vital that you understand all aspects of any potential final settlement being discussed before agreeing to any-thing. Remember, your attorney is your agent and should never act without your authority or try to coerce you into agreeing to something you believe not to be in your best interests. She should neither take a deal nor turn one down without first explaining it to you and obtaining your explicit permission to do so.

That said, your lawyer should also give you her informed opin-ion about what you should do. It is also wise to talk it over with a trusted confidante who is intimately familiar with your situa-tion. Ultimately, however, you are the only one who can make the final decision regarding any settlement offer. After all, you are the one who is going to have to live with the consequences.

When presented with a settlement offer, you may well be put in the position of having to decide—often very quickly—whether to make a concession to settle the issue (or the case) or to give some-thing in exchange for getting something. Sometimes, the deciding factor may be nothing more than realizing that the only benefits to settling are to gain your freedom and to save the time and expense of continuing the fight. Just keep in mind that, as difficult and lengthy and costly as a divorce may become, the decisions you make now will significantly impact you or your children for years to come. Discuss your case with your attorney before each con-ference, so that you can make these important decisions quickly and wisely. Consider all of the factors you and your attorney have analyzed throughout the process, including your immediate and future financial needs and the well-being of your children. Besides, if you reject an offer on the table once, there is no guarantee it will be an option later if you realize it really was a good choice.

Note of Issue

After financial disclosure is over and all the necessary apprais-als, settlement conferences, and court conferences have been completed, the plaintiff must usually file a *note of issue* and a *certificate of readiness* with the court. These documents, which are fairly standard forms your lawyer will draft, notify the judge that the parties are ready for trial. In legal lingo, "ready" means your lawyer has completed certain tasks. In an effort to avoid a lengthy and expensive trial, the judge will usually first hold a pretrial conference to make sure that both lawyers and their clients are really ready for trial. A note of issue, or the equivalent, is also typically required even if you and your husband have settled all issues out of court—whether through collaboration, mediation, or arbitration. This notifies the court to issue the final disposition without holding a trial.

Trial

If your case is not completely settled during or after the pretrial conference, the judge may schedule another pretrial conference if she believes the case is close to settling. Usually, however, the judge will schedule your case for trial. That does not mean your lawyer must, or should, stop settlement negotiations. Your case can be settled anytime before trial. It can settle the day the trial is scheduled to start; it can even settle during the trial. Regardless of whether settlement negotiations are continuing, once your case is scheduled for trial, your attorney must continue to prepare your case as if it were being tried to completion.

Because a trial can be a very extensive and serious undertaking and because your divorce judgment will depend on its outcome, your lawyer will likely do a huge amount of work to prepare for it. This is very time-consuming and will be costly, but it is imperative. Although it is good to hope and attempt to settle out of court, your attorney must be prepared for trial in the event it doesn't. You cannot afford for your lawyer to be caught unprepared for trial because she was too focused on a settlement that falls through at the last minute.

If your case goes to trial, be prepared for several days in court. A trial can last a few days, a couple of weeks, or even several months, depending on the complexity of the issues and the judge's schedule. Some judges will schedule the trial continuously for days at a time; others will space the trial dates apart. After extensive preparation with your lawyer, you will most likely be called as a witness to testify at your trial. Your lawyer will ask you questions during a session called a *direct examination*. Then your husband's lawyer will ask you questions, which is called *cross-examination*. Your lawyer should listen closely to the cross-examination and object to any improper questions, which you may not have to answer. Your spouse will likely be questioned in the same manner. The judge may also ask you and/or your spouse questions.

Other witnesses may include third-party experts, such as forensic accountants and psychologists. Sometimes business part-ners, personal accountants, neighbors, friends, family members, or lovers may be called as witnesses, if they have information on relevant financial, custody, or grounds for divorce issues. Docu-ments and photos may be submitted into evidence as *exhibits*.

Your and your husband's lawyer may each be given the oppor-tunity to make opening or closing statements, at the beginning or end of the trial, which may include the theory of the case. Sometimes the lawyer will also provide the judge with a written *brief*, or *memorandum*, which is a legal and argumentative essay that summarizes the testimony and relevant law.

The judge usually won't disclose his judgment on the spot. You may have to wait a few weeks or even months for a decision.

Final Disposition

Litigated divorce cases, like other civil (noncriminal) cases, are *disposed* (ended) through a *court order*. Most court decisions in litigated matrimonial cases are set forth in a formal written doc-ument, which is called a *judgment of divorce*. The judgment of divorce, which is signed by the judge, signifies that the divorce is official.

If a settlement agreement is reached at the last minute, just before the trial is over, rather than having the negotiated agreement written up, the court may make it official by *oral stipulation*. This may occur when both lawyers, along with you and your husband, speak in open court and say that you each accept the agreement worked out by the lawyers and the judge. When you speak in court, the judge may put you and your husband under oath and ask you questions, for which your lawyer should have prepared you. The statements will also be recorded by a court reporter so that it can be transcribed. The written version of the oral stipulation is then sent to the lawyers. You and your lawyer should check it over to make sure it is accurate. The terms and conditions of the judgment of your divorce to which you verbally agreed in court can then become part of the final judgment of divorce.

Of course, most cases end before going to trial, by the parties voluntarily and mutually reaching a settlement agreement through negotiations and conferences. When that happens, the lawyers will put the final agreement in writing, which will later be incorporated into the court's final judgment of divorce. Once such an agreement is fully executed by each party, meaning that everyone has signed and notarized several copies, the case is technically concluded in court.

If the case is settled in court or the attorneys and the parties want to put the settlement on the record, you and your husband may be required to appear in court with your lawyers, as a formality to officially wind up the case. The settlement will be read into the record in front of a judge and with a court reporter.

One or both of the opposing parties' lawyers then files the required documents with the court (or her designated *referee*) for the judge to review and sign.

Claiming Your Victory

Once the divorce has been finalized by the court and all of the assets and debts have been transferred according to the judgment or agreement, you can finally focus more of your attention on redefining and restructuring your life. Many people think of divorce as the death of a relationship, of a way of living in the world, and it is, but it is also a chance at a new life, and a rebirth for you.

One of the best ways to recover from divorce, which is usually a chaotic and disorienting experience, is to create order in your life. This is particularly important when you have children. This can be as simple as spending extra time with your kids, feathering your nest, creating a budget, and opening a savings account. It is also a good time to nurture yourself, strengthening your mind, body, and spirit for the journey ahead. You might join a divorced women's or single-parents' support group. Take up ballroom dancing or boxing. Get a new hairstyle or a new couch. Reconnect with old friends and make new ones. Get a new career, a new house, or a new boyfriend. Be good to yourself and patient with yourself. It takes time and effort.

No doubt, you fought the good fight to save your marriage and then fought a tough fight to end it as fairly as possible. But you've come out of it a champion. Now, it's time to put down the gloves and move on with your life—even if you have a contrite ex who's spoiling for a fight. Don't let him lure you back in the ring. There are other better ways to hit him where it hurts.

Making a Recalcitrant Ex Pay Up or Put Up

Just when you think the battle is over, your ex reneges on the postdivorce terms he agreed to or the judge ordered. As tempting as it might be to punch his lights out, you really can't do that. Besides, it's much more effective to take him back to court—as many times as necessary—so he gets the message that you're not going to let him off the hook.

He has to fork over assets that legally belong to you. He has to pay his child support and/or alimony, the full amount and on time. He has to make good on any debts and expenses he is legally liable to pay. He has to comply with child custody and visitation rules. The law says so. And there are legal channels available to enforce compliance and to get restitution: garnishment, property liens, judgments, etc.

Child support, custody, and visitation arrangements are not cast in stone, either, though these arrangements are usually more difficult to obtain after a divorce than during one. However, if there are significant changes in circumstances postdivorce that warrant more child support, a change from joint to sole custody, or restrictions in visitation, you can petition the court for the new arrangement. Of course, you'll need to file a new civil suit, and you'll probably need a good matrimonial lawyer. Treat your ex like a business; keep a file of letters, e-mail, and phone conversations between the two of you.

Daring to Love Again

Love is not necessarily easier the second (or even third) time around, but divorce can be if you take precautions before and during the marriage. First of all, when a new love comes into your life—as I certainly hope it does, hopeless romantic that I am, despite my twenty years as a divorce attorney, my own two divorces, and my parent's divorce—embrace it and enjoy it. Go with the passion, but be smart. Get to really know the guy and make sure he's financially responsible, hasn't worked over a former wife or girlfriend in a split, and understands that marriage is an economic as well as an emotional partnership. If you have children, keep the relationship to yourself first and then be careful not to step over any boundaries that might irk your ex-husband or make your kids uncomfortable.

If you decide to remarry, before saying "I do," discuss with your future husband your short- and long-term financial goals. Put your current financial cards on the table—your individual incomes, debts, assets, credit ratings, and spending and saving habits. Create a marital budget, deciding how much to allot to housing and other major expenses, daily expenses, and any luxury items. It is crucial to agree on which funds will be used to pay which bills. If there are children from previous marriages, talk about how to "blend" your two families. If you want children, discuss who will care for them and how you will allocate funds for their education, your retirement, and insurance. Of course, you should also decide a budget for your wedding.

Some couples are wise enough to enter into a premarriage agreement, also known as a *prenuptial* or *antenuptial* agreement. This is a legal contract that addresses financial and other issues that are important to you and your fiancé. These other issues may include children, religion, sharing housekeeping tasks, and career support. You should have your own matrimonial lawyer draw up the prenuptial agreement or at least review it before you sign it. Attached to the agreement should be a financial statement, listing all of your and your fiancé's assets, debts, and income. A prenuptial agreement ensures that promises made are promises kept. If both you and your future husband are willing to enter into a prenuptial agreement and mutually agree to all of the issues it addresses, it can free you to focus on and enjoy your marriage.

TKO!

DIVORCE MISTAKE #18

Failure to move on. You ended your marriage to step out of the ring and to make a better life for yourself and your family. Now that the divorce is final, give yourself some time to nurse your bruises and to mourn the inevitable loss that comes with freedom. Then ditch that heavy old gym bag stuffed with anger, hurt, frustration, disappointment, guilt, and resentment. Take a deep cleansing breath, give your muscles a loosening shake, and step into a new ring—your new life. Comfortable, confident, and strong. Ready, willing, and able to take on the world and not hold any punches.

Glossary of Matrimonial Law Terms

Action: A civil lawsuit or proceeding in a court of law

Adversarial: A matrimonial lawsuit having opposing parties, a plaintiff and a defendant

Affidavit: A voluntary, written or printed, and sworn declaration of facts; in a matrimonial case, affidavits usually accompany motions, so the party won't have to make a personal court appearance

Agreement: A decision made by mutual consent of the opposing parties involved in the suit

Alimony: After a divorce or separation, the money paid by one spouse, as either a lump sum or payments over time, to the other to fulfill the financial obligation conveyed by marriage; also called "maintenance" or "spousal support"

Allegation: A statement of the issues in a written document (a pleadings), which a person is prepared to prove in court

Answer: A formal, sworn and written response by the defendant in a lawsuit that answers each allegation contained in the complaint

Annulment: A legal decree stating a marriage was never valid; having the legal effect of establishing the marriage never existed

Appearance: The act of appearing in court as a party to a suit, either in person or through an attorney

Arbitration: An impartial hearing of a dispute by an impartial third party (chosen by the opposing parties in a suit), whose award the parties agree to accept

Assignment: The transfer to another person of any property, real or personal

Attachment: Taking a person's property to satisfy a court-ordered debt, such as attaching a spouse's wages to collect child support or alimony

Beneficiary: The person(s) named to receive property or benefits in a will or trust

Brief: A written argument by the lawyer arguing a case, containing a summary of the facts of the case, pertinent laws, and an argument of how the law applies to the fact situation

Case: An action, cause, suit, or controversy before a court of law

Chambers: The judge's private office; a hearing in chambers takes place outside the presence of the jury and the public

Child: Minor children (by birth or legal adoption) of two parties involved in a matrimonial action; depending on the state, "minor" may be defined as under eighteen or under twenty-one years of age

Child Support: Money one parent pays to the other parent for the basic living expenses of children, including housing, food, and clothing

Child Support Guidelines: Established by each state, a formula and rule for setting the amount of child support to be paid under normal circumstances, based on the payee's income

Civil Law: Relating to private rights and remedies sought by civil actions as contrasted with criminal proceedings

Collaborative Divorce: A nonadversarial process by which the opposing parties and their attorneys pledge to settle the matrimonial action collaboratively, using cooperative rather than adversarial tactics and litigation

Community Property: Property acquired by a couple during their marriage; the system in some states for dividing the couple's property in a matrimonial action or upon the death of one spouse; usually divided equally (fifty-fifty), regardless of who acquired and who benefited from

Contempt of Court: Willful disobedience of a judge's instruction or an official court order

Contested Divorce: Whereby the parties dispute one or more of the issues in a divorce

Continuance: Postponement of a legal proceeding to a later date

Counsel: A legal adviser; used to refer to lawyers in a case

Counterclaim: A claim made by the defendant in a civil lawsuit against the plaintiff

Court Costs: Expenses of prosecuting or defending a lawsuit, other than the attorney fees; an amount of money awarded to the successful party as reimbursement for court costs

Court Reporter: A person who records testimony, depositions, or other trial-related proceedings and transcribes them

Cross-Examination: The questioning of a witness produced by the other side

Custody Evaluator: A third party, usually a forensic psychologist, psychiatrist, or child therapist, who conducts a psychological evaluation to determine the custodial arrangement that is in the child(ren)'s best interests

Custodial Parent: The parent who has custody of the child at a particular time

Decision: The opinion of the court in concluding a case at law

Decree: An order of the court; a final decree is one that fully and finally disposes of the litigation

Default: Failure of the defendant to appear and answer the summons and complaint

Default Judgment: A judgment entered against a party who fails to appear in court or respond to the charges

Defendant: The person defending or denying a suit

Deposition: Testimony of a witness or a party taken under oath outside the courtroom, the transcript of which becomes a part of the court's file

Discovery: The name given pretrial devices for obtaining facts and information about the case

Dismissal: The termination of a lawsuit

Divorce: A legal judgment or order that ends the marriage between two people; also called "dissolution"

Equitable Distribution: The division of property and debts acquired during a marriage in a divorce

Estate: All of the property owned by a person or jointly by a married couple

Exhibit: A document or other item introduced as evidence during a trial or hearing

Ex Parte: On behalf of only one party, without notice to any other party

Fair Market Value: The value for which a reasonable seller would sell an item of property and for which a reasonable buyer would buy it

File: To place a paper in the official custody of the clerk of court/ court administrator to enter into the files or records of a case

Filing Fee: The fee required for filing various documents

Finding: Formal conclusion by a judge or regulatory agency on issues of fact; a conclusion by a jury regarding a fact

Grounds: Legally recognized (by the state in question) reasons why a person is seeking the matrimonial action

Hearing: A formal proceeding (generally less formal than a trial) with definite issues of law or of fact to be heard; hearings are used extensively by legislative and administrative agencies

Hold Harmless: An agreement by which one person assumes full responsibility for a financial obligation, thereby protecting the other from that liability

Intangible Assets: Nonphysical items that have value, such as stock certificates, bonds, bank accounts, and pension benefits, and that must be taken into account in a divorce or separation

Interrogatories: A set or series of written questions propounded to a party, witness, or other person having information or interest in a case; a discovery device

Joint Legal Custody: A legal agreement or order by which both parents have equal rights and responsibilities for major decisions concerning their minor children

Joint Physical Custody: A legal agreement or order by which the divorced couple's children reside with each parent an equal share of the time

Judgment: The official and authentic decision of a court of justice upon the rights and claims of parties to an action or suit submitted to the court for determination

Jurisdiction: The power or authority of a court to hear and try a case; the geographic area in which a court has power or the types of cases it has power to hear

Legal Separation: An order of the court determining the rights and responsibilities of a husband and wife that live apart and separate without dissolving the marriage

Marital Property: All property acquired during the marriage, regardless of which spouse paid for it, uses it, and to which it is titled

Matrimonial Law: Those areas of the law pertaining to families, including marriage, divorce, child custody, juvenile, paternity, etc.; also called "family law"

Mediation: A process by which an impartial third party facilitates a matrimonial action in which the opposing parties dispute issues

Motion: An application made to a court or judge that requests a ruling or order in favor of the applicant

Negotiation: The process of submission and consideration of offers until an acceptable offer is made and accepted

No-Fault Divorce: A type of divorce by which a marriage may be dissolved without the necessity to allege or prove marital misconduct on the part of either spouse

Noncustodial Parent: When one parent has sole or primary physical custody and the other parent has custody of the child less than half the time

Notice: Formal notification to the party that has been sued in a civil case of the fact that the lawsuit has been filed; any form of notification of a legal proceeding

Oath: A solemn pledge made under a sense of responsibility in attestation of the truth of a statement or in verification of a statement made

Objection: The process by which one party takes exception to some statement or procedure; an objection is either sustained (allowed) or overruled by the judge

Oral Argument: Presentation of a case before a court by spoken argument; usually with respect to a presentation of a case to an appellate court where a time limit might be set for oral argument

Order: A mandate, command, or direction authoritatively given; direction of a court or judge made in writing

Party: A person, business, or government agency actively involved in the prosecution or defense of a legal proceeding

Perjury: The criminal offense of making a false statement under oath

Personal Property: Anything a person (or couple) owns, other than real estate

Petition: The first document filed in court, requesting the matrimonial action and stating the facts of the case, allegations against the defendant, and the plaintiff's settlement requests

Plaintiff: A person who brings an action; the party who complains or sues in a civil action

Pleadings: The written statements of fact and law filed by the parties to a lawsuit

Prenuptial Agreement: A written and sworn contract between an unmarried couple that intends to marry, stipulating their individual rights to property, support, and/or inheritance brought to the marriage in the event of divorce or separation

Pretrial Conference: Conference among the opposing attorneys and the judge called at the discretion of the court to narrow the issues to be tried and to make a final effort to settle the case without a trial

Primary Caretaker: The parent who has provided and continues to provide the majority of the daily care of minor children

Pro Se: When a party represents him or herself in a legal proceeding, waiving legal counsel

Protective Order: An emergency remedy of brief duration issued by a court only in exceptional circumstances, usually when immediate or irreparable damages or loss might result before the opposition could take action

QDRO (Qualified Domestic Relations Order): In a matrimonial action, an order used to divide a pension or retirement plan owned by a spouse

Real Property: Land, buildings, and whatever is attached or affixed to the land; generally, "real estate"

Record: All of the documents, evidence, and transcripts of oral proceedings in a case

Reply: The response by a party to charges raised in a pleading by the other party

Request for Admission: Written statements of facts concerning a case that are submitted to an adverse party and to which that party must admit or deny; a discovery device

Request for Documents: A direction or command served upon another party for production of specified documents for review with respect to a suit; a discovery devise

Retainer: The act of employing legal counsel; the fee the client pays when he or she retains the attorney to act on his or her behalf

Service of Process: The act of hand-delivering writs, summonses, and subpoenas to the party named in the document; also called "service"

Separation Agreement: In a marital breakup, a document that outlines the terms of the couple's legal separation

Settlement: An agreement between the parties disposing of a lawsuit

Sole Custody: When one parent has full authority for all decisions regarding a minor child

Subpoena: A command to appear at a certain time and place to give testimony upon a certain matter

Summary Judgment: A judgment given on the basis of pleadings, affidavits, and exhibits presented for the record without any need for a trial; used when there is no dispute as to the facts of the case and one party is entitled to a judgment as a matter of law

Summons: A document that commences a civil action or special proceeding; the means of acquiring jurisdiction over a party

Temporary Relief: Any form of action by a court granting one of the parties an order to protect its interest pending further action by the court; also called "*pendente lite*"

Testimony: The evidence given by a witness under oath; does not pertain to evidence from documents and other physical evidence

Title: Legal ownership of property, usually real property or automobiles

Transcript: A word-for-word written record of what was said during a trial, hearing, or other proceeding that has been transcribed from a recording or from shorthand

Trial: A judicial examination of issues between parties to an action

Trial Brief: A written document prepared for and used by an attorney at trial, containing the issues to be tried, synopsis of evidence to be presented, and case and statutory authority to substantiate the attorney's position at trial

Uncontested Divorce: A divorce case in which there are no disputes between the two spouses and both parties mutually agree to divorce and to all terms of the settlement

Visitation: The time the noncustodial parent spends with the minor child

Witness: One who personally sees or perceives a thing; one who testifies as to what he has seen, heard, or otherwise observed

Appendix B

Forms and Worksheets

▶ MARITAL HISTORY WORKSHEET

Domestic Violence

If your husband has been abusive, please provide a factual, detailed, and unbiased account of each incident of his misconduct. If you cannot remember exact locations, dates, or times, provide as much detail as possible—for example, "early September, 1989, week night, evening" and "in parking lot of movie theater."

Date: _____ Time: _____ Place: _____

Witnesses: _____

Description of Incident: _____

Date: _____ Time: _____ Place: _____

Witnesses: _____

Description of Incident: _____

Use a blank sheet of paper and the above format to document any and all other incidents of domestic abuse.

Current Living Arrangement

_____ We are not yet separated.

_____ We are separated but have no financial arrangements at this time.

_____ We are separated and have a financial arrangement.

Current Financial Arrangement

1. Does your husband provide you with cash payments for your children's living expenses? _____

   If yes, how much per month: $_____

2. Does your husband provide you with cash payments for your (household) living expenses? _____

   If yes, how much per month: $_____

3. On a separate sheet of paper, list each expense (groceries, utilities, child care, tuition, etc.) and debt (mortgage, car payment, credit card, etc.) and record the amount paid, payment frequency (per day, week, month, quarter, year), and person who is paying. Attach to this document.

Other Arrangements of Separation (child custody, visitation, etc.)

_____ We have no such written or verbal agreements.

_____ We have a written agreement.
(Attach the agreement to this worksheet.)

_____ We have a verbal agreement or understanding.
(Describe on separate sheet of paper and attach.)

Pending Issues and Questions

1. I foresee the following problems in dealing with my spouse (for example, fear, distrust, dishonesty, unwillingness to compromise, using children as a weapon, violence, etc.).

   _____

2. I have the following questions and issues I would like to explore:

   _____

3. I have already made some decisions about the outcome I would like with respect to property, children, support, or goals and conduct of this case, as follows:

   _____

Use a blank sheet of paper to continue recording your responses to the above numbered statement. Indicate the corresponding.

▶ EMERGENCY RELIEF CHECKLIST

Check the following *Pendente Lite* relief that you feel you need:

- ❑ Visitation
- ❑ Child Custody
- ❑ No Removal of Child from Jurisdiction
- ❑ No Disparaging of Other Parent to Child
- ❑ Support. Specify the type of support needed:
  - ○ Child Support
  - ○ Family/Spousal Support
  - ○ Insurance Coverage (medical, life, auto, homeowner, rental)
  - ○ Education
  - ○ Child care
  - ○ Other (specify) _____
- ❑ Protective Order (domestic violence, child abuse)
- ❑ Exclusion of Other Spouse from Residence
- ❑ Sever Joint Tenancy of Marital Residence (or other real Property)
- ❑ Possession of Property Other Than Residence (business)
- ❑ Payment of Debts
- ❑ Payment of Attorney's Fees and Legal Costs: $_____
- ❑ Payment of Expert Fees:
  - ○ Accountant. For which asset: _____ $_____
  - ○ Appraiser. For which property: _____ $_____
  - ○ Evaluator. For which asset: _____ $_____

- ❏ Production of Financial Documents or Other Paper Before Hearing
- ❏ Demand for Statement of Net Worth
- ❏ Personal Property Removal (or to neutral place)
- ❏ Regular Accounting of Business and/or Accounts
- ❏ Division of Business Income
- ❏ Lis Pendence (Pending Lawsuit)
- ❏ Restraint of Assets. Specify the type of restraint needed:
  - ○ Transfer and/or Dissipation of Property
  - ○ Use of Credit Cards
  - ○ Encumbering or Liquidating Life Insurance Policies
  - ○ Canceling or Changing Beneficiaries on Insurance Plans (medical, life, etc.)
  - ○ Block on Joint Accounts
- ❏ Reinstatement of Credit Card (if frozen)
- ❏ Income Execution Order (Garnishment of Wages, for example, for Child Support)

▶ STATEMENT OF MARITAL WORTH

SUPREME COURT OF THE STATE OF _____

COUNTY OF_____

Date of commencement of action _____

I, [NAME], the Plaintiff herein, being duly sworn, depose and say that the following is an accurate statement as of [DATE], of my net worth (assets of whatsoever kind and nature and wherever situate minus liabilities), statement of income from all sources and statement of assets transferred of whatsoever kind and nature and wherever situated:

I. Family Data

Husband's age:_____

Wife's age:_____

Date married:_____

Date separated:_____

Number of dependent children under 21 years: _____

Names and birth dates of children: _____

Custody of children: ❑ Husband ❑ Wife ❑ Joint

Minor children of prior marriage: ❑ Husband ❑ Wife

Husband/Wife paying/receiving $_____ as alimony (maintenance) and/or $_____ as child support in connection with prior marriage

Custody of children of prior marriage: ❑ Husband ❑ Wife

Marital residence occupied by: ❑ Husband ❑ Wife ❑ Both ❑ Neither

Husband's present address: _____

Wife's present address:_____

Occupation of husband:_____

Husband's employer:_____

Occupation of wife:_____

Wife's employer:_____

Husband's education, training and skills:_____

Wife's education, training and skills:_____

Husband's health:_____

Wife's health: _____

Children's health: _____

II. Expenses

(You may elect to list all expenses on a weekly basis or all expenses on a monthly basis, however, you must be consistent. If any items are paid on a monthly basis, divide by 4.3 to obtain weekly payments; if any items are paid on a weekly basis, multiply by 4.3 to obtain monthly payment. Attach additional sheet, if needed. Items included under "Other" should be listed separately with separate dollar amounts.)

Expenses listed: ❑ weekly   ❑ monthly

A. Housing
1. Rent: _____
2. Mortgage and amortization: _____
3. Real estate taxes: _____
4. Condominium charges: _____
5. Cooperative apartment: _____
Total Housing: $_____

B. Utilities
   1. Fuel oil: _____
   2. Gas: _____
   3. Electricity: _____
   4. Telephone: _____
   5. Water: _____
   Total Utilities: $_____

C. Food
   1. Groceries: _____
   2. School lunches: _____
   3. Lunches at work: _____
   4. Dining out: _____
   5. Liquor/alcohol: _____
   6. Home entertainment: _____
   7. Other: _____
   Total Food: $_____

D. Clothing
   1. Husband: _____
   2. Wife: _____
   3. Children: _____
   4. Other (i.e., children from previous marriage): _____
   Total Clothing: $_____

E. Laundry
   1. Laundry: _____
   2. Dry cleaning: _____
   3. Other: _____
   Total Laundry: $_____

F. Insurance
   1. Life: _____
   2. Homeowner's/tenant's: _____
   3. Fire, flood, theft, liability: _____
   4. Automotive: _____
   5. Umbrella policy: _____

6. Medical plan: _____

7. Pharmaceutical plan: _____

8. Dental plan: _____

9. Optical plan: _____

10. Disability: _____

11. Worker's Compensation: _____

12. Other: _____

Total Insurance: $_____

G. Unreimbursed Medical

1. Medical: _____

2. Dental: _____

3. Optical: _____

4. Pharmaceutical: _____

5. Surgical, nursing, hospital: _____

6. Other: _____

Total Unreimbursed Medical: $_____

H. Household Maintenance

1. Repairs: _____

2. Furniture, furnishings, housewares: _____

3. Cleaning supplies: _____

4. Appliances, including maintenance: _____

5. Painting: _____

6. Sanitation/carting: _____

7. Gardening/landscaping: _____

8. Snow removal: _____

9. Extermination: _____

10. Other: _____

Total Household Maintenance: $_____

I. Household Help

1. Babysitter: _____

2. Domestic *(housekeeper, maid, etc.)*: _____

3. Other *(i.e., petsitter, gardener)*: _____

Total Household Help: $_____

J. Automotive
   Year: ___ Make: _____ ❑ Personal ❑ Business
   1. Payments:
   2. Fuel and fluids: _____
      (engine oil, brake, transmission)
   3. Repairs: _____
   4. Car wash: _____
   5. Registration and license: _____
   6. Parking and tolls: _____
   7. Other: _____
   Total Automotive: $_____

K. Educational
   1. Nursery and preschool: _____
   2. Primary and secondary: _____
   3. College: _____
   4. Postgraduate: _____
   5. Religious instruction: _____
   6. School transportation: _____
   7. School supplies/books: _____
   8. Tutoring/homeschooling: _____
   9. School events: _____
   10. Other: _____
   Total Educational: $_____

L. Recreational
   1. Summer camp: _____
   2. Vacations: _____
   3. Movies: _____
   4. Theatre, ballet, etc.:   _____
   5. Video rentals: _____
   6. Tapes, CDs, etc.:   _____
   7. Cable television: _____
   8. Team sports: _____
   9. Country club/pool club: _____
   10. Health club: _____
   11. Sporting goods: _____
   12. Hobbies: _____

13. Lessons *(music, dance, art, sports, etc.)*: _____
14. Birthday/holiday parties: _____
15. Other: _____
Total Recreation: $_____

M. Income Taxes
   1. Federal: _____
   2. State: _____
   3. City: _____
   4. Social Security and Medicare: _____
Total Income Taxes: $_____

N. Miscellaneous
   1. Beauty parlor/barber: _____
   2. Beauty aids/cosmetics, drug items: _____
   3. Cigarettes/tobacco: _____
   4. Books, magazines, newspapers: _____
   5. Children's allowances: _____
   6. Gifts: _____
   7. Charitable contributions: _____
   8. Religious organization: _____
   9. Union organization: _____
   10. Commutation and transportation: _____
   11. Veterinarian/pet expenses: _____
   12. Child support payments: _____
   13. Alimony and maintenance payments: _____
   (prior marriage)
   14. Loan payments: _____
   15. Unreimbursed business expenses: _____
Total Miscellaneous: $_____

O. Other Expenses
   1. _____: _____
   2. _____: _____
   3. _____: _____
Total Other Expenses: $_____

Total Expenses: $_____

III. Gross Income

(State source of income and annual amount. Attach additional sheet, if needed.)

A. Salary or Wages: $_____

B. Has income changed during the preceding date of this affidavit: ❑ Yes ❑ No

    (If yes, set forth name and address of all employers during preceding year and average weekly wage paid by each. Indicate overtime earnings separately. Attach previous year's W-2 or income tax return.)

    _____

C. Pay Period: ❑ Weekly ❑ Biweekly ❑ Monthly

    ❑ Other _____

D. Deductions

    1. Federal tax: $_____
    2. State tax: $_____
    3. Local tax: $_____
    4. Social Security: $_____
    5. Medicare: $_____
    6. Other payroll deductions (specify):

    _____ $_____

    _____ $_____

E. Social Security Number: _____

F. Number of Dependents Claimed: _____

G. Names of Dependents Claimed: _____

    _____

    _____

H. Bonus, Commissions, Fringe Benefits (use of auto, memberships, etc.): $_____

I. Partnership, Royalties, Sale of Assets (income and installment payments): $_____

J. Taxable Dividends and Interest: $_____

K. Nontaxable Dividends and Interest: $_____

L. Real Estate (income only): $_____

M. Trust, Profit Sharing, Annuities (principal distribution and income): $_____

N. Pension (income only): $_____

O. Taxable Awards, Prizes, Grants: $_____

P. Nontaxable Awards, Prizes, Grants: $_____

Q. Bequests, Legacies, Gifts: $_____

R. Other Income (from all other sources):

_____ $_____

_____ $_____

S. Tax Preference Items

1. Long term capital gain deduction: $_____
2. Depreciation, amortization, or depletion: $_____
3. Stock options (excess of fair market value over amount paid): $_____

T. Income of Other Members of Household: $_____

If any child or other member of your household is employed, set forth name and that person's annual income:

_____ $_____

U. Social Security: $_____

V. Disability Benefits: $_____

W. Public Assistance: $_____

X. Other:

_____ $_____

Total Income: $_____

IV. Assets

(If any asset is held jointly with spouse or another, so state, and set forth your respective shares. Attach additional sheets, if needed.

A. Cash Accounts

1. Cash
   a. Location:
   b. Source of funds:
   c. Amount: $_____

2. Checking accounts
   Financial institution:
   Account number:
   Title holder:
   Date opened:
   Source of Funds:
   Balance: $_____

   Total checking accounts: $_____
   See additional checking accounts on attached sheet.

3. Savings accounts (individual, joint, totter trust, certificates of deposit, treasury notes)
   Financial institution:
   Account number:
   Title holder:
   Type of account:
   Date opened;
   Source of funds:
   Balance: $_____

   Total savings accounts: $_____
   See additional savings accounts on attached sheet.

4. Security deposits
   Location:
   Title owner:
   Type of deposit:
   Source of funds:
   Date of deposit:
   Amount: $_____

Total securities: $_____
See additional security accounts on attached sheet.

5. Other cash accounts
   Location:
   Title owner:
   Type of account:
   Source of funds:
   Date of deposit:
   Amount: $_____

   Total other accounts: $_____
   See additional other cash accounts on attached sheet.

Total Cash Accounts: $_____

B. Securities

1. Bonds, notes, mortgages
   Description of security:
   Title holder:
   Location:
   Date of acquisition:
   Original price or value:
   Source of funds to acquire:
   Current value: $_____

   Total bonds, notes, mortgages: $_____
   See additional bonds, notes, mortgages on attached sheet.

2. Stocks, options, and commodities contracts
   Description of security:
   Title holder:
   Location:
   Date of acquisition:
   Original price or value:
   Source of funds to acquire:
   Current value: $_____

   Total stocks, options, commodities: $_____
   See additional stocks, options, commodities on attached sheet.

3. Broker margin accounts
   Name and address of broker:
   Title holder:
   Date account opened:
   Original value of account:
   Source of funds:
   Current value: $_____

   Total broker margin accounts: $_____
   See additional broker margin accounts on attached sheet.

Total Securities: $ _____

C. Loans to Others and Accounts Receivable
   Debtor's name and address:
   Original amount of loan or debt:
   Source of funds from which loan made
        or origin of debt:
   Date payment(s) due:
   Current amount due: $_____

   **Total loans to others and accounts receivable:
   $_____**
   See additional loans to others' accounts receivable on attached sheet.

D. Value of Interest in Business
   Name and address of business:
   Type of business:
   Capital contribution:
   Percentage of interest:
   Date of acquisition:
   Original price or value:
   Source of funds to acquire:
   Method of valuation:
   Other relevant information:
   Current net worth of business:

   Total business interest: $_____
   See additional business interests on attached sheet.

E. Cash Surrender Value of Life Insurance
Insurer's name and address:
Name of insured:
Policy number:
Face amount of policy: $_____
Policy owner:
Date of acquisition:
Source of funding to acquire:
Current cash surrender value: $_____

Total life insurance cash surrender value: $_____
See additional insurance policies with cash surrender value on attached sheet.

F. Vehicles (automobile, boat, plane, truck, camper, etc.)
Description:
Title owner:
Date of acquisition:
Original price: $_____
Source of funds to acquire:
Amount of current lien unpaid: $_____
Current fair market value: $_____

Total vehicles: $_____
See additional vehicles on attached sheet.

G. Real Property
(including real property, leaseholds, life estates, etc., at market value; do not deduct any mortgage)
Description:
Title owner:
Date of acquisition:
Original price: $_____
Source of funds to acquire:
Amount of mortgage or lien unpaid: $_____
Estimated current market value: $_____

Total real property: $_____
See additional real property on attached sheet.

H. Vested Interests in Trusts, Pensions, Profit Sharing, Legacies, Deferred Compensation, Etc.
Description of trust:
Location of assets:
Title owner:
Date of acquisition:
Original investment: $_____
Source of funds:
Amount of unpaid liens: $_____
Current value: $_____

Total vested interests: $_____
See additional vested interests on attached sheet.

I. Contingent Interests
(stock options, interests subject to life estates, prospective inheritances, etc.)
Description:
Location:
Date of vesting:
Title owner:
Date of acquisition:
Original price or value: $_____
Source of funds to acquire:
Method of valuation:
Current value: $_____

Total contingent interests: $_____
See additional contingent interests on attached sheet.

J. Household Furnishings
Description:
Location:
Title owner:
Original price: $_____
Source of funds to acquire:
Amount of lien unpaid: $_____
Current value: $_____

Total household furnishings: $_____
See additional household furnishings on attached sheet.

K. Valuables

(jewelry, art, antiques, gold and precious metals, and other items valued at more than $500)

Description:

Title owner:

Location:

Original price or value: $_____

Source of funds to acquire:

Amount of lien unpaid: $_____

Current value: $_____

Total valuables: $_____

See additional household furnishings on attached sheet.

L. Other Assets

(tax shelter investments, collections, judgments, causes of action, patents, trademarks, copyrights, and any other asset not hereinabove itemized)

Description:

Title owner:

Location:

Original price or value: $_____

Source of funds to acquire:

Amount of lien unpaid: $_____

Current value: $_____

Total other assets: $_____

See additional other assets on attached sheet.

Total Assets: $_____

V. Liabilities

A. Accounts Payable

Name and address of creditor:

Debtor:

Amount of original debt: $_____

Date of incurring debt:

Purpose:

Monthly or other periodic payment: $_____

Amount of current debt: $_____

Total accounts payable: $_____

See additional accounts payable on attached sheet.

B. Notes Payable
Name and address of creditor:
Debtor:
Amount of original debt: $_____
Date of incurring debt:
Purpose:
Monthly or other periodic payment: $_____
Amount of current debt: $_____

Total notes payable: $_____
See additional notes payable on attached sheet.

C. Installment Accounts Payable (security agreements, chattel mortgages)
Name and address of creditor:
Debtor:
Amount of original debt: $_____
Date of incurring debt:
Purpose:
Monthly or other periodic payment: $_____
Amount of current debt: $_____

Total installment accounts payable: $_____
See additional installment accounts payable on attached sheet.

D. Broker Margin Accounts
Name and address of broker:
Amount of original debt: $_____
Date of incurring debt:
Purpose:
Monthly or other periodic payment: $_____
Amount of current debt: $_____

Total broker margin accounts: $_____
See additional broker margin accounts on attached sheet.

E. Mortgages Payable on Real Estate
Name and address of mortgagee:
Address of property mortgaged:
Mortgagor(s):
Original debt: $_____
Date of incurring debt:

Monthly or other periodic payment: $_____
Maturity date:
Amount of current debt: $_____

Total mortgages payable on real estate: $_____
See additional mortgages payable on attached sheet.

F. Taxes Payable
Description of tax:
Amount of tax: $_____
Date due:

Total taxes payable: $_____
See additional taxes payable on attached sheet.

G. Loans on Life Insurance Policies
Name and address of insurer:
Amount of loan: $_____
Date incurred:
Purpose:
Name of borrower:
Monthly or other periodic payment: $_____
Amount of current debt: $_____

Total life insurance loans: $_____
See additional life insurance loans on attached sheet.

H. Other Liabilities
Description:
Name and address of creditor:
Debtor:
Original amount of debt: $_____
Date incurred:
Purpose:
Monthly or other periodic payment: $_____
Amount of current debt: $_____

Total other liabilities: $_____
See additional other liabilities on attached sheet.

Total Liabilities: $_____

Net Worth *(total assets – total liabilities)*: **$_____**

VI. Assets Transferred

List all assets transferred in any manner during the preceding three years, or length of the marriage, whichever is shorter. Transfers in the routine course of business that resulted in an exchange of assets of substantially equivalent value need not be specifically disclosed where such assets are otherwise identified in the statement of net worth.

Description of property:

_____

To whom transferred and relationship to transferee:

_____

Date of transfer:

_____

Transfer value:

_____

See additional assets transferred on attached sheet.

Total Value of Transferred Assets: $_____

VII. Support Requirements

A. Deponent received/paid support prior to separation:
❑ Yes   ❑ No
Purpose/type:
Amount: $_____
Frequency: per   ❑ week   ❑ month
These payments were voluntary: ❑ Yes   ❑ No
Amount in arrears: $_____

B. Deponent is currently receiving/paying support:
❑ Yes   ❑ No
Purpose/type:_____
Amount: $_____
Frequency: per   ❑ week   ❑ month

These payments are being made voluntarily?
❑ Yes ❑ No
Amount in arrears: $_____

C. Deponent requests support for children:
❑ Yes ❑ No
Amount: $_____
Frequency: per ❑ week ❑ month
Date/day of payment: 1st of month

D. Deponent requests support for self:
❑ Yes ❑ No
Amount: $_____
Frequency: per ❑ week ❑ month
Date/day of payment: 1st of month

VIII. Counsel Fee Requirements

A. Deponent requests for counsel fee and disbursements, the sum of which is to be determined.

B. Deponent requests reimbursement of monies paid to counsel in the amount of: $

C. Deponent has agreed with counsel concerning fees:
1. Per the attached retainer agreement.
2. A copy of the retainer agreement must be annexed.

IX. Accountant and Appraisal Fees Requirement

A. Deponent requests for accountants' fees and disbursements, the sum of which is to be determined.

B. Deponent requests for appraisal fees and disbursements, the sum of which is to be determined.

C. Deponent requires the services of an accountant for the following reasons: to be determined

D. Deponent requires the services of an appraiser for the following reasons: to be determined

X. **Other Data Concerning the Financial Circumstances of the Parties That Should Be Brought to the Attention of the Court Are:**

_____

_____

_____

_____

_____

_____

_____

_____

_____

_____

_____

Certification of Plaintiff:

The foregoing statements and a rider consisting of ____ pages, annexed hereto and made part hereof, have been carefully read by the undersigned, who states that they are true and correct.

_____
[NAME]

Sworn to before me this _____ day of [MONTH], 20_____

_____
[NOTARY PUBLIC]

Certification of Attorney:

I hereby certify under penalty of perjury and as an officer of the court that I have no knowledge that the substance of any of the factual submissions contained in this document is false.

_____
[NAME OF ATTORNEY]

Index